RAMBLING
RECOLLECTIONS
OF
FLYING & FLYERS

MUNCIE HAS a long history of interest in aviation. For example, a letter found in a collection of old documents, dated August 31, 1848, predicted man's travel by air. The author was Mr. Carleton M. Shipley, a prominent Muncie lawyer, politician, businessman and obviously a person of vision and great imagination. In flowery, almost poetical style, he wrote a thesis on "the powers and possibilities of the human mind." His rather lengthy and imaginative treatise concludes with the thought that "may we not reasonably predict 'ere the close of his journey here in the imitation of birds of the air he will journey by the aid of artificial wings?"

The letter was published as a feature article in the Muncie Morning Star, *March 26, 1922.*

DESCRIPTIONS OF AIRCRAFT ON COVER
Selected as of significance out of twenty-seven aircraft pastels, by Reed Kinnett

From left to right and downward:

1. NC9831–Travel Air Open Cockpit OX-5–90 HP engine, cruise speed 85 MPH, Edmund F. Ball soloed October 7, 1929, Silver Fox Airport, Yorktown, Indiana.
2. NC11252 Waco F Three-Place Open Cockpit, 125 MPH Kinner engine, cruising speed 110 MPH, June 19, 1932–May 3, 1935. First airplane owned by Edmund F. Ball
3. NC12460 Waco A, Two-Place Enclosed Cockpit, 170 HP Jacobs engine, cruise speed 130 MPH, June 25, 1932–July 15, 1932. First plane stolen in Michigan, totalled by Barney Galowski at Traverse City, Michigan.
4. NC14012 Waco C, Four-Place Cabin Plane, 210 HP Continental engine, cruise speed 140 MPH, May 5, 1934–September 8, 1937. Wedding trip to Galveston and New Orleans, January 11, 1936. First cabin plane owned by Edmund F. Ball.
5. NC18043 Stagger-Wing Beech, Four-Place " E-1-7-B," 285 HP Jacobs engine, cruise speed 145 MPH, November 1, 1937 to June 23, 1938.
6. N5173C Beechcraft V-Tail, B-35, Four-Place Cabin, 210 HP Lycoming engine, cruise speed 155 MPH, October 2, 1951–March 6, 1955. Wedding trip June 28, 1952, Dallas; Santa Fe; Pebble Beach, California; Grants Pass, Oregon; Las Vegas, Nevada, to Muncie, July 1952.
7. NC1630 Cessna F-50, Five-Place Cabin, Edmund F. Ball's first twin-engine plane, twin 225 HP Jacobs engines, cruising speed 145 MPH, November 24, 1940–September 30, 1941. Plane requisitioned by United States Army Air Corps, sank on board ship in North Atlantic en route to North Africa for transitional training in World War II.
8. N5246Y Piper Aztec, Six-Place, twin 250 HP Lycoming engines. Flown 1,260 hours October 1, 1963–January 10, 1968. Typical of several owned and flown.
9. N20BZ Piper Aerostar Model PA-60-602P, Six-Place pressurized cabin to 25,000 feet, twin 350 HP Lycoming engines, cruising speed 205 knots. Purchased from Ball Corporation by Muncie Aviation Company April 30, 1984, leased to Edmund F. Ball and Virginia B. Ball.

©1993 by Edmund F. Ball. All rights reserved.
Printed in the United States of America
Library of Congress Catalog Card No. 93–078596
ISBN 0–9623291–8–5

CONTENTS

Chapter I

HISTORY

Chapter II

EARLY EXPERIENCES

Chapter III

MEMORABLE EXPERIENCES

Chapter IV

THE PIONEERS

Chapter V

THOSE HALCYON YEARS
—PROMOTING AVIATION—

Chapter V

Chapter VI

THE ENDURANCE FLYERS

Chapter VII

PILOTS OF NOTE

Delaware County, Indiana

Chapter VIII

CONCLUSION

List of Illustrations

Chapter I

Chapter II

Chapter III

Chapter V

List of Maps

Chapter II

Edmund F. Ball, License Number P14861, July 16, 1930.

RAMBLING
RECOLLECTIONS
OF
FLYING & FLYERS

VOLUME I

By

Edmund F. Ball

Reed Kinnett

REED KINNETT, from Richmond, Indiana, flew with us on numerous air tours back in the 1930s. He became a well-known aviation artist and illustrated several books on aviation. One of his own, entitled *Our War Birds,* was published by Macmillan Company of New York in 1946, of which I have an autographed copy.

I think that I was his first customer. It was a conceptual picture of the Travel Air in which I made my first solo. The plane itself had been previously demolished, killing Harry White, my instructor, and his student pilot, Paul Karleen.

Virginia continued the tradition until Reed's death. The last of his drawings in my collection is of my Piper Aztec N5426Y in 1968.

Several of his drawings are used as illustrations and on the cover of these *Recollections.*

PREFACE

Rambling Recollections of Aviation In and Around Muncie and Elsewhere

THIS ACCOUNT of aviation history began in response to requests by a few family members and friends for a record of my adventures and misadventures as a pilot. To refresh my memory of dates and events, I visited the Muncie Public Library which has an amazingly good card index on various subjects of local interest, including aviation. This index was compiled as the result of a Works Progress Administration (WPA) project undertaken in Muncie during the Great Depression in the early 1930s.

I quickly became intrigued with these reminders of so many people and events connected with aviation in Indiana and particularly about aviation in Muncie. In fact, I got carried away! Research was irresistible. One subject led to another to the point where my original plan to relate a few interesting and amusing experiences quickly grew into a much larger study.

Readers of this chronicle should know that I have been a licensed aircraft pilot for over six decades and, in addition, have enjoyed the good fortune to know a good number of aviators in Indiana. Through such organizations as Quiet Birdmen (QBs), the OX-5 Pioneers, the UFO (United Flying Octogenarians), and as a charter member of both AOPA (Aircraft Owners and Pilots Association) and SPA (Sportsman Pilots Association) and also through my business interests with Muncie Airport, Incorporated and the Muncie Aviation Company (of which I am a surviving founder), I have been privileged to participate in much of Indiana's aviation history.

So, a study which began as a simple account of a few personal experiences has turned into a potpourri of *Rambling Recollections,* not only of mine, but also those of many others. The accounts of my fellow pilots certainly add great interest as well as historical importance to this study. Undoubtedly, I could include the recollections of many other pilots, but time and space make such a task impossible. So I offer my apologies to those aviation pioneers not included in this account.

I express my sincerest gratitude to all who have helped to give these Recollections some semblance of historic significance.

Edmund F. Ball

Edmund F. Ball
Muncie, Indiana

Special Acknowledgements and Special Thanks

MY SPECIAL THANKS to so many special people.

First and foremost is my secretary, Sarah Wanthal, and her marvelous word processor. Without them, there is no way whatsoever that this book could ever have been attempted and much less completed. To her, my very special thanks.

Then there would be Bruce Geelhoed of Ball State University for his interviewing people and pilots and preparing autobiographies and for his editing.

Dr. John J. Pruis, retired President of Ball State University and second career retiree from Ball Corporation's Vice President for Corporate Relations, and Douglas A. Bakken with his secretary Judy LaCasse have contributed enormously with final editing, corrections, and suggestions.

Paul Antrim, for his knowledge of photography and his capability to convert a miscellaneous collection of photographs, some of dubious quality, and drawings to reproducible material likely to be of more general interest than the script.

Denise Jones, also of Ball State University, did a magnificent job of layout, design and composition that has made this publication a masterpiece of appearance, if not so much of content.

Heather Davis, of Minnetrista Cultural Center, tenaciously collected photographs and materials from such varied sources as the Smithsonian Air and Space Museum in Washington, historical societies, libraries and out of albums and collections like Roger Pelham's, Bill Moffitt's, Orv Knarr's, Jim Belknap's and many others.

Kerry Shaw of Ball Corporation did the cover and drawing of the homemade artificial horizon and bank and turn instrument. And Sam Clemmons helped with transparencies of maps and provided technical advice when asked. Professor Alten F. Grandt of Purdue University School of Aeronautics and Astronautics, thanks for technical information and historic photographs.

Christine Olson, a Minnetrista Cultural Center intern from Ball State University's graphic arts program, worked the maps and precisely laid out the routes of some of our more interesting flying ventures.

I've tried to give credit to each individual who has contributed personal information concerning their own careers or careers of others they knew. Their knowledge and valued reminiscences have added fascinating dimensions to these *Recollections*.

For whatever historic value this publication may have, I am indebted to them all for their generous responses to my inquiries and requests for help.

To all of them, I owe a debt of gratitude beyond any ability to fully express. I'm immensely grateful to them all.

Sincerely,

Edmund F. Ball

Dedicated to

My All-Time Favorite Pilot
Virginia B. Ball

INTRODUCTION

ALTHOUGH this book started to be a published collection of his personal experiences as a pilot for the past 63 years, Edmund F. Ball tells us "one thing led to another" until *Rambling Recollections* became a comprehensive history of the development of the aviation industry, principally in Delaware County and East Central Indiana.

Drawing on results of research in many areas, as well as his own experiences, Ed Ball has blended the information about "People, Places, and Things" into extremely interesting reading about aviation in his home town, Muncie, Indiana, and elsewhere from the early years of the twentieth century up to the present day.

Ed and his wife, Virginia, have flown in far-off places—Australia, New Zealand, South Africa, Alaska, The Bahamas and Mexico—and he has recorded them in his "Ramblings."

Ed has named the "People," the men and women who have figured prominently in molding the industry as we know it today in East Central Indiana—the flight instructors and the pilots they trained, the administrators and the businessmen who had the foresight to recognize what the future of aviation might have in store for this community and who were willing to invest their money in the potential it promised.

He also named the "Places" where it all happened—from the first airports, The Silver Fox Airport where he soloed in 1929 and Wall Field, the original Delaware County Airport (now Johnson Field) where commuter airline service is available to nearby metropolitan cities, and where the latest in FAA navigational aids have been installed. (Five airports have flourished in Delaware County along with numerous "flying farmer" landing strips on private property.)

Last, but not least, Ed Ball has referred to the "Things" which made it all happen—the airplanes, from what might be called the first "kit plane" which was built by Muncie residents in 1910 to the modern business jets which are locally owned and hangared at the Delaware County Johnson Field Airport.

Of special interest to aviation "buffs" and enthusiasts is the large number of photographs and artist's drawings which depict the span of the author's aviation experiences. They cover the period from his first solo flight in 1929 in an OX-5 powered Travel Air, open-cockpit bi-plane to the present. Some of the pictures are of aircraft which belonged to other family members and friends. He has also included details of the tool and die shop's owner, George Kemp's, invention of an "aeroplane tractor," an engine mounted on the nose of the aircraft *pulling* it forward. Kemp produced these in small numbers in 1914 and shipped them to many points throughout the nation. In comparison to this item, Ed Ball has drawn an interesting parallel with his reference to the production of rotor blades for jet engines in the 1990s by another Muncie manufacturer.

The author is the son of the late Edmund B. Ball, one of the glass industry's five founding Ball Brothers. He has been affiliated with the company all of his life, starting in 1928 "in the ranks" with various manufacturing assignments before assuming management positions. He is now an honorary director of Ball Corporation and retired President and Chairman of the Board. He presently serves as Chairman Emeritus of the Executive Committee.

Ed was a co-founder of Muncie Airport, Incorporated, and of Muncie Aviation Corporation in 1932 and continues his interest as Chairman Emeritus of the Board. His son, Frank Ball, the current President, continues the tradition.

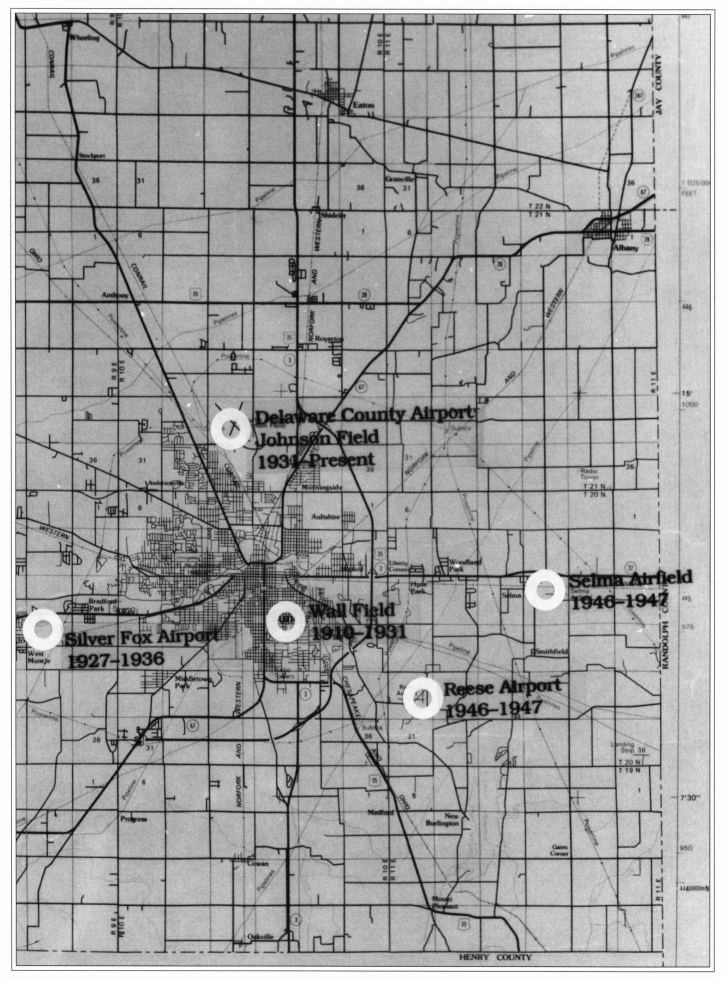

Primarily an industrialist, the author is equally well-known as a humanitarian and civic-minded philanthropist. He has taken an active part on the boards of many organizations and institutions—educational, industrial, and fraternal—and he has served his country militarily in peace time and in war. Early in World War II, he was called to active duty as a Lieutenant and was promoted to the rank of Major with a Service Pilot Rating. Overseas in the Mediterranean Theater, he participated in the planning and execution of three military D-Day landings in Sicily, Salerno and Anzio.

Ed Ball has also taken an active role in Masonic work and is an honorary member of the Supreme Council Scottish Rite 33rd Degree.

As a pilot, the author holds a commercial pilot's license for single- and multi-engine aircraft, gliders and instrument rating. He has flown more than 12,000 hours as pilot-in-command. He is a member of the United Flying Octogenarians. In order to qualify, a pilot must fly and hold a valid FAA pilot's license after the age of 80. He also is a member of the Quiet Birdmen, the Sportman Pilots Association, the OX-5 Aviation Pioneers and is enshrined in the OX-5 Hall of Fame in San Diego, California, and the Aircraft Owners and Pilots Association.

His life has spanned an exciting period in history, a time that might well be called the period when aviation moved from "Jennies to Jets," in which Edmund F. Ball has played a major part.

—BILL JAMIESON
*Aviation Columnist
for* The Muncie Star

Bill Jamieson, in his Introduction, reminds us that the Muncie Community has been served by five different airports: Wall Field on South Hackley Street, 1910–1931; The Silver Fox Airport, 1927–1936; Delaware County Airport (Johnson Field), 1931–present; Reese Flying Service Airport, 1946/47–present; and Selma Airport, 1946/47 to approximately 1985.

*The Blieriot Monoplane in which he,
Blieriot, flew the English Channel,
July 25, 1909, after which Arthur
Humfeld, Arthur Ford, and Vincent
Fox patterned their aircraft in 1910.*

*Blieriot Monoplane with GNOME 50
HP motor achieved speeds of 50 MPH.*

CHAPTER I

HISTORY

Muncie's Early Interest in Aviation

O N NOVEMBER 1, 1910, only seven years after the Wright brothers' first flight at Kitty Hawk, North Carolina, the issue of the *Muncie Morning Star* showed photographs of a homemade monoplane reported to be the first of its kind to be built in Indiana.

Courtesy of Purdue University Special Collections
Blieriot Monoplane with original ANZANI 25 HP motor which achieved speed of 34 MPH in a race.

The craft was designed and built by Arthur Humfeld, Arthur Ford, and Vincent Fox, three well-known mechanics employed by the High Wheel Auto Parts Company. In the photograph, Fox sits in the pilot's seat "at the wheel."

The aircraft reportedly weighed about 600 pounds and was built along the lines of the Blieriot

© 1910, *The Muncie Star*
The aircraft built by Humfeld, Ford, and Fox in Muncie in 1910 and Vincent Fox at the controls.

Monoplane "with several new and original ideas of the young constructors." Humfeld whittled out the propeller by hand. The aircraft was a single seater but the designers planned to build a plane which carried at least two passengers, after they successfully completed the testing of their first model. It was possibly a Kemp engine (made by a local manufacturer, George Kemp) which provided the power source for the aircraft. However, there seems to be no confirmed record of Kemp having built a three-cylinder engine which appears to have been used on the aircraft as mentioned in the second attempt two weeks later. There was an Orville Wright three-cylinder engine on display at Oshkosh Air Shop which might have been the one on the experimental plane built by the employees of Wheel Auto Parts Company.

The *Star* reported that, in a test run that day, Mr. Fox succeeded in getting the machine a few inches off the ground and might have "moved to greater heights" had not one of the wheels hit a stump in the field causing the engine to reverse and the machine to "lower." After the flight, the young "builders" planned a later flight, probably sometime for the following week. In the meantime, they displayed their machine in the Interstate Automobile sales window in the Pall Building on East Main Street.

On Sunday, November 14th, the three aviators attempted another test flight, this one at the Stephen Streeter Farm at the north end of Elm Street. A crowd of about five hundred people had gathered to see the trial flight. A failure of the engine to function properly aborted the attempt, however. In spite of several adjustments, one of the aircraft's three cylinders would not "hit" properly. Since the engine had worked perfectly indoors, its failure was attributed to outside weather conditions. The inventors had made several alterations on the machine itself since the first trial, including a lever instead of a wheel to control the plane. Also, they needed to whittle a new propeller for the next test.

© 1910, *The Muncie Star*
Rear view of plane, showing rudder and surface.

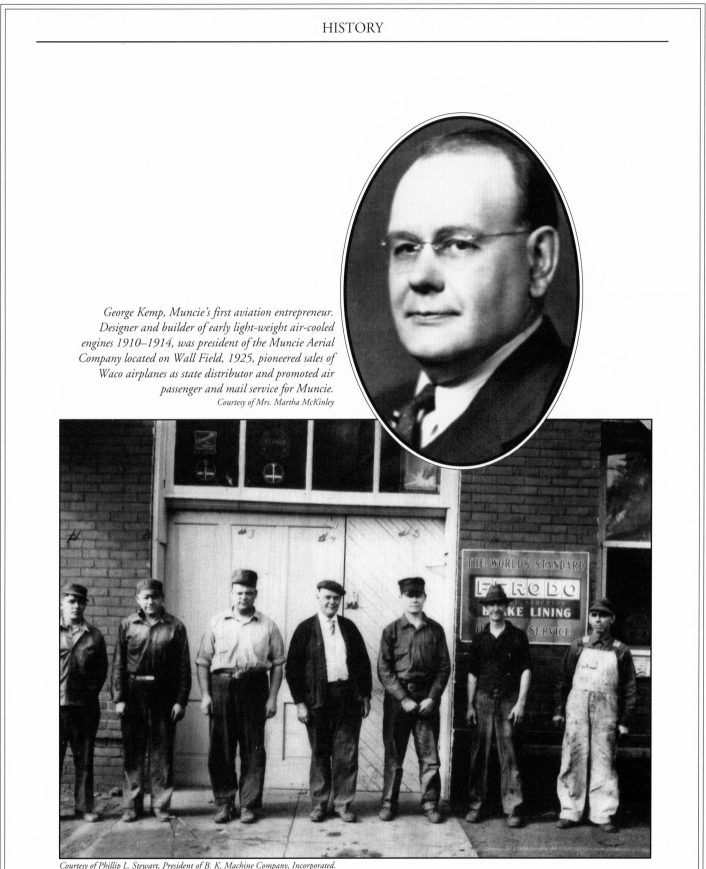

George Kemp, Muncie's first aviation entrepreneur. Designer and builder of early light-weight air-cooled engines 1910–1914, was president of the Muncie Aerial Company located on Wall Field, 1925, pioneered sales of Waco airplanes as state distributor and promoted air passenger and mail service for Muncie.
Courtesy of Mrs. Martha McKinley

Courtesy of Phillip L. Stewart, President of B. K. Machine Company, Incorporated.
Kemp shop employees circa 1910.

Courtesy of Mrs. Martha McKinley

George Kemp and his brother-in-law, Harve Kratzer, a mechanic at the Bell Machine and Engineering Company, in 1913 created a strange automobile powered by a Kemp engine and propeller, mounted on an Interstate car chassis. Along the River Road to Yorktown, they approached a farmer driving a horse and buggy. The horse went through the fence, taking the buggy and farmer with him as far as the river bank where the frightened horse stood still, quivering, and the farmer was so bruised and dazed, he didn't know what happened.

Later, in 1916, they mounted the engine and propeller on a bobsled and tried it again using the siding on Walnut Street where streetcars ran. A newspaper article reported that they hit a rut in the track throwing "George and Harve off on their own, sliding on the ice almost to 6th Street." That was the end of their experimenting with propeller driven vehicles.

Although disappointed by this failure, the young men said they were continuing to learn and predicted that they would finally succeed.

On August 28, 1912, the *Muncie Star* reported that an "airplane club" had been organized. The club had about twenty-five members and George W. Kemp was elected its President. One of the club's first items of business dealt with "establishing a permanent flying field to serve Muncie."

George W. Kemp was unquestionably Muncie's first entrepreneur in the aviation industry. He founded, in 1905, the Kemp Machine Works, later changed to the B&K Machine Shop. He designed what is thought to be one of the very first light-weight, air-cooled combustion, piston engines.

Bill Jamieson, Muncie's best-known aviation writer and historian, wrote about him in one of his columns in the *Muncie Star* under the heading of

"Vapor Trails" back in the 1970s. He recorded that there was more than one model of the Kemp air-cooled engine. A Kemp catalog, dated 1915, offered a two-cylinder, horizontal opposed cylinder engine for "boats, motors, sleighs and ice boats." The most popular engine was the four-cylinder, in-line, and there was also a V-8 engine available. They were the "tractor" type, that is, designed to pull an aircraft forward with its propeller pulling it through the air rather than a "pusher" with the engine mounted rearward, the propeller pushing it forward through the air. Engines were reported being sold to customers as far away as California and Alaska. They operated at the *fantastic* speed of 1150 RPMs. The price for the larger engine was $450. Several engines were manufactured for World War I airplanes. Kemp also invented a shoulder harness with which the pilot could "warp" the wings to correct a roll instead of hinged aelirons. His shop also produced "blades" which might be considered the generic forerunner of the high-tech rotor blades later manufactured for modern jet engines by Ontario Corporation here in Muncie.

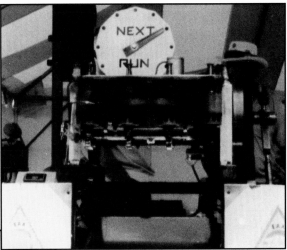

Courtesy of Edmund F. Ball
A Wright 1902 4-Cylinder Engine (above) on display at Oshkosh 1992. Wright also manufactured a 3-cylinder such as Humfeld, Ford, and Fox used on their experimental 1910 aircraft.

Courtesy of Phillip L. Stewart, President of B. K. Machine Company, Incorporated
The Kemp 1914 Aircraft Engine on display at the Minnetrista Cultural Center in 1992. It still runs! Kemp also made a three-cycle engine which is likely the one used by Humfeld, Ford, and Fox.

A Humiliating Experience

ON AUGUST 18, 1918, two military planes flying from Dayton *en route* to Indianapolis passed over Muncie and "thrilled spectators with their maneuvers." It was the first flight which Muncie's people had ever witnessed in their home city. Automobiles followed the aircraft to the northeast where the pilots landed, one on ground owned by Thomas Weir and the other about a mile further northeast in a wheat field. A large crowd assembled to greet the flyers and increased so rapidly that it was necessary for "police and members of the local militia to form safety lines to keep people back from the machines."

After getting a supply of gasoline, the pilots took off and performed a few stunts to thrill the spectators. Now that Muncie had been "discovered," Munsonians believed that more flights would likely be passing over *en route* from Dayton to Indianapolis with some possibly even landing again. As a result of this first flight, Mayor Rollin H. Bunch invited the aviators to return to Muncie for the Labor Day celebration.

Not long afterwards, one of those same planes *en route* from Dayton to Indianapolis landed on a field northeast of Muncie, which led to one of my most humiliating childhood experiences. Although it happened seventy-five years ago, the incident made such a great impression that, today, I remember it with more amusement than humility.

I don't recall whether the plane had landed intentionally or because of a mechanical problem. At any rate, the pilot indicated that the plane would remain there overnight. Quite a crowd of curious spectators had gathered. The authorities determined that the plane should be guarded to prevent accidental damage or possibly vandalism. Someone in the community then suggested that the Boy Scout Troop, of which I happened to be a member, should receive the high honor and important responsibility of guard duty during the night. Our dubious parents drove several of us Boy Scouts to the temporary airfield where the Scout Master in charge explained the importance of our assignment. We didn't have any provisions for an overnight mission—food, shelter, blankets—and by that time, the crowd had mostly departed. We deployed ourselves around the aircraft in some semblance of a protecting circle. With nothing much to do, we soon became bored.

Now, a bunch of twelve- to thirteen-year old boys could not be restrained from satisfying their curiosities about this wonderful flying machine within their reach, so we started to climb around the airplane. The scoutmaster tried valiantly to keep us off the plane and out of the cockpit. I recall that one Scout punched a small hole in the lower wing when he tried to sneak a peek into the cockpit.

As the scoutmaster struggled to keep his boys away from the plane, he happened to notice a glow coming from the cockpit. The glow was caused by the phosphorescent paint on the instruments, but in his distressed state of mind, he thought that one of the boys had accidentally hit a switch and turned on the lights. Certain that serious damage had been done, he sent for help to higher authority. Before long, our families arrived to take us home. We were disgraced, humiliated that we had failed in our responsibility and were replaced by uniformed officers from the local police force. I suspect that our parents were relieved to have us safely home and spared the all-night vigil for which we were ill-prepared. But for our scoutmaster, it was an experience that he would long remember, but probably like to forget.

Muncie's First Airport–Wall Field

1910–1931

R. H. Pelham Photo
Ernie Basham, on right, Muncie's first professional, commercial pilot, with O. Sackstetter, an early supporter of aviation as passenger, with an OX-5 powered "Jenny" JN4D.

MUNCIE'S first airport, identified as Wall Field, was located on South Hackley Street between 18th and 26th Streets. It had a north-south sod runway of about 1,200 feet, bordered on the west by Hackley Street and an east-west runway probably about half that length. Tall oak trees grew alongside both runways, not exactly an ideal airport by modern standards. The field was first operated as a business venture by The Muncie Aerial Company in 1910. Wall Field had recently been designated as a Class-A airfield by Captain L. G. Meister and Lieutenant H. F. Hetkert of McComb Field, Dayton.

On July 24, 1925, the officers of the Muncie Aerial Company, George W. Kemp, President; C. G. Wood, Vice President; and Paul Meredith, Secretary, held a meeting with the Muncie Chamber of Commerce at which they announced a big step toward making Muncie the "Airport of Indiana." Meredith stated that Wall Field had been offered to the National Aeronautics Association for use in cross country flights starting on Labor Day. Such an event might help to stimulate more interest in aeronautics in Muncie. At the time, one plane operated daily from the field, taking up passengers, and it was reported that a local businessman had used it one day for a business trip to Union City. E. E. "Ernie" Bashem, believed to be Muncie's first commercial pilot, was the company's chief pilot.

George Kemp reported to a meeting of the Commercial Club that the Muncie Aerial Company would become the Indiana distributor for Waco aircraft manufactured in Troy, Ohio, by the Advanced Aircraft Company. Kemp estimated that, given good quality and prompt production, his company could sell twelve planes per year in Indiana. Aviation observers believed that the Muncie firm's location on Wall Field was an excellent facility and that Muncie could become the "premier clearing house" for the sale

and distribution of aircraft throughout Indiana and the Midwest.

In June 1925, the Aerial Company contracted with Will Eppards to move a large tobacco warehouse north of the Wall Street field to be used as a hangar. The plan called for making other improvements in the building, including a concession stand. If all plans went forward, the new hangar would be dedicated in July. (Several years later, after the demise of Silver Fox Airport in 1930, I kept my plane hangared there until the new hangar at the Muncie Airport north of town, was available.) After all the improvements planned for Wall Field had been completed, arrangements were made for its dedication on September 18, 1925.

The Dedication of Wall Field

1925

WALL FIELD was officially and impressively dedicated on September 17, 1925. Local newspapers reported that almost 25,000 people attended the ceremony, an obvious show of interest in aviation. Flying in a cabin plane taking off from nearby Silver Fox Field, Mayor John C. Hampton led the parade of aircraft. For safer control of traffic, planes had been directed to fly a precise route falling into line over Richmond, then in single file to Hagerstown, and directly in to Muncie. As each plane landed, it was described by an announcer and flagged into the parking area.

Twenty-one aviators took part in the event. Among the participants were listed Lieutenant Clyde Shockley, L. I. "Cap" Aretz of Kokomo and Sidney A. Stout of Indianapolis, all of whom would become important figures in the history of Indiana aviation. A giant Martin bomber also flew in from Langley Field

near Washington. It had a wing span of sixty feet and was a feature of the event. The bomber was too large to fit in the hangar, so it was planned to be placed outside under police guard for the night. (This time, not with Boy Scouts, however!) John R. Drumm and John A. Collins with Technical Sergeant Ross Cooper as mechanic were the flight crew for the Martin. In charge of the plane and the events of the day was Lieutenant Commander P. M. Bates of the United States Navy.

The pilots' various types of demonstrations, included individual exhibits of flying skills. A Lieutenant C. A. Moffat from McComb Field, Dayton, thrilled the crowd with his high-powered pursuit plane capable of flying at a top speed of 190 miles-per-hour (MPH).

Another feature was the arrival of a Ford Tri-Motor plane carrying a load of passengers, and a

Lindbergh (left) ready to depart in his "Spirit of St. Louis" from Roosevelt Field, New York, Paris, May 20, 1927 at 7:52 A.M. He landed at La Bourget Field about 10:00 P.M. Paris time (5:00 P.M. New York time) on May 21, officially 33-1/2 hours.

© Wide World Photos

© Underwood

Lindbergh with his Ryan Monoplane "Spirit of St. Louis," 1927, before solo flight across the Atlantic to Paris.

reporter from an Evansville newspaper. The Tri-Motor was powered by three Wright Whirlwind engines totalling 1,400 horse power.

Brigadier General William G. Everson of Muncie, Commander of the 76th Infantry Brigade, gave the principal address, pointing out the need of Muncie citizens to cooperate in promoting aeronautical activities in Muncie. He asked his audience to remember only ten years previously, when the automobile was in its early stages of development, and to think ahead for another ten years concerning the development of the airplane. Actually, it would be another seventeen eventful years before the airport north of Muncie would be dedicated and finally become Muncie's official municipal airport.

The potential advantages of flight did not escape the attention of local law enforcement, either. A rather innovative scheme was reported on April 7, 1926, when Ernie Bashem, then chief pilot of Muncie Airport, joined the Delaware County law enforcement body after being appointed as Deputy Sheriff by Sheriff Harry McCawley. Tom Inlow, an Army aviator "capable of soaring to heights of heaven in an airplane," was also named a "high-flying deputy." The deputies would be equipped with hand grenades as a means of coping with miscreants attempting to escape the town in high powered motor cars. The Sheriff stated that with this arrangement, a complete circle of Muncie could be made in fifteen minutes. The airborne deputies could spot speeding criminals from the air using high powered glasses, and then drop grenades on the fleeing cars. The traffic in

those days was limited and a large car speeding out of Muncie could easily be identified and apprehended.

Sheriff McCawley viewed this scheme as having great potential and looked forward to his first flight to become accustomed to air travel should his official duties require such action.

On Monday, July 16, 1928, an organization named the Muncie Air Service Company was formed by a group of Anderson investors. It assumed control of the hangar, two airplanes, and all the equipment at the Wall Field formerly belonging to Muncie Aerial Company which had gone into receivership. The Muncie Aerial Company was organized in 1925 when it assumed the operation of the South Hackley Street facility.

The Muncie Air Service Company, which also planned to operate an aviation school and provide inter-city passenger service, employed Harry L. White, a World War I-trained pilot who had been in charge of the field under the ownership of the failed company. The new company also entertained high hopes for the development of air mail services, encouraged by a visit of Mr. A. P. Talliferro, aviation expert from the Aeronautical Section of the Department of Commerce in Washington, D.C.

On the same day, South Bend reported celebrating the commencement of air service from South Bend-LaPorte on a Chicago-Michigan route serving Kalamazoo.

Lindbergh's solo flight over the Atlantic in 1927 created a wave of curiosity and excitement about aviation and its future. Then a junior in college, I was mildly interested.

The Last Event at Wall Field
and
The Dedication of Silver Fox Airport

September 1929

ON SEPTEMBER 12, 1929, Munsonians received the news that the old airport, Wall Field on South Hackley Street, would be closed—but not before it had one final party.

Frank N. Reed, Chairman of the Chamber of Commerce Airport Committee, had spent a day in Indianapolis completing the arrangements. Almost simultaneously, Munsonians learned that work on an air field would be started as soon as crops had been harvested on the Ault farm north of Muncie which Abbott Johnson, Muncie businessman and aviation enthusiast, had purchased and donated to the city. The City Council had appropriated $10,000 to be used on the airport and a tax would provide approximately $6,000 of additional income. The city administration at the time, led by Mayor George Dale, refused to move ahead on the airport matter and so Johnson had his land returned. In spite of this setback, many aviation enthusiasts in Muncie continued to plan for a future which included a municipal airport.

Lester Bush, Secretary of the Muncie Chamber of Commerce, announced on September 29th that arrangements had been made for a flight of twenty to twenty-five planes making a circuit of the state to fly over Muncie. It would plan to land on old Wall Field.

Muncie would have its first opportunity to see a large fleet of planes flying overhead in formation. Included in the formation would be two of Ford Motor Company's Tri-Motor, six-passenger aircraft. By the time it reached Muncie, the caravan had grown to fifty-five planes flown by experienced pilots who were thoroughly briefed as to landing procedures and parking arrangements in order to handle that large number of arriving aircraft. There were plans for a reception when the caravan arrived.

The formation flew over the city so that school children could see them without being dismissed from their studies for any length of time. Frank Allen, superintendent of Muncie schools, had requested this arrangement so that the children would be in no danger of landing aircraft at the airport. Large crowds of spectators assembled at the field and the police prepared for any difficulty in keeping citizens and children away from the runways.

Fred Wertz, always the entrepreneur, using the public interest stimulated by the Wall Field Event, on the 29th organized the dedication of his Silver Fox Airport near Yorktown on Highway 67. There would be balloon-bursting contests, dead-stick landings, stunt flying, races, wing-walking, and a parachute jump made by Pat Blancett, a stunt man from Winchester. The Collins Boys Band would give a concert and all sorts of activities were planned which would draw a large crowd.

The first plane arriving was flown by C. F. Carter and D. E. Berger of Danville, Illinois, and piloting the second to land was Mike Murphy, then of Lafayette. (Murphy later rose to the rank of colonel in World War II. After the war, he was employed to head up Marathon Oil's Aviation Division located in Lima, Ohio.)

Mike, a well-known stunt flyer, put his Cub plane, hangared at the Muncie Airport, through a series of stunts to entertain the crowd. An opportunity was given to inspect a new United States Army observation plane flown by Captain J. H. Dulligan, instructor for the 38th Aviation Division.

Harry McClain and Harry White, two of the Silver Fox's pilots, flying in Travel Airs, won first and second place, respectively, in the balloon-bursting contest. (Balloons were of the children's small display type, rubber balloons filled with gas and released from the ground.) Planes were maneuvered so as to hit the elusive targets with their props, a real test of piloting skill.

Planes flew in from as far away as Cleveland, Cincinnati, Joliet, Illinois, and various places in Indiana. It was customary in those early days of promoting aviation for pilots to attend and participate from places far away from the site of the exhibition.

In spite of the closing of Wall Field, the opening of Silver Fox Airport and the confusion as to whether Abbott Johnson's gift to the city would actually be developed as an airport, Muncie's interest in aviation continued at a high level.

At its meeting on March 14, 1930, the Muncie Chamber of Commerce's Aviation Committee and its ten members unanimously declared that Muncie and Delaware County needed a municipal airport if it expected to keep pace with surrounding counties. A. F. Youngberg, a Chicago Airport Engineer employed by the newly-appointed Muncie Aviation Commission, presented general plans for the development of the field and stated that it was an ideal site. Subsequently, the Commission proposed to issue

© The Muncie Star

Muncie group meeting first interstate passengers on Continental Airways ship to Columbus, Ohio, and return at Wall Field, February 12, 1931. Aircraft a seven-passenger Ryan Monoplane flown by "Sad" Sam Jones, pilot, and Pete Williams, Co-pilot. Pictured (left to right) Frank N. Reed, F. D. Rose, Mrs. F. D. Rose, Lester C. Bush, Abbott L. Johnson, Mayor Jack Edwards of Marion, Mrs. George R. Dale, Mayor George R. Dale, Victor C. Hutzel, Frank A. Hanley, Dr. Howard E. Hill, and Paul C. Stubbs.

$125,000 of bonds for the development of the real estate which Abbott Johnson previously had given to the City.

On March 5th, the *Muncie Morning Star* reported a heated discussion at which Abbott Johnson defended his gift to the City and elaborated on Muncie's need for an airport. Johnson's opponents made strong arguments against the airport idea. Two Councilmen, one understandably opposed, being Fred Wertz, owner of the Silver Fox Airport, and Robert Tumelson "on behalf of the people" spoke vociferously against the development of the Johnson property. The opponents would eventually prevail.

In spite of the confusion about airports, in February of 1931, Muncie was placed on a Continental Airways route using Wall Field. Planes were to stop here daily en route between Chicago and Columbus, Ohio. Arrangements were made by President Anderson of the Chamber of Commerce and General Manager Mann of Continental Airlines based on authority that had been granted by the Aeronautics Division of the Department of Commerce. Daily service would be provided to and from Chicago and Columbus and intermediate points connecting with Trans-Continental-Western Airlines for Pittsburgh, Philadelphia, New York, St. Louis, Tulsa, and Los Angeles.

On February 9th, the *Muncie Evening Press* reported that, by using proposed schedules, passengers might travel from Muncie to New York in six hours and connections could be made there for west-bound through Chicago, Omaha, and Salt Lake City to arrive in San Francisco the following day. Chairman Reed was also negotiating for the inclusion of Air Mail as well as passenger and cargo services being available in Muncie.

Muncie's Airport, Wall Field, would be used as the local facility. On February 12th, Sam (Sad Sam) Jones, the manager of Wall Field, would handle ticket sales. Seven-passenger Ryan Monoplanes would be used. Mr. Bush, Secretary of the Chamber of Commerce, and Frank Reed, Chairman of the Chamber's Aviation Committee, were the first passengers, flown by Jones as pilot and Pete Williams, co-pilot. The flight to Chicago lasted two hours and five minutes because of headwinds. The return flight lasted one hour and thirty-seven minutes with a stop in Kokomo to confer with Clyde Shockley, the airport's General Manager.

On the weekend June 30, 1931, Muncie hosted a State Air Tour. Thirty planes participated from all across Indiana. The Indiana Aircraft Trades Association sponsored the event. The planes landed at Wall Field which had been officially closed in 1929. Participants were entertained at a banquet at the Roberts Hotel. Walker Winslow, president of the Association, gave a short talk at the banquet supporting the need for a municipal airport for Muncie and praised Abbott Johnson for his generosity and foresight in donating the land to the City. Frank Hanley was toast master at the meeting and Mayor George Dale welcomed the members of the tour and invited them to return.

In spite of the Mayor's offer of hospitality, his administration later declined to proceed with the field's development. It would be left to private individuals to assume responsibility and complete the project in 1932.

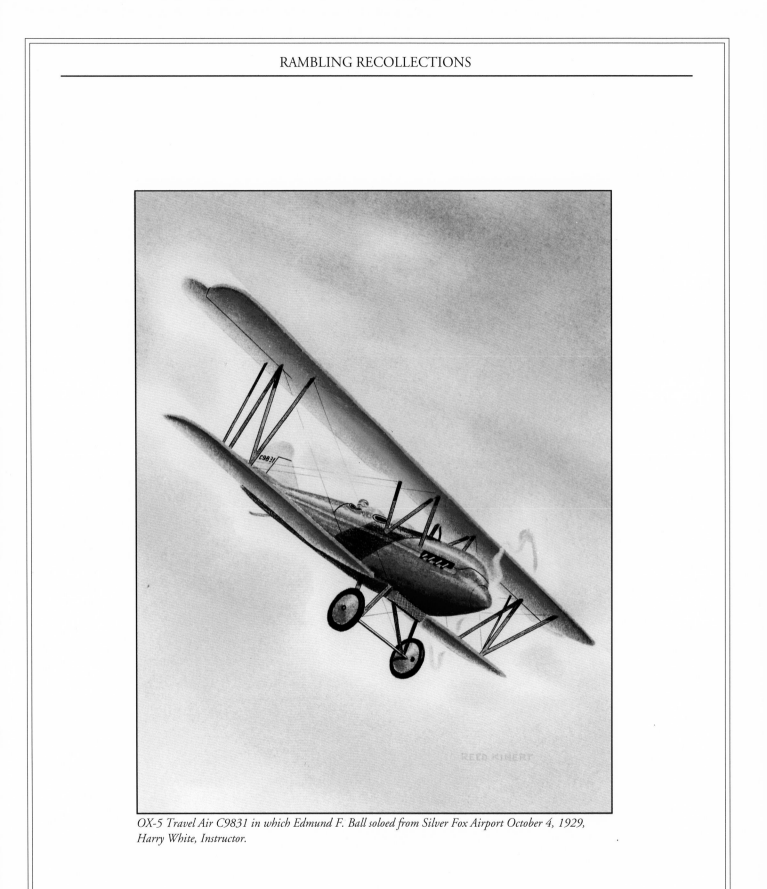

OX-5 Travel Air C9831 in which Edmund F. Ball soloed from Silver Fox Airport October 4, 1929, Harry White, Instructor.

The Silver Fox Airport

1927-1936

SOMETIME in 1928, Fred Wertz, a Muncie business entrepreneur with interests in several unusual enterprises, including a company called "Gay Games" which made tip books, a somewhat dubious motel on the banks of the White River half way between Muncie and Yorktown, and a silver fox farm south of Highway 67 with adjacent land available, decided to go into the aviation business. He bought a couple of OX-5 Travel Air open cockpit bi-planes, hired Harry White as pilot-instructor, built a hangar, and opened an airport. Located on Pershing Road off Highway 67, the airport was named the Silver Fox Flying Service and offered sight-seeing rides, air transportation, and flight instruction. Guy Noel, who managed several of Wertz' enterprises, was named manager. I knew them only by name before I started my own flying career.

In mid–1929, out of curiosity, I stopped by the Silver Fox Airport just to look around. Guy Noel spotted me and introduced me to Harry White. Both Noel and White were good salesmen. The result was an appointment with Dr. Karl Brown, long-time Civil Aeronautics Medical Examiner, for my first of many succeeding years of physical examinations. I was issued a Student Pilot's Permit and bought a helmet and goggles, without realizing at the time that I was embarked on a lifetime avocation in aviation.

My next trip a day or two later to the airport resulted in my first lesson. Unfortunately, the precise date is missing as are all of my student records which were lost in the demise of the Silver Fox Flying Service and School.

Shortly after beginning my instructions, longtime friend Abbott Johnson and I discovered each other engaged surreptitiously in this dangerous and considered by some the foolhardy business of learning to fly. To prevent the rumor spreading that we might have lost our sanity, we swore each other to secrecy until we had earned our licenses, or had come to our senses and given up the whole idea.

My first log book actually begins with an entry on October 9, 1929, when, after an early morning telephone call from Harry White that he considered I was ready, the weather was perfect, and if I came to the airport promptly I would solo!

Quietly and a bit nervously, I slipped out of the house before breakfast, drove to the airport, and climbed into the cockpit of an OX-5 powered Travel Air C-9831. After a few last minute instructions, and an explanation of the maneuvers chosen for me, Harry spun the prop, the engine caught and it was too late to change my mind. As I taxied out to the runway, that front seat looked mighty empty as I checked the mags and prepared for take-off.

It was a perfect day, a one-hour-and-eleven minute thrilling experience by myself in the air and I was hooked!

I had only logged two hours and nineteen minutes of solo time after my initial flight when Harry White and his student Paul Karleen were tragically killed in the same airplane in which I had soloed just eleven days before. The cause of the crash was never definitely determined.

Harry L. White

Pilot and Instructor

Harry White, Instructor, Silver Fox Air Lines, Yorktown, Indiana, soloed Edmund F. Ball October 7, 1929, in this plane, NC9831, an OX-5, 90 HP liquid cooled, three place, open cockpit Travel Air. White lost his life in this plane as did student Paul Karleen, Jr. October 18, 1929.

HARRY L. WHITE enlisted as a mechanic in the Army Air Corps in World War I and later was sent to Flight School for his pilot's rating. Prior to coming to Muncie, he had worked for the Orin Welch Aircraft Company in Anderson before being transferred to Muncie and placed in charge of Wall Field.

White was a proponent of safety. His contention was that airplanes were equally safe, or safer, than automobiles if operated by competent pilots who flew cautiously. He had a reputation for carefully instructing his students on air traffic rules and, under no circumstances, to attempt maneuvers in which they had not been thoroughly instructed.

He instructed Abbott Johnson and accompanied him on a trip to Akron, Ohio, where Abbott purchased a new airplane, a Warner engine-powered Bird. At the time, Abbott was President of the short-lived Muncie Aviation Commission; Frank A. Hanley,

President of Hanley Auto Sales, another of Harry's students, served as the Commission's vice president. All who flew with or were instructed by Harry White considered him to be an excellent instructor as well as a competent pilot.

He was always concerned for his students' safety.

It was because of his concern for the safety of his students that he flew with Paul Karleen, Jr. on October 18, 1929. There was a strong cross wind blowing and he felt that student Karleen might not be up to handling the plane safely under those conditions.

An article in the *Muncie Evening Press* Thursday, July 26, 1929, written by Jim Kimbrough, tells about Harry White, his adventures and experiences before coming to Muncie, and his efforts to advance aviation and safer flying.

White began his career as an aviator in 1924 when, as the author said, the world was just beginning to feel the impetus given to flying by World War I.

His first solo flight was made from an "island" in West Virginia where he said a landing shortly after takeoff would force the flyer to choose a spot between the Ohio River and the mountains of West Virginia.

White had experienced a forced landing or two, as was normal in those days, but had only one serious accident in which his injuries were not serious. It occurred in Muncie as White, with two passengers, was landing at the old Hackley Street Airport (Wall Field) when some children ran out on the field and caused Harry to make a violent side slip maneuver to avoid them. He stated that he was glad that he had experienced this wreck since it brought forcefully to his attention the necessity for care and safety at all times. He thought that civilian flying was coming as surely as the automobile. He told all of his students his experiences, some caused by carelessness, so that they would not make the same mistakes. He hoped that by benefiting from his experiences their flying record would be safer and better than his.

From the newspaper report:

"Harry L. White, 38, Chief Pilot at the Silver Fox Airport, and his student Paul Karleen, Jr. were killed when the airplane in which they were flying crashed and burned on the Mort Carpenter farm five miles west of Muncie on the River Road. It appeared that White had been killed instantly on impact, but that Karleen, although fatally burned, survived the wreck but died that evening at the hospital. In the meantime he was conscious and coherent enough to say that the motor cut out when they were about fifty feet above ground, that everything had been going smoothly until then, and that 'we just got a bad break. We had to make a forced landing and when we hit, she caught fire. I got out, then I started back after Harry, but someone took me away.'"

Bill Osburn, mechanic at the field, said that the airplane was in good condition. He had helped White and Karleen roll it out of the hangar, fuel it with twenty gallons of gasoline and "prop the engine to get it started" with Harry then at the controls.

After it had warmed up a bit, Harry moved to the front cockpit, the instructor's seat, with Karleen in the rear. They took off at 11:00 A.M. as logged by Guy Noel, Field Manager.

Witnesses reported that about 12:00 noon they saw the plane flying unusually low and "when it fell, it went straight down, not landing on its nose" (pancaked). The wings collapsed, the gasoline tank was ruptured and burst into flames as the fuel poured over the hot engine.

It was noted that the ignition switch, which was located in the rear cockpit, was in the off position indicating that Karleen had sufficient presence of mind to do as he had been instructed, that is, turn off the switch in case of an impending crash to reduce the danger of fire.

Now, almost seven decades later, it is futile to speculate as to the cause of the accident, but my analysis would be that it was not because the student pilot "froze on the controls," as was sometimes used in an instructor-student related accident where there seemed to be no other apparent cause.

Ironically, there was an article in the same newspaper reporting the accident quoting Charles Lindbergh, "the silent man of the air," as saying that "safer airplanes were coming soon and that the forced landing is doomed and soon would be a thing of the past."

Lindbergh had just come back from an inspection flight for Pan American Airways, visiting twenty-one countries around the Caribbean, and predicted that in five years "airplanes simply won't land when you don't want them to." And, they'll be able to take off in fog in New York and land in fog in Chicago and that radio would help to improve safety immensely.

It is sad to think that Harry White, student Paul Karleen, and so many others in those early days of flying did not live to see Lindbergh's predictions materialize.

White's accident was a tragic and untimely ending of a likeable, highly respected and competent pilot and for his student, devastating to their respective families, and a blow to the advancement of aviation in Muncie.

Abbott Johnson, Frank Hanley, and one or two other of White's students, and I, served as Harry's pall bearers for his funeral and burial at the Mount Pleasant Cemetery north of Daleville.

The shock of this accident and the thought that I had soloed in this same plane only eleven days previously seriously threatened my interest in continuing flying.

This tragedy ended my flying until March 9, 1930, when I could no longer resist the urge to fly again. I went to Indianapolis where I took three hours of flying with Bob Shank in his Travel Air C-9831 from his airport located close to the Speedway. Bob was credited with having been the first Air Mail Pilot in the United States back sometime in the early 1920s.

He operated his airport for many years before yielding to the enticements of real estate developers, sometime in the mid–1950s.

Shank's partner and Number 1 Instructor was Ned Bottoms, a perfectionist. Nothing but perfect was good enough for him. His admonition was, "Your first mistake can be your last."

Those Were the Days!

Early in 1920, the United States Air Mail Service issued a set of rules and instructions for pilots to follow in the regular operation of their aircraft. Through the rules sound almost ludicrous in contemporary terms, they were taken quite seriously by Post Office Department pilots, and others, who realized that deviation from carefully established procedures could be a rather serious matter on the transcontinental air mail route.

Don't take the machine in the air unless you are satisfied that it will fly.

Never leave the ground with the motor leaking. Don't turn sharply when taxiing. Instead of turning short, have someone lift the tail around.

Never get out of the machine with the motor running unless the pilot relieving you can reach the engine controls.

Pilots should carry hankies in a handy position to wipe off goggles.

Riding on the steps, wings or tail of a machine is prohibited.

In case the engine fails on take-off, land straight ahead regardless of obstacles.

No machine must taxi faster than a man can walk.

Do not trust altitude instruments.

If you see another machine near you, get out of its way.

Before you begin a landing glide, see that no machines are under you.

Hedge-hopping will not be tolerated.

No spins on back or tail slides will be indulged in as they unnecessarily strain the machine.

Pilots will not wear spurs while flying.

If an emergency occurs while flying, land as soon as you can.

One other rule established a priority system that delighted the schedule-bound air mail pilot: Pilots landing with mail should have the right of way over all others.

From Air Mail, an illustrated History 1793–1981,
by Donald B. Holmes, 1981.
The American Philatelist

Abbott L. Johnson

ABBOTT L. JOHNSON had started his flight instruction lessons at the Silver Fox Airport some time before I had and accumulated enough hours to qualify for his pilot's license before Harry White's fatal accident. Anticipating his solo, with White's help and advice, Abbott had purchased a beautiful new Bruner-Windle Model Bird B, three-place open cockpit bi-plane, license NC80F powered by a Kinner 90 HP engine, air speed 120 MPH. It was the envy of all of us. He planned to use it for traveling on business trips for the Warner Gear Company, with which he was then associated.

Abbott, with Harry, landed in a cleared place on the land Abbott had purchased to give to the city which was being prepared for an airport, appropriately the first plane to do so. He soloed that same day off the Silver Fox Airport witnessed by his wife and a group of friends.

Abbott flew his plane one weekend to Northport, Michigan, where he had a summer cottage. Unfortunately for the airplane and Abbott's active participation in aviation as a pilot, he neglected to turn on the gasoline when he took off for a brief sight-seeing trip around the area, the result being an extremely short flight which ended in some trees at the end of the runway. Fortunately Abbott was not injured, but the plane was badly damaged.

This accident terminated his career in aviation as a pilot. However, it did not diminish his interest in aviation. A couple of years previously, he had purchased the one square mile Ault farm north of Muncie, now the location of the present Muncie–

Abbott Johnson Collection, courtesy of Joan Johnson Douglass
Invoice for purchase, price $5,376.50, May 3, 1930.

Delaware County airport. In the first administration of John C. Hampton, Abbott had given the property to the city of Muncie to be developed as an airport, but with the provision that it was to be returned to him if not used for that purpose.

A photograph of Muncie's first and only Aviation Commission, appointed by Mayor Hampton to develop the airfield, was shown in the Friday, September 9, 1930, edition of the *Muncie Star*. A bond issue of $125,000 was to be appropriated to provide money for its construction, first supported but later vetoed by Mayor George Dale and the Commission abolished. The membership of this first Commission included Abbott L. Johnson, Chairman

Frank A. Hanley, Vice Chairman Victor Hutzel, Joseph Broderick, and former City Clerk Maynel Dalby.

The city fathers, feeling that there were much more important uses for taxpayers money in those Depression days than constructing an airport, had failed to develop the property. Abbott requested and was successful in having the property returned to him.

When the new airport was ready for business under the ownership of Muncie Airport, Incorporated, the County organized an Aviation Commission, of which Abbott served effectively as Chairman for many years.

Minnetrista Cultural Foundation, Incorporated. Gift of Abbott Johnson
Abbott Johnson with his newly acquired Kinner Bird Aircraft, advertising Warner Gear Company. Johnson's intention was to use this airplane for transportation on Warner Gear business as well as for personal trips.

My License and Another Tragedy

© *Smithsonian Institute photo number 92-15637*

After loss of OX-5 Silver Fox Airport in Harry White's fatal accident, Fred Wertz replaced it with a 90 HP Warner Engine powered GAC Cadet high-wing monoplane and employed Paul Peters as pilot and instructor. Edmund F. Ball soloed the plane on May 1, 1930, and flew it for his private pilots license test on June 10, 1930, License number P14861, issued July 16, 1930.

WHILE White's accident had shaken me considerably, the flying bug had bitten deeply. When Fred Wertz reopened the Silver Fox Airport with a sleek looking Warner 90 horsepowered GAC Cadet high wing monoplane to replace the destroyed Travel Air and employed a new instructor, Paul Peters, I couldn't resist the urge to fly. On May 1, 1930, I first recorded soloing GAC Cadet NC49OK.

I flew Bob Shank's OX-5 Travel Air in Indianapolis a few more hours, but then stayed with Silver Fox's GAC Cadet until I had logged eight hours and fifty-five minutes. On June 20, 1930, in a forty-minute flight, I earned my Private Pilot's License, P14861. The Department of Commercial Aeronautics Branch Examiner Joe Shumate was convinced that I could fly well enough to qualify. By that time, with an estimated fourteen hours of dual instruction and fifteen hours and fifteen minutes solo, I had accumulated a grand total of twenty-nine hours and fifteen minutes. My license was not actually issued from Washington until July 6, thus cheating me out of almost a month's seniority as a licensed pilot. Interspersed with short flights in a Kinner powered Fleet aircraft, an OX-5 Travel Air and an Inland Sport, I mostly flew the Cadet 490K.

Edmund F. Ball's first airplane purchased from Clyde Shockley, May 3, 1931. It was a Waco Model F, three-place open cockpit plane powered by a Kinner 125HP engine, cruising speed (advertised) 110 MPH. It was sold June 19, 1932, and replaced by a Waco A, later described.

Once again, my flying career might well have ended as the result of another fatal accident.

Paul Peters, age 24, was a likeable, competent pilot holding a transport and an instructor's license, but had a youthful tendency to show off at times. Some of us "hangar flyers" thought Peters was a bit reckless. He and a student, Kenneth Helms, 22, were killed on February 10, 1932, and the Cadet de-molished when they failed to recover from a spin before striking the ground and crashing on the airport as newspapers reported:

"WHEN THE MONOPLANE GOES INTO SPIRALING DIVE AT 1,000 FEET ALTITUDE, flying from its base on Silver Fox Airport."

Courtesy of Edmund F. Ball

Edmund F. Ball's first private pilot's license number 14861 issued July 16, 1930, by United States Department of Commerce, Aeronautics Branch, signed by Joe F. Shumate, Inspector, authorized by Clarence M. Young, Assistant Secretary of Commerce.

Courtesy of Edmund F. Ball

Federal Communications Commission Aircraft Radio Operator's License required by all pilots using a radio. Edmund F. Ball made a special trip to Chicago to take the examination.

Peters was reported to have taken the plane aloft to test a new set of spark plugs. Whether Helms was simply a passenger or a student at the time was not clear.

A single witness said the engine had not failed before the accident, that Peters had battled the plane to gain control until the ship crashed on the airport killing both persons.

At that time, recovery from a spin was a qualifying maneuver in order to obtain a license. (My qualifying spins and recoveries were done in the OX-5 Travel Air.) It was always practiced at a fairly high altitude in order to have plenty of space in which to make a recovery—"engine to idle, nose down to regain speed, and hard opposite rudder." I have a recollection that the GAC cadet had a reputation for slow recovery from a spin. Obviously in this case there had not been sufficient altitude before it struck the ground.

It was a sad blow to the young men's families and a fatal one to Fred Wertz' Silver Fox Flying Service.

These were the fourth fatalities within a few months in the process of flight instruction in Muncie, yet another reminder that flying could be hazardous. Was it worth the risk? Another dilemma.

Clyde Shockley, "The Flying Farmer from Kokomo," persuaded me to buy my own plane. On May 3, 1931, he sold me a beautiful, little, red Waco F Bi-Plane NC11252 powered by a Kinner B-5 120 HP engine, the latest and safest plane on the market! I kept it at Wall Field.

After that second fatal accident at Silver Fox Airport, the field closed all operations. I had moved to Wall Field. It was so conveniently close to the Ball factory, that I could slip over there at lunch time and after work in the evening to "Hangar Fly" or maybe take a short hop in my plane. The land north of town which had been reacquired from the city was available for use, but had no facilities for service, parking and hangaring. We flew there occasionally to practice landings and take-offs.

Muncie Aviation Corporation and Muncie Airport Incorporated

Subscription of Shares of Capital Stock
Muncie Aviation Corporation

The undersigned, for value received, hereby severally subscribe and agree to pay $100.00 per share for the number of shares set opposite their respective names of the no par value capital stock of Muncie Aviation Corporation, a corporation, to be organized under the laws of the State of Indiana, with an authorized capital stock of one thousand (1,000) shares without par or nominal value, said shares of stock to be issued by said corporation for such an amount of consideration as the board of directors of said corporation may deem best, which said consideration may be paid in whole or in part, in money, in other property, tangible or intangible, or in labor actually performed for, or services actually rendered to the corporation, all as may be fixed and determined by the board of directors, and all of said capital stock when issued to be fully paid and non-assessable.

Subscriptions for said shares of stock shall be paid to the treasurer of the corporation at such time or times, in such installments or calls and upon such terms as shall be determined by the board of directors.

Dated at Muncie, Indiana, this 9th day of March, 1932.

MUNCIE AVIATION CORPORATION was organized on April 14, 1932. My Waco F as a demonstrator, Clyde Shockley's Model F Waco for general use, a Ford Model T truck, a desk, and two wooden file cabinets which he brought with him from Kokomo comprised its total net tangible assets.

Clyde had been persuaded to come to Muncie and join my cousin, Frank E. Ball, and me as major stockholders, and eight others to found Muncie Aviation Corporation. The original incorporators holding one share each were: James E. Kennedy, Andrew W. Rose, Lester M. Milligan, Victor C. Hutzel, Karl S. Thornberg, Frank N. Reed, Frank E. Hanley, and Abbott L. Johnson. Frank and I held twenty-six shares each and Clyde Shockley, forty shares.

Just prior to the organization, Frank and I purchased from Abbott the land he had reacquired.

Frank and I also jointly built and paid for the original hangar, which, along with the land became the first fixed, tangible assets owned by Muncie Airport, Incorporated. We were the only shareholders in this corporation, owning equal numbers of shares.

Several things needed to be done on the field to make it qualify as a fully operational airport. Riggin's Ditch, running through the field, needed to be replaced with a buried cement culvert the full length of the field east to west large enough to take care of flood waters. It was built by WPA labor and provided much-needed jobs during the Depression in the early 1930s. Only the north half of the field was originally used as an airport. The other half was planted in soybeans which became the airport's principal source of income for several years since, its only tenant, Muncie Aviation Corporation, was often slow and poor pay.

The Dedication of Muncie's New Municipal Airport

Muncie Airport original hangar, 1932, Waco Aircraft Distributor.

AN ARTICLE appearing in the *Muncie Morning Star* September 9, 1932, reported that Frank E. Ball spoke at the Altrusa Club. The Club was presided over by President Mrs. Edmund B. (Bertha) Ball (my mother). He was introduced by Mrs. Harriet Johnson (an insurance company executive).

Frank spoke of the development of airplanes and suggested that it might have come about much earlier had not, in the fifteenth century, the artist, sculptor, scientist, and inventor Leonardo da Vinci's assistant tried to fly his experimental aircraft too soon, resulting in his death. This accident discouraged the multi-talented Leonardo from further experimentation with

flying devices, thus perhaps setting back aircraft development several centuries.

He reminded the audience that imaginative flight by human beings and gods were recorded in both Greek and Roman legends and mythologies.

He pointed out that rapid development had taken place following World War I. He presented figures showing substantial increases in passenger, mail and cargo transportation by air with a comparatively small number of deaths from accidents.

The meeting was closed by an invitation from Frank A. Hanley, a director of Muncie Aviation Corporation and General Chairman of the dedications who outlined the program and urged attendance at this interesting and important event planned for the weekend. Members of the Club were invited to attend the dedication of the new Muncie Airport.

Headlines in the *Muncie Morning Star* that same day were "Stunt Flying Exhibition to Open Program, Dedication of Muncie Airport Would Start Next Day" (Saturday).

The event was expected to attract hundreds of visitors to Muncie. It would be the first major air show to be given in eastern Indiana and would provide memorable and thrilling experiences to the expected crowd.

Dick Young, test pilot of Waco Aircraft, from Troy, Ohio, would open the event with "an exhibition of fancy flying" at 11:30 A.M.

There would be a parade of aircraft over the city. Air races and formations of eighteen Army planes from Dayton would fly formations. There would be dead-stick landing contests, parachute spot landing contests and demonstrations of an auto gyro aircraft-not a helicopter.

President Lemuel Pittinger of Ball State University would give the principal address, to be followed by brief remarks from representatives of the municipal administration and of the Aviation Corporation.

A large number of pilots were expected to fly in a number of aircraft of many different types.

Bus services were available from the Delaware County Courthouse to the airfield and parking space provided for automobiles. There would be aircraft rides from dawn to dusk and the Goodyear Blimp would also be offering rides throughout the day.

Visiting pilots would be put up at the Roberts Hotel with a dinner-dance planned for the evening.

Frank A. Hanley, General Chairman, said that all committees had planned their various responsibilities in detail with the hopes of making this an outstanding event with everything working out perfectly.

The Program Committee was: Clyde E. Shockley, Airport Manager; Frank E. Ball, President Muncie Aviation Corporation; and Edmund F. Ball, Vice President, Muncie Aviation Corporation.

R. H. Pelham Photo
Muncie Airport hangar with paved ramp. Muncie Aviation Corporation, a Beechcraft Distributor, 1938.

Lester Bush, Secretary of the Muncie Chamber of Commerce, served as Secretary.

Lester Milligan, appropriately, was in charge of entertainment; L. S. Gantor, in charge of traffic; Ray Applegate, publicity; James Kennedy, finance; Andrew Rose, reception and registration; Frank Reed, transportation.

The *Muncie Evening Press* carried similar reports featuring a front-page picture of the new hangar and of Frank E. Ball, President; Edmund F. Ball, Vice President; and Clyde E. Shockley, Chief Pilot and General Manager of Muncie Aviation Corporation and Muncie Airport, Incorporated. A tabloid edition also appeared with the issue containing pictures and stories about various events, participants and types of aircraft that would be involved. It stated plans had been in progress for several months and that it most certainly would be the greatest air show that Muncie

had ever seen. There would be a special race for aircraft powered by OX-5 World War I government surplus engines around pylons about a mile apart, the same as in national air race shows. There would be Pony Express races using aircraft instead of ponies. Pilots would be tested for skills as they landed to pick up the "mail" for the next leg of the race.

Major James Doolittle, holder of the world's speed record of 296 miles-per-hour, was expected to attend.

The Muncie Airport was officially opened and dedicated on Saturday, September 10, 1932. We spread the word around the industry that free gasoline and free parking would be offered and that there would be a banquet at the Hotel Roberts one night for the participants.

We expected perhaps twenty, maybe at the most thirty, airplanes to show up. But the pilots and their

Muncie Aviation Corporation

Registration platform at the dedication. At the right, Arthur Meeks. From right to left, unidentified; 3rd, Dave Meeks; Andy Rose; at far right at microphone, probably Jimmy Fiddler; next, unidentified. Seated below, left to right: Mary Bostwick reporter from the Indianapolis Star, *who was an avid reporter on all major aviation events in Indiana; unidentified; 3rd, Pete Williams; 4th, Edmund F. Ball, 5th, Frank Hanley; 6th, Clyde Shockley.*

airplanes came from all over Indiana, from Ohio, Illinois, from Michigan and Wisconsin. There were National Guard planes from Fort Benjamin Harrison and Mars Hill (Schoen Field) in Indianapolis and Army Air Corps planes from Wright–Patterson Field in Dayton. The pilots flew formations over the field before landing and their planes were open for inspection by the public. The United States Navy "Hell Divers" gave exhibitions of bombing tactics.

Darwin Andrews (in booth) was the civilian in charge of public relations at Wright–Patterson Air Base in Dayton, Ohio, during World War II. Left to right, seated in front of booth, unidentified, Joe Stipp, Chief of Police, and Edmund F. Ball.

A Goodyear blimp from Akron showed up and did a capacity business hauling passengers at the southeast corner of the airport.

There were exhibitions of dead stick landings; contests with engines cut off over the field within gliding distance of the field; prizes were given for pilots' coming to a complete stop next to a circle in the middle of the field. Then there was aerial bombing with paper bags filled with flour. When the bags hit the ground, they would, of course, burst with a spectacular display of a plume of flour rising into the air and the points where the "bomb" hit were measured from the center of the target. The pilots did aerobatics, and five-minute rides over the airport were available at $2 per person. There was stunt flying, air races by vintage OX-5's, formation flying and demonstrations of various types of aircraft. The aircraft ranged from small low wing speeders to luxurious cabin planes. Powell Crosley, Jr., President of Crosley Radio Corporation, was departing Cincinnati in his twin amphibian when an emergency call that his father was seriously ill caused him to cancel his flight.

Major Jimmy Doolittle, holder of the world's speed record, was scheduled to attend but forced to cancel. Jimmy Haizlip, an equally famous flyer, holder of the world's transcontinental speed record of ten hours and eighteen minutes averaging 240 MPH, was dispatched by Shell Oil to take the other "Jimmy's" place. Haizlip was equally famous as Doolittle at the time. He had soloed in 1917, trained with the French during World War I, and devoted his entire life to aviation. It was said: "No one had done more to advance aviation in the last ten years than Haizlip." His wife was also a competent pilot.

Probably the most memorable event was the first airplane ride of the "100-year old lady." We had persuaded Dick Young, test pilot of Waco Aircraft, to dress up like a little, old lady, complete with black dress, sunbonnet and apron. Clyde Shockley was to be her pilot. "She" was helped into the front seat of the open cockpit aircraft with great care and considerable conversation over the loudspeaker by the announcer. "Her" goggles were placed carefully under her sunbonnet. Just as Clyde was beginning to taxi out to take off, a messenger ran out to the plane and advised that he had an emergency telephone call at the announcer's booth. Jimmy Fiddler, the announcer, played it up most realistically. Clyde got out of the pilot's seat in the rear cockpit, leaving the engine idling, and trotted towards the stand. Slowly at first and then with the engine revving up more rapidly, the aircraft began to move, apparently without a pilot. Clyde assumed great alarm and tried to run out to catch the moving aircraft, but, of course, was unable to get there in time. The "little, old lady" had apparently hit the throttle and the aircraft was moving and the announcer said that he feared that something terrible, he was afraid, was going to happen. The aircraft, as it gained speed, went careening across the field, first on one wheel and then the other, bouncing, turning and straightening out briefly and finally becoming airborne. Fiddler, the announcer, played up the scene on the mike calling for rescue crews, an ambulance to stand by and trying to persuade a pilot to volunteer to go up in another aircraft and see if he could transfer into the out of control airplane and bring both it and "the little old lady" safely back to earth. After a few erratic movements, wide skidding turns, dangerous to any but a skillful pilot, the aircraft turned back across the field at a low altitude, and headed directly for the grandstand which was being frantically evacuated by the alarmed spectators.

Fortunately, no one was injured as the plane roared over the almost empty stand, clearing it by fifteen or twenty feet. After a few spectacular maneuvers, the plane landed first on one wheel and then another, taxied up in front of the slowly refilling grandstand to the applause of a still somewhat confused but thoroughly thrilled audience.

Later, Dick Young (the "little, old lady") was introduced to the crowd to loud applause and a few friendly fist shakings at having been at the same time fooled, frightened but entertained by a skillful bit of flying demonstrating how *not* to do it. Today he would likely be greeted by infuriated Federal Aviation authorities and a few lawyers looking for damage claims from the frightened spectators.

Marjorie Kitselman, a sixteen-year old, received her pilot's license September 16, 1932. She was thought to be the youngest licensed pilot in Indiana

Marjorie Kitselman, youngest female pilot in Indiana, daughter of Mr. and Mrs. A. L. Kitselman, standing in front of Waco F open cockpit training plane at airport dedication, 1932.

and the Muncie Airport's first student. She was the daughter of Mr. and Mrs. A. L. Kitselman, her father one of three brothers, founders of the Kitselman Brothers Manufacturing Company.

Her parents did not know about their daughter's having learned to fly until it was announced at the airport dedication and that she would take a plane aloft to demonstrate the thoroughness of her training. This announcement about Marjorie was the first time that Mr. and Mrs. Kitselman were aware of their daughter's interest in aviation and they were delighted to learn of this exciting news.

Much to the consternation of the sheriff's department and local residents trying to get home, traffic was backed up on North Walnut Street halfway south of the bridge almost to the county courthouse.

Amidst all the confusion, Mary Helen Sullivan, Clyde Shockley's wonderful Girl Friday, who did everything from keeping the books to answering telephones, handling correspondence, and keeping creditors reasonably assured of payment, came to me with the exciting information that our woefully inadequate toilet facilities had overflowed and there was about an inch of effluent all over the floor of the hangar.

The next day, newspapers were expansive in reporting the number of planes and pilots performing before a crowd estimated in the thousands.

Andy Rose, Chairman of the Registration Committee, recorded 158 pilots by late afternoon with more still coming.

At the banquet that evening, an eloquent but somewhat lengthy and poorly informed Judge was the principal speaker, extolling the accomplishments of that intrepid aviator Charles "Lind*en*bergh" for flying solo across the Atlantic to Paris.

But putting it all together, Muncie Airport was without question duly, officially dedicated, without a single accident, and memorably embarked on its now sixty and over years of service to Muncie and East Central Indiana.

Courtesy of William E. Moffitt
Mary Helen Sullivan

From time to time over the years, several tee hangars housing individual aircraft were added as required. The heating system was changed from the original coal fired boiler in the hangar to gas heaters. Shops were added on the west side of the hangar. A parachute packing loft was added overhead. Several tee hangars were replaced by larger hangars to accommodate larger private and corporate aircraft. A large pole-barn type hangar was built to the north; then a hangar was added to the east using the space previously occupied by classrooms and office for service department offices and modest overnight facilities for transient pilots. Finally, the large hangar near the terminal and control tower was built to house the Aircraft Distributors organization in conformance with government and Piper Aircraft legal requirements. (This is the hangar now occupied by Ball Corporation.)

In the meantime, a little building, located where the parking lot for the Administration and restaurant building now stands, called the "Spin Inn," served home cooked food to employees, transients, local

Muncie Aviation Corporation
Seated left to right: Bill Mueller, W. T. Piper, Clyde Shockley, Howard Gregory. First row, left to right: W. C. Smith, Lou Dominico, Ed McCready, Gene Netzley, Ralph Graham, Felix Jackson, Bob Hudgens, Paul Rupprecht. Second row, left to right: Lloyd Brown, Walt Carr, Edd Pyland, Dan Mueller, April 16, 1964.

pilots and visitors. It was the locale for many hours of "hangar flying." The "Spin Inn" was the forerunner of today's Vince's Gallery.

All of the above were accomplished with funds internally generated and from private sources at no cost to the taxpayers.

First a small asphalt SE/NW runway was built with private funds. After the County Aviation Commission purchased land for airport improvements and expansion with funds from the Federal Aviation development funds, it was eventually replaced by an asphalt 6,500' x 150' Runway 32/14 and crossway Runway 20/02, 5,000' x 100' with adjacent taxi strips.

The terminal building was added in 1957 and the control tower in 1963. Instrument landing systems and field lighting were installed to FAA specifications.

Delaware County Airport holds a United States Department of Transportation, Federal Aviation Administration Airport Operating Certificate for a General Aviation Airport. Facilities include: a Control Tower, full Instrument Approach Systems, Aircraft Rescue and Fire Fighting Equipment with over 2,500 Air Carrier Operations per year qualifying it as a Commercial Airport.

It is Muncie's, Delaware County's and East Central Indiana's principal airport and a favorite stop for transients flyers and casual visitors.

For the original boundary lights, Ball Wide-Mouth Mason Fruit Jars were used, screwed into threads in specially made iron castings which housed the bulb socket. The seal against moisture was attained by using an ordinary Ball rubber fruit jar sealing gasket. These served quite adequately for a number of years. The cost of replacements was about twenty-five cents each. New lights required now by FAA for field approved for night operations cost several hundred dollars each.

The airport beacon is still operating on the abandoned airways beacon tower which Shockley bought for the cost of removal.

The next major important event was reported in the *Muncie Evening Press* on April 29, 1970. It was the dedication of the new 9,000 square foot administration building and transit pilot lounge of Muncie Aviation Company. The building cost $250,000. It would also house the Flight Deck restaurant as well as other facilities, a far cry from the minimal buildings that had housed the company's operations since 1932.

John W. Fisher, President of Muncie Aviation, reminded the persons attending the dedication ceremonies that the company had started with a working capital of $10,000 and equipment. He commented that Clyde Shockley, who was the first manager, brought with him from Kokomo an ancient pickup truck, a desk, some small wooden filing cabinets and a dream. Shockley was one of the original ten incorporators of the firm. Fisher said that the payroll now was more than $1,500,000 annually and a similar amount was spent to pay taxes, carry inventories, and other costs of doing business.

William T. Piper, Jr., President and Chief Executive Officer of Piper Aircraft Corporation, flew to Muncie for the ceremony, in a new Piper pressurized, twin-engine 7-9 passenger Navajo. It was the first public showing of the aircraft in the United States. Piper stated that public aviation handles much more passenger traffic than is generally realized. He said airlines serve only major cities and about ninety percent of the passengers are served in less than one hundred airports in the nation. He went on to say that air-taxi, general aviation, charter and feeder airlines are the "collecting agencies" at smaller airports delivering passengers to the larger airports for cross-country flight.

Larry Hirschinger, Vice President of Muncie Aviation, remarked that "talk about crowded airways is a myth. There is room for all of us in the air. Most traffic delays around the major airports are caused by airline scheduling."

Hirschinger went on to remark that during the recent "sick-in" of the air controllers of major airports, it was proven that general aviation doesn't need all the fancy equipment. We (MAC) flew passengers to small airports within a ten minute taxi ride of O'Hare in Chicago and landed without delay.

Edmund F. Ball, Chairman of the Board of Muncie Aviation and the only surviving member of the original group of stockholders, was on hand to greet Mr. Piper and reminisce with him about "Mr. Piper and his Cubs."

A Visit by Chuck Yeager

MAC—A Fifty Year Distributor of Piper Aircraft

© *The Muncie Star*

General Chuck Yeager, representing Piper Aircraft Corporation, with Edmund F. Ball, Chairman of the Board of Muncie Aviation Company on the occasion recognizing 50 years of dealership relationship.

ON WEDNESDAY, July 25, 1986, officials from the Piper Aircraft Company visited Muncie to present a plaque in recognition of the half century of Muncie Aviation Company's[1] association with Piper as a distributor, during which time it had been successful in selling hundreds of Piper aircraft amounting to several million dollars.

To add memorable interest to the occasion, Chuck Yeager, the retired Air Force Brigadier General, was a featured guest at the ceremony. He had been trained as a fighter pilot during World War II, became responsible for testing of aircraft saving the lives of countless United States Air Force pilots as he worked out aircraft engineering and construction flaws in new types of aircraft. He was the first to break the sound barrier on October 14, 1947, and was, of course, the inspiration for the best seller, *The Right Stuff.* He was a fascinating visitor who left lasting memories in the history of Muncie Airport.

To meet him, and exchange stories for the first time, was like meeting an old friend—easy to talk to seriously or joking. No wonder he is such a popular celebrity.

Yeager's entertaining book, *Yeager, An Auto-biography,* personally autographed, sold like hot cakes on a cold day.

Flying Piper's new Cheyenne IV for demonstrations, he returned to Washington, D.C., establishing a world's record for fastest flight of a piston driven engine aircraft over this particular route. Good publicity!

[1]*Formerly Muncie Aviation Corporation until becoming a division of Minnetrista Corporation.*

Dedication of Johnson Field

Gala scene at dedication of Johnson Field ceremony.

© The Muncie Star
Abbott Johnson receives a plaque from Vice President Nixon on which the names of the County Aviation Commissioners is engraved.

THURSDAY, September 30, 1958, was a gala day in the history of aviation in Muncie, Delaware County, and East Central Indiana.

It was the culmination of years of effort to provide the community with a top-level airport and air transport services.

The weather blessed the occasion with clear skies, brilliant sunshine and a brisk, cool breeze. The field would be named Johnson Field after Abbott L. Johnson, long-time moving spirit in the advancement of aviation. Appropriately so, because it was the result of Abbott's vision in 1929 when he had purchased the site as the best location for an airport and given it to the City with the one proviso, that it be developed as an airport or returned to him. The Depression of the

Minnetrista Cultural Foundation, Incorporated. Gift of Abbott Johnson
Abbott Johnson with Rear Admiral Ernest P. Forestall, Commander of the 9th Naval Base at Great Lakes, Illinois.

© *The Muncie Star*
Vice President Nixon at microphone. Seated left to right, Mrs. Pat Nixon, Congressman Ralph Harvey, Mrs. Harvey, Abbott Johnson, Mrs. Betty Johnson, and Gwinn Hicks, President of Lake Central Airlines.

Minnetrista Cultural Foundation, Incorporated. Gift of Abbott Johnson
Vice President Nixon presents American flag which flew over the Capitol building to Abbott Johnson.

1930s and a negative vote from the City Council had smothered possibilities for public funds, and the property had been returned to Johnson. With private financing, principally from Frank E. Ball and myself, but with others in support, and limited public funds as they became available over the years, this splendid facility had finally emerged.

All through those difficult years, Abbott Johnson had played a dogged leadership role as Chairman of the Delaware County Board of Aviation Commissioners. It was timely and fitting that the field should memorialize his name.

Elaborate preparations were made for the dedication. Vice President Richard M. Nixon, who had been urged to attend by Congressman Ralph Harvey, was the principal speaker.

A large crowd of several thousand people attended, many arriving before noon to find a desirable location to view the events.

The chartered Lake Central plane carrying the Vice President, his charming wife, Pat, and accompanying passengers, circled the field a couple of times, landed and taxied close to the reviewing stand. Mayor Arthur Tuhey and Mrs. Inah Lambert, President of the Delaware County Commissioners, met and escorted the Vice President and his wife to the stand to the tune of "Back Home Again in Indiana" played by the Ball State Teacher's College Band. Abbott greeted them on the platform.

Dr. Lewis Gishler, pastor of First Presbyterian Church, gave the invocation. Johnson spoke of incidents relating to the field's history and persons responsible for the airfield. Dick Jennings, President of the Chamber of Commerce, introduced those seated on the platform and called on Congressman Harvey to introduce the Vice President.

Nixon spoke for about fifteen minutes, complimented the Board of Commissioners, congratulated the community on the opening of its fine commercial airport, and elaborated on its importance to the community.

At the conclusion of his comments, the plaque carrying the names of those principally responsible for the field was presented to Johnson by the Vice President along with an American flag that had flown over the Capitol.

Burnham Holmes, Vice President Ball Corporation, and Chairman of the Chamber of Commerce Aviation Committee with Commander Tom Quillman, at Johnson Field dedication September 30, 1958.

Accompanying the Vice President was Rear Admiral Ernest P. Forrestal, Commander of the Ninth Naval District at Great Lakes, Illinois, and Commander Tom Quillmann, a close friend of Johnson's.

The Nixons lived up to all the past publicity as they returned to the plane for departure, graciously shaking hands with all they could reach and signing autographs.

It was a proud day for Abbott Johnson and a memorable one for the community.

Resolution Determining Official Name of Delaware County Airport to be Johnson Field

Abbott L. Johnson has actively promoted and lend every major effort to bring scheduled airline service to Muncie and Delaware County, and for thirty years, has been a member of all official bodies formulated to advance such efforts.

In 1928, Mr. Johnson was appointed chairman of the first Aviation Committee of the Muncie Chamber of Commerce, which was created to promote aviation in the county, and during the year 1929, qualified for the first private pilot's license issued to a resident of this county. During the years 1928 and 1929, Mr. Johnson served on Muncie's Inter-Club Aviation Committee and participated as a pilot in the second all-Indiana air tour during the year 1930. During these same years, Mr. Johnson promoted the organization of a commercial airline between St. Louis and Cleveland, which was to serve this community. Such service was premature, and gave the way to the Columbus–St. Louis section of the initial air-rail transcontinental route.

On June 14, 1929, Mr. Johnson was appointed president of the first Aviation Commission of the City of Muncie, by John C. Hampton, then Mayor of said city. In 1943, Mr. Johnson was appointed a member of the Tri-City Aviation Commission, Which was created to build an airfield to serve the cities of Muncie, New Castle, and Anderson. He served as a member and president of said Tri-City Aviation Commission until 1947, when said Commission was dissolved. Thereupon, the Twin-City Aviation Commission was organized to establish commercial aviation facilities for the Cities of Muncie and Anderson. Mr. Johnson served as a member and president of the Twin-City Aviation Commission during its entire existence.

Mr. Johnson has been a member and president of the Delaware County Aviation Commission since its creation in 1955. In such capacities, he has supplied the leadership that has been so essential in obtaining the necessary funds, acquiring the property and in successfully promotion the construction of an adequate public airport, and in obtaining scheduled airline service for this county.

In all of his official capacities in advancing commercial aviation for this community, Mr. Johnson has unselfishly given of his time and substance without thought of personal reward. As the goal of his interest, efforts and persistence of thirty years is soon to be realized by the inauguration of scheduled airline service to this county, we declare that the field that has been created for such purpose should be named in his honor.

IT IS, THEREFORE, RESOLVED BY THE BOARD OF COMMISSIONERS OF DELAWARE COUNTY, INDIANA, That the Delaware County Airport be, and the same shall be hereafter, named Johnson Field.

Passed this 25th day of July, 1958.

BOARD OF COMMISSIONERS OF DELAWARE COUNTY, INDIANA

Clyde E. Shockley

CLYDE E. SHOCKLEY was a pioneer in the history of Indiana aviation. He was born in Kokomo, Indiana, in 1897 and became known as "Mr. Aviation" and as a "one kind of guy, respected all over the country."

Lawrence ("Cap") Aretz, later of Lafayette, a World War I pilot and member of the National Guard, whose biography is included later in these *Ramblings*, soloed Clyde in Kokomo in 1921. Clyde was briefly a Lieutenant in the Indiana National Guard. He sold his farm in 1926 and started his own small airport near Kokomo from which he gained his reputation as a pilot, nicknamed "The Flying Farmer."

He told me, ruefully, of how his career as a farmer and a pilot almost ended when in 1924 he flew his recently acquired Canuck World War I OX-5 powered "Jenny" home to show his bride Ruth, and landed in a field close to the house. Taking off, their brood sow ran in front of the plane; he hit it, killed it, and wrecked his airplane. The accident almost ended his career both as a farmer and an aviator.

Clyde was a very quiet but determined and persuasive person. He became well-known for his piloting skills and his success as an aircraft salesman throughout the state. As a publicity stunt for the Indiana State Fair, for example, he flew low around the Indianapolis Monument Circle, landed at the State Fair Grounds and was promptly arrested by the local sheriff for exceeding the speed limit around the circle.

In these early years of the Muncie Aviation Corporation, cash was a very important commodity and hard to come by. Clyde would take off barnstorming in southern Indiana, around Nashville, in Brown County, and come home with enough cash to make the payroll and pay the fuel bill. I went with him a time or two, flying my Waco F, but very quickly

decided that for $2 a ride, I was not cut out to be a barnstormer.

One of his favorite places was in the hills of Tennessee where he went barnstorming when cash was badly needed. He might spend a week or ten days at a time, then return with a substantial roll mostly of dollar bills which he had accumulated by giving sightseeing rides for $2 per ride. Once he brought back with him two handsome, young men, Garland Park and Clyde Havens, who were willing to work to learn to fly in lieu of pay. Both worked on the line at Muncie Airport for enough time to learn to fly and

Courtesy of the family of Clyde E. Shockley
Clyde E. Shockley, July 13, 1897–December 2, 1973, the "Flying Farmer," "Mr. Aviation." Co-founder of Muncie Aviation Corporation and Muncie Airport, Incorporated, the "Consummate Salesman" and one of Indiana's premier pioneer pilots.

Courtesy of Muncie Aviation Corporation and the family of Clyde E. Shockley
Clyde and Ruth Shockley with Clyde's first airplane, World War I Canuck, powered by OX-5 engine, JN4D, "Jenny," 1924.

fact, Clyde had parachuted and had watched his plane crash and burn as he floated down, landing safely in a cornfield. Somewhat to his amazement, he determined that he was unhurt, and trudged back to the Country Club carrying his parachute while I, with others, continued to search for him in vain. As one of his partners in the aviation business, and by then a close friend, I cannot describe my relief when I returned to the Country Club to find him sitting in the locker room, drinking a cold beer.

This was the demise of unlucky Waco F-2 N11487, a beautiful airplane—fun to fly but with a sad ending. Its damaged engine, with one cylinder cross-sectioned so the working of the pistons, valves and connecting rods could be seen, was used for several years in the Muncie Aviation Corporation's pilot training and mechanics school to teach the operations of a radial aircraft engine.

earn their licenses. Both men eventually won jobs on airlines and became long-time career airline pilots. Clyde Havens flew for Pan American Airlines. Mysteriously and tragically, on his last flight to the Pacific Islands, on departure after take-off, turning on course, Clyde's aircraft apparently lost power and crashed into the ocean. All on board perished.

From Frank Ball's airplane, Waco F-2, on July 4, 1935, Clyde Shockley became a member of the "Caterpillar Club," an exclusive organization of pilots who have parachuted safely to ground from a distressed aircraft. It happened in this fashion: Clyde had contracted with the Delaware Country Club to fly the 4th of July aerial fireworks display over the Club. Presumably a "safe" system of fireworks was attached to the wings and struts of the airplane which could be ignited from the cockpit. The result was intended to be a spectacular display of trailing fireworks and smoke as the plane looped and rolled and turned overhead.

It turned out to be entirely too spectacular. A firing malfunction resulted in a strut and large section of the right wing being blown off. The plane crashed and burned in a nearby cornfield. In the darkness, it was not possible to see whether or not Clyde had successfully ejected. Clyde seldom wore a parachute, so it was impossible to know whether he was safe. In

Courtesy of Muncie Aviation Corporation and the family of Clyde E. Shockley
Clyde Shockley, 1929

40

MR. SHOCKLEY, THE AVIATOR!

CLYDE SHOCKLEY, manager of the Muncie airport, is alive today because he is a flier capable of manning an airplane with an iron nerve. He added to his reputation as a pilot Thursday night by the way he maneuvered his airplane after it had caught fire while he was entertaining members of the Delaware Country Club with an aerial display of fireworks. One wing was torn off his ship by the premature discharge of the pyro-technics but it apparently did not unnerve him. He leveled his plane as best he could and then leaped to safety with the aid of a parachute. As he floated down to earth he watched his ship spiral in a blazing mass into territory far distant from any of the thousands of people who sat in automobiles parked on roads in the vicinity to share the Fourth of July thrills he had arranged for the entertainment of the Country Club members. While searchers were scouring the clubhouse and whispered to a few of his close friends that his ship caught fire.

Shockley came to Muncie three years ago as the manager of the Muncie airport when it was dedicated. He is probably one of the best known pilots operating in Indiana and his intimate friends say he has had more hours in the air in six months of this year than he has experienced in any like period. While his accident added chills to the thrills he had already furnished the countryside, he proved himself competent. He is to be complimented for his ability to serve a world that is becoming air-minded. The Muncie airport is fortunate in having such a man in its organization.

Editorial from the Muncie Morning Star,
July 5, 1935

Clyde and Ruth Shockley (left) posing before a Waco Cabin plane circa 1935. Shockley (below) demonstrating by reflection his tradition of excellent maintenance.

R. H. Pelham Photo

Courtesy of the family of Clyde E. Shockley

Clyde moved to Muncie in 1932 when he joined us in the formation of Muncie Aviation Corporation, of which he was appointed Manager and given a forty percent stock interest. He brought with him his Waco F airplane, a Model T Ford pickup truck and two wooden file cabinets which, along with my Waco F he had recently sold me, became the first and only fixed assets of the new company formed on March 9, 1932.

Muncie Airport, Incorporated was the sister company which owned the land and buildings (hangar) which Clyde managed but held no stock interest.

He managed these operations for thirty years, building a reputation from coast to coast for operating clean, well maintained facilities, and providing good and friendly service to all who came. Even today, the reputation which he created remains a tradition and hallmark of Muncie Aviation's operations.

When Jimmy Haizlip, holder of many international speed records, representing Shell Gasoline Company, visited Muncie on February 24, 1933, he praised the Airport and spoke highly of Clyde Shockley, the Manager. He said, "Whenever we think of aviation in Indiana, we think of Clyde Shockley."

Clyde believed that anyone could learn to fly. He was an expert instructor, approaching each student with that philosophy.

Clyde Shockley with Paul Rupprecht and a Commanche 400 at Muncie Airport in the 1960s. Rupprecht was a protege of Clyde's, a great salesman and fine pilot. He deserves a separate biography in this book, but it was not available. He is referred to briefly in Alaska 2nd Trip Number II in Volume II.

A Hunting Incident in Canada

1958

CLYDE AND his friend Loren Yohey from Muncie experienced an unexpected end to a moose hunting trip in Canada. They had flown from the little community of Chapleau, near Sudbury, Northern Ontario, to an island in Wabus Lake where, on the first day, they bagged a moose, dressed it out and butchered it. They planned to fly back to Chapleau and advise the White River Flying Service that their hunt had been successful and to pick up the meat which was too heavy for their small plane to carry.

Clyde and Loren had left Muncie at the end of September, 1958, in a Piper Cub equipped with pontoons, flown to Chapleau, picked up supplies and camping equipment, and arrived on the island on October 2nd.

After the successful hunt, they taxied across the lake from the camp to head into the wind for take-off.

As Clyde described it, just as they reached takeoff speed, a freak gust of wind struck them sideways, suddenly tipping the aircraft so that the left wing and pontoon caught in the water. The plane cartwheeled and overturned. Clyde and Loren were unhurt and were able to escape from the cabin and cling to the overturned pontoons. Shockley could not swim and Yohey was not a strong enough swimmer to tow Clyde ashore. Clyde hung tightly to the pontoon and was reluctant to let go. Yohey swam ashore, found a log he could float out to Clyde so that he could paddle into shallow water and wade safely ashore.

They decided it was too far to swim back to camp or paddle a log that far. So with food and shelter in sight but out of reach, they set out to make the best of a bad situation.

They had planned a week's hunting trip. They would not be missed for several days. With a lake full of fresh water, they wouldn't die of thirst, but, otherwise, everything else was either in the back of the plane where they could not reach it or, by that time, on the bottom of the lake. A small pocket knife was their only tool—their entire survival kit.

They built a lean-to shelter out of branches and made mattresses from evergreen boughs. They brewed a tea from some leaves, boiled some roots and bulbs from plants in a tin can.

Though their clothes eventually dried out, they had no other means of keeping warm and there was nothing for them to do but to settle down and wait for a search and rescue. Then, the weather turned foul.

They said that they heard planes flying in the area, but none came close enough to see them. Clyde and Loren were stranded.

Continuing their search for food, they came across a supply of nuts stored by a squirrel for the winter. The squirrel wound up in short supply, needless to say.

They found a few berries, tried to hit a squirrel and a rabbit with stones, but neither of them were big league pitchers and always missed by a mile. Clyde said that by the third day, they were amazed that they had lost their hunger pangs and survived without too much difficulty on water and their brew of leaves and roots.

On their seventh day in their wilderness, they found a muskrat in a trap and prepared for the first meat in a week. They had just tasted the first bite when a plane came in sight. It was flown by a friend, Gil Wells from Gaylord, Michigan, who spotted the overturned aircraft in the water and, at first seeing no survivors, imagined the worst. Gil had planned to join his friends at Chapleau but when he arrived there and not finding them as expected, set out to search. Fortunately, he spotted them on the shore, wildly waving their arms to attract his attention. He returned to Chapleau and arranged for a rescue plane to pick them up. The search and rescue plane retrieved the two with no harm or damage, only a few pounds lighter and very tired from loss of sleep. The greatest permanent loss was their camping equipment, guns and the moose meat.

Clyde, the consummate salesman, was able to sell the submerged aircraft "where is and how is." The ingenious recovery of the aircraft by the purchaser is another story, but was, nevertheless, completely successful. After righting it, drying out the electrical equipment and replacing the battery, he flew the plane off the lake to another destination with no problem. This experience was another Shockley saga.

Shockley and the Sikorsky S-39 Amphibian

LATE IN 1933, Shockley, always the salesman, took a Sikorsky S-39 Amphibian in on a trade. I was both amused and concerned. What in the world would we do in Muncie, Indiana, with a lumbering, old, monstrosity like that? You could not argue very much with Clyde. He would just clam up, maybe mumble a few words about fishing trips, and go on with his business.

Clyde flew a few prospective passengers around, but mostly the plane just sat in the hangar. He convinced me it was simple to fly, checked me out on it at the airport, and I flew it briefly, mostly as a novelty. One thing about the plane was its consistency: it took off at 80 MPH, cruised at 80 MPH, and landed at 80 MPH. The wheels were lowered or raised for land or water operations by use of a hand pump operated by working a lever vigorously back and forth. Flying in the all metal cabin-boat combination was like sitting inside a sheet iron shed in a hurricane: you conversed by shouts and hand signals only.

The Sikorsky was powered by a Wasp Jr., which I believe was rated at 350 HP.

In landing this monster, the procedure consisted of flying fairly close to the point at which a landing was intended, either on a field or at the end of the runway at around 300 feet, point the nose straight down, throttle back the engine and at about ten feet above the ground, close the throttle, pull back heavily on the elevators, make a final check to be sure that the

A Sikorsky Amphibian airplane such as Clyde Shockley and Edmund F. Ball flew to Lake Wawasee for a water landing lesson.

wheels were down, shut your eyes, and wait for a crash! If you did all that correctly, the result was usually a surprisingly good landing.

A couple of times I flew it to Troy, Ohio, with Andy Rose and perhaps Dave Meeks as passengers to show it off to some of my friends at Waco Aircraft.

One weekend Clyde persuaded me to fly the Sikorsky up to Lake Wawasee with him to check out on water landings. This, of course, was long before the development of Prairie Creek in Muncie and Lake Wawasee was the closest water available. I flew the left seat with Clyde in the right as instructor. We had pumped up the wheels in proper position for a landing on the water and Clyde instructed me down to a fairly decent first attempt at a splash landing. He thought I ought to make another one which seemed reasonable, so I immediately gave it full throttle, took off and circled around this time for an unassisted landing. This time, though, was a near disaster! The plane started skipping across the water like a flat stone, but each skip seemed to toss it higher into the air and into a more precarious attitude, approaching a stall. The landing was aborted and Clyde suggested we trade positions and he would show me how to do it. I was happy to comply so Clyde and I exchanged seats. He made an approach very similar to mine and touched down onto the water, which resulted in the same antics as my attempt, only his bounces seemed higher and more alarming. He gave it full throttle to gain flying speed and aborted the attempt. We looked at each other, shrugged our shoulders and, without a word, headed south for Muncie. That was my first, last and only attempt to land an amphibious aircraft, and I think it was the same for Clyde.

Clyde, still the ultimate salesman, immediately went to work to convert this expensive plaything into a money-making operation. He employed a young man by the name of Kenneth Jackson, who wanted to get enough flying time and earn enough money to pay for his air transport license to qualify for a job on an airline. He worked the Sikorsky all summer at Wawasee, flying sight-seeing passengers at something like $10 apiece for a ten-minute ride. He usually had a full load of five passengers on each flight during weekends. In five hours of flying each day, he was taking in about $3,000 per weekend. He split his "take" with Muncie Aviation Corporation on a 50-50 basis—not too bad a deal on a $3,500 investment.

Jackson later went to work for United Airlines and became its chief competency check pilot for all of its pilots.

Clyde worked out the same arrangement with a young man by the name of Bob Bolyard who flew the plane for two summers, again at Wawasee, with the same terms. Bob understandably became bored with the repetition of take-offs, short flights and landings, so after two summers he gave it up. By that time he had enough money stashed away to pay for his air transport pilot license, got a job with American Airlines and flew as a Captain for many years. At retirement, Bob was one of its very senior captains with flights logged to the far corners of the world, and thousands of hours of accident-free flight time recorded.

Clyde finally sold the Sikorsky for about what he had paid for it, having earned a very good profit on the investment during its three years of service.

Again the consummate salesman, Clyde had a knack for turning what might seem to be a very bad deal into a very good one.

Clyde never quite recovered from the loss of his son, John E. Shockley, an experienced World War II pilot who died in a plane crash in 1954. John was flight testing a new plane in Dayton, Ohio, at the time. The cause of the accident was never satisfactorily determined.

Clyde Shockley died on December 5, 1973, survived by his wife, Ruth, two daughters, seven grandchildren, five great-grandchildren, and a place of honor in the annals of aviation pioneers.

Frank E. Ball

Courtesy of Muncie Aviation Corporation and Edmund F. Ball
Frank E. Ball, March 26, 1903–May 28, 1936, at Muncie Aviation Corporation hangar with his new Waco C cabin plane.

MY COUSIN, Frank E. Ball, and I had grown up together. We were neighbors. We did many things together. He was a few months older than I and often took the lead in some of our ventures, but my interest in aviation preceded his.

After I got my pilot's license in 1930 and purchased an airplane, he was not long to follow.

Clyde Shockley was his instructor. As soon as Frank qualified for his pilot's license, Clyde sold him an airplane—a Waco F-2—a bit larger and a bit faster than mine. Frank enjoyed flying, I think, as much as I did. He flew on long adventuresome trips before I felt I was experienced enough to undertake them.

We flew on many short trips together, participated in state air tours, flew to Florida to attend air meets, were charter members of the Sportsman Pilots Association, the AOPA and various trade associations. Frank was elected president of the Indiana Aircraft Trade Association. He was an emerging figure of significance in the business world, in the Masonic fraternity, in community affairs and aviation.

On a business trip, May 28, 1936, he flew to Toledo, Ohio; Wheeling, West Virginia; and Lancaster, Ohio. He landed at Findlay, Ohio, to make a telephone call to conclude a business matter affecting the entire glass container industry.

He took off for the short ninety miles or so flight to Muncie. He was flying his newly acquired Waco cabin plane, the latest model in the industry. I had flown it with my wife, Isabel, and another couple to South Bend the week before.

Shortly after Frank took off, a faultily designed wing fitting failed and the wing collapsed. Unmanageable, the aircraft simply fell out of the sky, crashed and burned. Frank was instantly killed.

It was my sad duty to drive to Findlay that night to confirm the identity of my long-time friend and associate in so many things, including our venture in aviation.

The third fatality in seven short, eventful years, of people I had known and in aircraft which I had flown.

The first was an OX-5 Travel Air in which I soloed only eleven days before it crashed with my instructor and his student. The second was the aircraft in which I qualified for my pilot's license, a GAC Cadet, which crashed killing the instructor and his student, three months after my qualifying flight. Now the third plane I had flown quite recently crashed. All were tragic, but this last one, because of our lifetime association was most serious and difficult to rationalize; devastating.

At first I suffered an emotional reaction bordering on guilt. If I had not permitted myself to become so involved in this hazardous business of flying, if I had not encouraged Frank to join me, if I had not . . . and so on and so on.

Many of my friends and associates were certain that I would give up this dangerous business and devote my time and what talents and abilities I had to more conventional, less dangerous undertakings.

I wrestled with a decision for several weeks, but gradually—finally I made the decision to continue. I felt it was my responsibility to take over as best I could the things in which Frank had participated. I had a very positive feeling that he would want me to do so. He was an adventuresome pioneer in an exciting and rapidly growing new industry that would change the course of the world. As pioneer adventurers and explorers before had faced dangers, sailed unknown seas, explored the outbacks of civilization, Frank had lost his life pioneering the vast frontiers of space.

Frank leads my list of pioneer pilots I have known.

I'm grateful to my family, my wife, Isabel, my mother, my sisters and others who supported me and encouraged me to continue my interest in the aviation industry, and as a pilot, now for well on to seven decades.

CHAPTER II

EARLY
EXPERIENCES

$\mathcal{M}$Y parents,
Edmund B. Ball and Bertha Crosley Ball,
had early fascinations for aviation and were
pioneer passengers.

Edmund Burke Ball
October 24, 1853–March 8, 1925

Mrs. Bertha Crosley Ball
February 11, 1875–October 7, 1957

Courtesy of Edmund F. Ball

My First Flight

Daytona Beach, Florida–1914

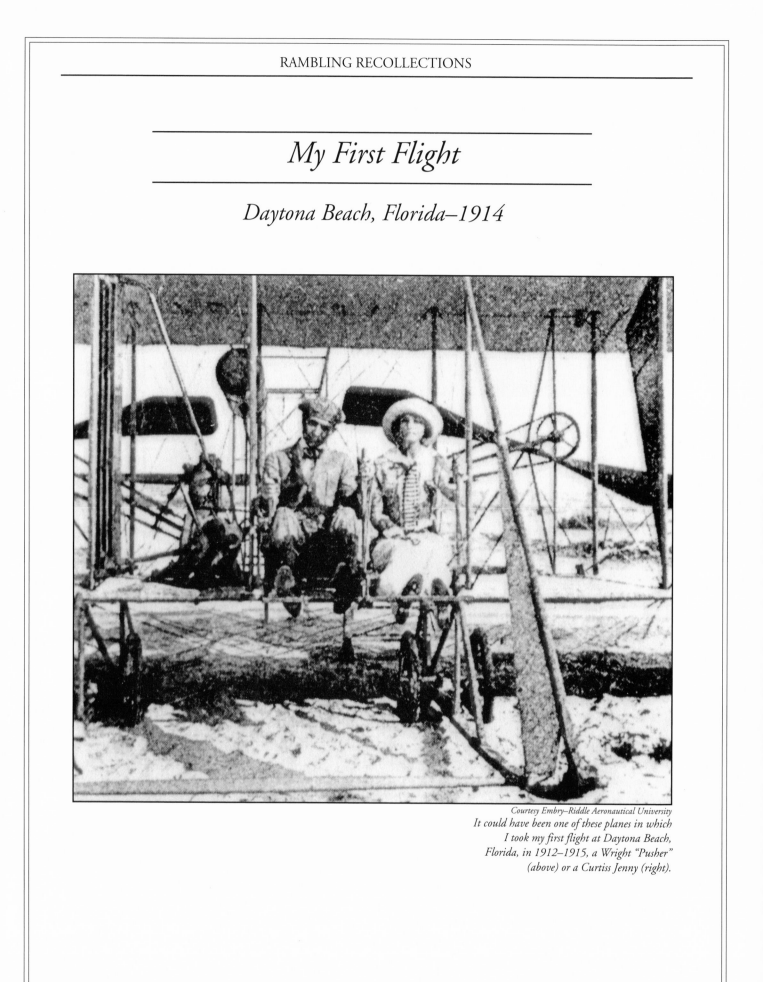

Courtesy Embry–Riddle Aeronautical University
It could have been one of these planes in which
I took my first flight at Daytona Beach,
Florida, in 1912–1915, a Wright "Pusher"
(above) or a Curtiss Jenny (right).

MY FIRST recollection of a flight was off the beach at Daytona Beach, Florida, somewhere around 1912 to 1915. After they had safely flown, my father and mother sent me off alone, strapped to a seat in an open plane without cowling or windscreen—only goggles. I wish I could remember the plane and type of aircraft, but I cannot. I'm guessing that it might have been one of those pictured herewith, courtesy of the Daytona Beach Historical Society. I cannot imagine, however, that it was quite as primitive as the one pictured of a Wright Pusher. Probably more likely a bit more advanced airplane, but still back in the "stone age" as far as aviation and aircraft is concerned.

Courtesy of Halifax Historical Society

Across the English Channel

1925

Ball Aerospace Collection, School of Aeronautics and Astronautics, Purdue University
A Fokker tri-motor aircraft such as Mother, Mrs. Bertha C. Ball,
sisters Adelia and Janice and I flew the Channel from Croydon
Field, London, to Amsterdam in 1925.

Ball Aerospace Collection, School of Aeronautics and Astronautics,
Purdue University
A Fokker pilot cockpit arrangement.

AFTER OUR father died in 1925, Mother took us three children—my sisters Adelia (Diggie) (Mrs. Robert M. Morris), Janice (Mrs. John W. Fisher) and me—to Europe, by boat of course. There were no overseas flights until many years later, but we did fly in one of the earlier commercial flights across the English Channel from London to Amsterdam in a KLM Fokker airplane. Passengers were seated in comfortable wicker chairs much like those in the illustrations.

Ball Aerospace Collection, School of Aeronautics and Astronautics, Purdue University
A Fokker F-5 passenger seating arrangement such as I remember.

Ball Aerospace Collection, School of Aeronautics and Astronautics, Purdue University
Interiors of aircraft (above) carrying passengers circa 1925 were designed for passenger confidence and comfort, using familiar sitting room type chairs for seats and lightweight materials, usually wicker.

Ball Aerospace Collection, School of Aeronautics and Astronautics, Purdue University
Seating arrangement of an Aeromarine flying Cruiser which saw considerable service in the United States. (Not in England, but typical of air transports in the 1920s.)

54

Pan American Clipper Ship Hawaii

Honolulu to San Francisco, 1938

MY MOTHER and Janice were early passengers on a Pan American Airways "Clipper Ship" in 1938. It was an eighteen-hour flight from Honolulu to San Francisco where they met the Meeks family, whom they had seen off on a steamship back to San Francisco, two or three days before. Mother wrote a letter to me about watching the moon rise over the Pacific Ocean through a porthole from her comfortable *bunk bed* before going to sleep. Janice clearly recalls the flight and has the same recollection of the moonrise. She also recalls looking down on the ocean at night as they flew over the *Lorilee* steamship of the Mattson Steamship Line Company, fully lighted for their special benefit, as they passed it overhead.

Research of dates indicates that Mother and Janice flew in Martin M-130 NC14714, christened and named the *Hawaii Clipper,* built in 1936. There were only three of this type of aircraft built. It was powered by four 800 HP Pratt and Whitney engines,

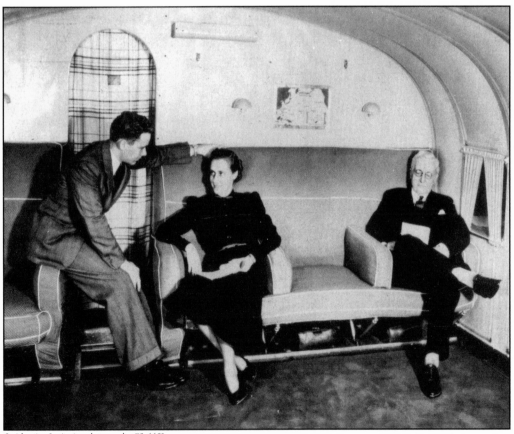

Smithsonian Institution photo number 75-4462
Clipper Ship passengers lounge area converted to berths at night.

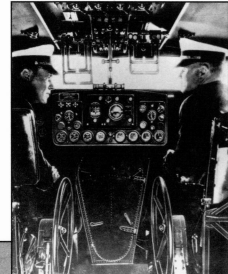

Cockpit of a Martin 130 (left), Captain E. Musick on left and Second Officer R. Sullivan, co-pilot. Captain Musick was the most famous of the Clipper Ship captains. He was involved in an air/sea rescue following crash of his ship at sea. A famous singer, Jane Froman, was on board. Musick held her aloft for many hours before rescue. They were married later. Musick was lost in one of the fatal crashes of the three Clipper Ships, causes unknown.
Smithsonian Institution photo number 91-6279

Smithsonian Institution photo number 77-5799
Clipper ship cut-away of NC14714 showing crew, passenger accommodations and storage areas. Note entrance stairway for passengers, at the rear as Janice remembers it.

the top speed was 180 MPH, but the cruising speed was only 130 MPH. Its range was 3,200 miles. Its wingspan was 130 feet. It was ninety feet, ten inches long and twenty-four feet high. It carried a crew of five to seven persons, with accommodations for thirty-six passengers with bunks for eighteen.

All of these aircraft came to tragic ends. The sister ship NC14715, the *Philippine Clipper,* crashed in San Francisco harbor in 1943. The *China Clipper,* NC14716, crashed in Trinidad in 1945. The *Hawaii Clipper,* in which Mother and Janice flew, was presumed to have crashed in the Pacific sometime later in 1938. There was speculation, never substantiated, that the aircraft had been hijacked by Japanese shortly before the war, not only to learn the secrets of its design, but because there was reported to have been several million dollars of gold in the cargo intended for the Chinese Nationalists.

My Mother was my first passenger after getting my license. Janice was my first cross-country passenger, flying with me in my open cockpit Waco F to Columbus, Ohio, and return.

A bit of memorabilia trivia: Frank E. Ball and I flew to Washington, D.C. a few times to participate in organizing agencies to sponsor legislation and plans to protect the interests of private flyers and their aircraft. Commercial air lines were being formed, and there was a fight brewing as to who would control the skies. Two of these organizations still survive, the Aircraft Owners and Pilots Association (AOPA) and the Sportsman Pilots Association (SPA).

I logged two flights to Washington, D.C., in 1934 and two in 1937. I wonder how many people remember that the original Washington, D.C., airport was located on the site now occupied by the Pentagon. There was one east-west runway only partially paved as I remember. North-south National Highway Number One from Maine to Florida crossed the east end of the runway. When a plane landed or took off, a stop-light was turned to red and automobile traffic stopped and waited until the plane had cleared! I never was able to find out who operated the light. I think it must have been by someone looking out the window of the little operations office building.

Smithsonian Institution photo number 92-933
Hawaiian Clipper Ship M-130, NC14714, on the water ready for boarding.

Primitive Flight Instruments

Navigation Procedures in 1920's–1930's

FOLLOWING World War I, the aircraft industry began to switch from aircraft built solely for military use to meet a civilian market. Flight instruments were woefully lacking, as were aerial maps that could be used for cross country navigation.

The magnetic compass, an altimeter, and the basic engine monitoring instruments: the RPM tachometer, temperature and oil pressure gauges plus a turn and bank indicator were about all there were on the instrument panel.

Some early innovative pilots made a crude horizon, bank and turn indicator of their own design using the principles of gravity and centrifugal force, the same as modern instruments to accomplish their objective: to maintain a controlled flight without visual reference to the horizon or the ground. Early attempts to "fly blind" in clouds and obscurements found that even the best of pilots would become disoriented in a matter of seconds attempting to fly "by the seat of their pants." The result often was a tight spiraling turn or a spin out of the clouds which were fatal unless there was sufficient altitude below the clouds to recover before striking the ground.

One crude "homemade" artificial horizon consisted of a glass jar, such as a fruit jar (preferably Ball) half-filled with a semi-viscous material such as light weight oil so it would not splash around too much in turbulent weather. A straight horizontal line would be painted across the middle of the jar at the level of the liquid, and a second vertical line painted down the center of the jar crossing at the liquid level. A plumb bob suspended on a string fastened above the jar and lined up with the vertical line on the jar controlled by centrifugal force in a turn would identify a skidding or a slipping turn. The level of the liquid in the jar as related to the black horizontal line served as the artificial horizon. Below the line indicated a climb, above the line a descent, banking for a turn indicated—dip to the left, left turn; to the right, right turn; level flight, liquid level with the black line.

The trick was to keep the string over the vertical line using reference to the liquid level in the jar as the horizon.

With practice and concentration it worked!

See diagram herewith.

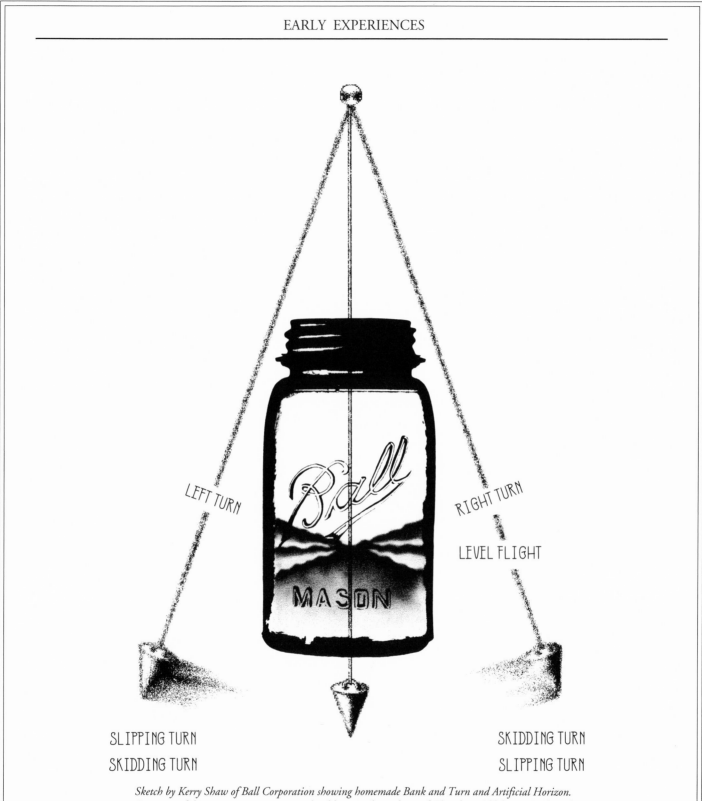

LEFT TURN

RIGHT TURN

LEVEL FLIGHT

SLIPPING TURN

SKIDDING TURN

SKIDDING TURN

SLIPPING TURN

Sketch by Kerry Shaw of Ball Corporation showing homemade Bank and Turn and Artificial Horizon.
I saw one of these ingenious creations at the old airport located east of Okmulgee, Oklahoma, made and
used effectively by Jack Russell, pilot and airport operator, sometime between 1929 and 1936, before the
new Okmulgee field was built north of town. Jack helped me de-ice my plane with a carefully applied
blow torch after I picked up heavy ice shortly after leaving Okmulgee for Wichita Falls, Texas.
I returned to Okmulgee and landed with full power.

Navigation Maps

THE ONLY maps available in those earlier years that could be used for cross country navigation were Rand McNally railroad maps on which airports were designated by red dots or red circles indicating the type of airport. There were no sectional maps indicating topography such as we have today so a cross country flight might involve the use of several state maps, each likely using a different scale. In plotting a cross country trip, "point to point" navigation was used drawing a line across the map from one distinguishable object such as a town, lake or river to another and verified whenever possible by references to the "iron compass," railroad tracks. General direction or compass heading of the flight could be estimated by referring to the "compass rose" imprinted in red at the top of the maps. It was always tricky to know exactly where a state line was crossed, which, perhaps might require a new compass heading adjustment and a different scale.

The copy of the State of Minnesota's railroad map altered for aviation navigation shown herewith will clearly illustrate the problem.

Location identification and confirmation were often determined by buzzing a small community in order to read its name on a water tank or even low enough to catch its name on the railroad station. It's no wonder that pilots frequently landed simply to verify their position and "What state am I in?" was not a facetious question.

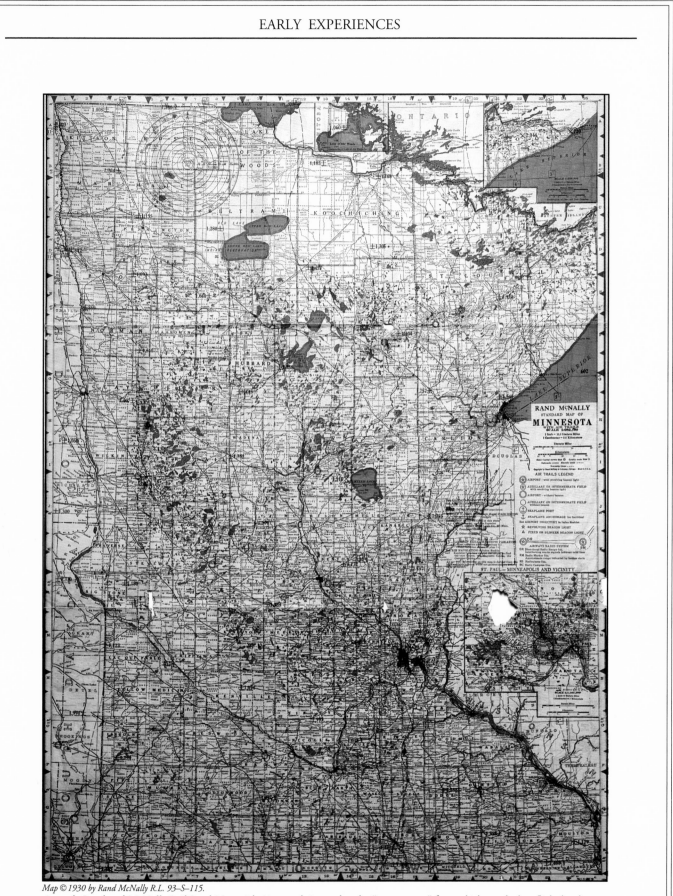

Map © 1930 by Rand McNally R.L. 93–S–115.
An early Rand and McNally Rail Road Map with Airports designated and a "compass rose" from which to calculate flight headings.
Only aerial maps available in the 1920s and early '30s.

CHAPTER III

MEMORABLE EXPERIENCES

Edmund F. Ball
A restored Waco F-2 (right) at Oshkosh, 1992.

First Try for California

April 1932—Unsuccessful

ON APRIL 20, 1932, I began my first long trip from Muncie in my relatively new Waco F airplane, which had a top speed of about 90 miles-per-hour. In those days, trips very far from the local airport were considered quite adventuresome. Rand McNally Railroad state maps were the only ones available; likewise, one obtained weather reports from newspapers and *The Farmer's Almanac,* and airport information by hearsay. My destination was San Diego, California, where my sister Adelia (Diggie) Morris was expecting a baby. The expected baby is now Mrs. James (Patsy) Gantor, mother of Patty Pelizzari, whose son, Jimmy, made my sister a great-grandmother, and me a great-grand uncle. The baby that I went to see in California is now a grandmother. Time flies as well as airplanes!

But I never made it further than El Paso.

From Kokomo, where my plane was hangared temporarily after the demise of Silver Fox Airport, I flew to Okmulgee, Oklahoma, where Ball Brothers operated a glass plant acquired in 1929. Refueling stops were made *en route* in St. Louis and Springfield, Missouri. I visited the plant, stayed overnight, then flew to Wichita Falls, Texas to visit the glass plant which Ball Brothers had operated there since 1913. Tom Smock, an institution in his own right, a Spanish-American War veteran who proudly wore his campaign hat, presided as Plant Superintendent. Thence, I proceeded to Dallas, where I first became acquainted with David, the newly arrived son of Colonel Alvin and Lucy Ball Owsley. David's older brother, Alvin, now Chairman of the Board of Ball Corporation, was then six years old. Then I flew westward, with refueling stops en route at Sweetwater and Midland. The route was Guadalupe Pass to El Paso, where my flight involuntarily terminated.

At Midland, I was told that approaching El Capitan at Guadalupe Pass, if I circled a lonesome ranch house there, an accommodating rancher would wave me on if the pass was clear. Unfortunately, he didn't know what the weather would be in El Paso.

Without radio or weather information, I arrived in El Paso in a 40/50 MPH wind and dust storm. After a rough landing, while attempting to taxi to the safety of the flight line for tie down, a gust of wind picked up my little plane (landing speed about 30 MPH) and flopped it over on its back. No injury to me, but sufficient damage to the plane to require major repairs—prop, motor mount and tail section. I took a taxi across the Rio Grande to Juarez to settle my nerves with a couple of shots of tequila and a Mexican meal with Cerveza. At the bar, I overheard a couple of young *Americanos* discussing the small airplane blown over in the wind in the El Paso Airport and wondering whether the pilot was injured. I assured them he was not! I continued the trip commercially. Clyde Shockley arranged for aircraft repairs and either he or Pete Williams, another early Muncie pilot, flew it back to Muncie. This is another event that might well have terminated my interest in flying. In this case, however, it only increased my determination to keep flying!

First Plane Stolen in Michigan

June 1932

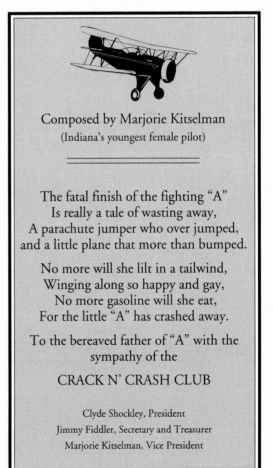

AFTER REPAIRS to the Waco F and its return to Muncie, I flew it on several flights, mostly to Indiana cities. In June, 1932, Clyde sold my "demonstrator," which was replaced by a side-by-side, two-seater Model A, NC12460, cockpit enclosed by a plastic or pyroline cover, referred to as a "celluloid solarium," powered by a Jacobs 170 HP seven cylinder radial engine. After flying it a few hours, mostly locally, I flew it to Traverse City on July 16, 1932, where it came to an untimely end. I had broken my record flying time from Muncie, making it non-stop in three hours and fifty minutes. (Compared to an hour and twenty minutes today!)

I landed at the original Traverse City airport located south of town. A traveling air show was performing at the time, headlining a daring parachute jumper, one Barney Galowski. The next morning, I was playing golf on the Leland golf course where two State Troopers found me, identified me as the owner and advised that my aircraft had been taken for a joy ride early that morning by Barney Galowski (a non-pilot) who had appropriated it and put on quite a show over Traverse City just at dawn. In a low pass, he caught its landing gear in a fence at the top of a hill a half mile or so from the airport, causing the aircraft to do cartwheels down the side of the hill, completely demolishing the aircraft. Amazingly, there was little or no damage to the pilot, whose alcohol content was judged to be at a very high octane level.

The Troopers said that, to their knowledge, this was the first airplane stolen in Michigan and that their charges against Galowski and expected jail sentence would not only keep him from skydiving soon again, but would also be a deterrent to others who might fancy a similar undertaking. And that was the last I ever heard of Mr. Galowski.

Until a replacement could be acquired. I flew my old Model F, NC11252, which Clyde and Muncie Aviation had been using for flying passengers, as a demonstrator and a training plane.

Composed by Marjorie Kitselman
(Indiana's youngest female pilot)

The fatal finish of the fighting "A"
Is really a tale of wasting away,
A parachute jumper who over jumped,
and a little plane that more than bumped.

No more will she lilt in a tailwind,
Winging along so happy and gay,
No more gasoline will she eat,
For the little "A" has crashed away.

To the bereaved father of "A" with the sympathy of the

CRACK N' CRASH CLUB

Clyde Shockley, President
Jimmy Fiddler, Secretary and Treasurer
Marjorie Kitselman, Vice President

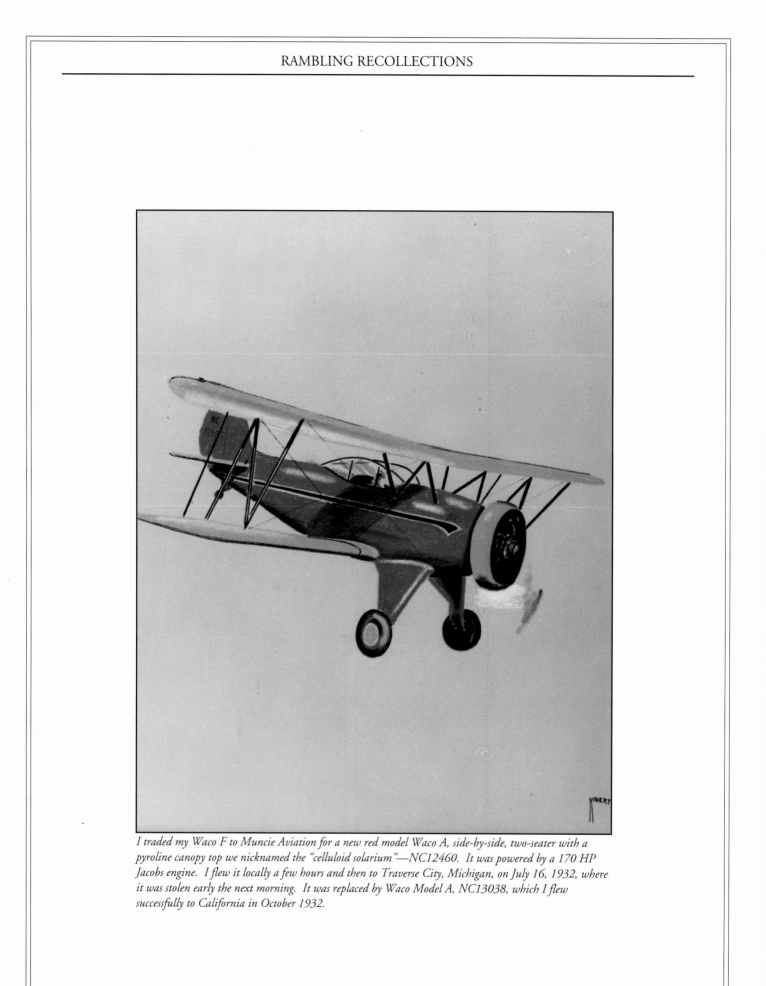

I traded my Waco F to Muncie Aviation for a new red model Waco A, side-by-side, two-seater with a pyroline canopy top we nicknamed the "celluloid solarium"—NC12460. It was powered by a 170 HP Jacobs engine. I flew it locally a few hours and then to Traverse City, Michigan, on July 16, 1932, where it was stolen early the next morning. It was replaced by Waco Model A, NC13038, which I flew successfully to California in October 1932.

The fatal finish of the fighting "A"
Is really a tale of wasting away,
A parachute jumper who overjumped,
And a little plane that more than bumped.

No more will she lilt in a tailwind,
Winging along so happy and gay,
No more gasoline will she eat,
For the little "A" has crashed away.

To the bereaved father of "A"
with the sympathy of the
CRACK N' CRASH CLUB
Clyde Shockley,Pres.
Jimmy Fidler,Secy & Treas.
Marjorie Kitselman,Vice Pres.

Waco A NC12460, stolen and wrecked by one Barney Galowski, the plane obviously totalled. Barney, a small scratch over his eye. The photography, drawing and poem composed by Marjorie Kitselman. (She, when she soloed at the dedication of Muncie Airport, was the youngest female pilot in Indiana.)

"Black Cat" Roy

July 1932

ROY LOVE was Ball Brothers' bricklayer foreman of furnace construction and rebuilds. The Wichita Falls, Texas, glass plant was in the process of rebuilding, so I offered to fly him down to take over supervision. This was in July 1932. I had about 300 hours logged by that time and was feeling quite competent as a pilot.

Roy had two great "colored roustabouts," as these African-Americans were then called in the factory, brothers Ernie and Monroe Modoc, both exceptionally strong men. Roy would good naturedly pit one against the other to see which could carry the most bricks up the ladder to service the brick masons. Roy would tell Ernie that Monroe had carried up twenty bricks, so Ernie would say, "If Monroe can carry up twenty bricks, I can carry up twenty-five." Ernie could well have played wide receiver on anybody's football team today and Monroe, nose tackle.

Roy told them he was flying with me to Texas and Monroe, who Roy jokingly referred to as his "Secretary," remarked, "Mr. Roy, remember you is always a black cat."

My Waco A had just been stolen and wrecked and not yet replaced, so I borrowed Frank's Waco F-2 for the trip. It was July 24th.

We left Muncie about 8:30 in the morning, planning to refuel in St. Louis. Near Brazil, Indiana, the engine began to cough and sputter. It was sort of intermittent, clearing itself with a bang and then smoothing out for a while, and then repeating the

Edmund F. Ball

same symptom once again. I picked a reasonably good pasture with no cows in it, landed and walked to the nearest farmhouse to telephone Muncie. Pete Williams, MAC's all around pilot, instructor and mechanic, agreed to fly down to my improvised landing field and try to diagnose the problem. In less than an hour Pete arrived in another Waco F, landed, looked everything over and could find nothing amiss or hanging loose, started the engine up and it ran beautifully. We thought it might be some water in the fuel or an anomaly that would not occur again. I took off and headed for St. Louis with no reoccurrence of the problem.

We, or at least I, didn't know enough in those days to realize the problem was simply a case of the carburetor icing up, quickly cured by opening up the carburetor heat for a few moments, a thing we soon learned to do routinely until engines were converted from carburetor to fuel injection systems.

After St. Louis, we flew to Springfield, Missouri, for refueling and thence uneventfully over the Ozarks to Okmulgee for a plant visit and overnight. The next day we took off for Wichita Falls. We crossed the Red River, where, by then-existing law, fishing for whales was forbidden, into Texas, with Wichita Falls a short ten miles away. It had begun to drizzle a bit and finally rain, but visibility remained reasonably good under a fairly low overcast.

Without warning, the engine became very rough and, in spite of Wichita Falls airport being just a few miles away, I picked a clear patch between cactus and mesquite trees to land. As we came to a stop and I cut the engine, Roy turned around the cockpit and said, "By God, I guess Monroe was right. I am a black cat!"

Just before landing, I had spotted a farmhouse about half a mile away which couldn't be seen from the ground, so we took off in the general direction carrying our bags with a light drizzle falling. As we neared the house, we saw a lady, who didn't see us at the time, headed for the outhouse, the house obviously having no indoor plumbing. We politely went to the front door and waited a reasonable time to let the lady return to the house before knocking on the door. It seemed a long time before she answered, and when she did was obviously and understandably startled to see two strange men standing there in the rain carrying suitcases and a long ways off from any highway.

Although it was raining, she didn't invite us in. In response to our inquiry how we might get a ride to town, she said she had no vehicle, that the mailman only came twice a week and he had come yesterday, and the dairy truck came by every day or so on an irregular schedule. She didn't know when it might be back. "Well, how far was it to the dairy?" She thought it might be three or four miles down the road "that-a-way." So much for Texas hospitality.

We walked down the road "that-a-way" for a mile or two, picking up great globs of Texas gumbo on our shoes at every step, until finally we came to a small dairy. After some negotiations, we got a ride to town in a typical, beat-up ranch pickup truck. Roy and bags were dropped off at the old Kemp Hotel, while I went on to the airport to try to locate a mechanic.

I was able to find a mechanic who agreed to go out with me and take a look at my grounded aircraft and fix it if he could. We left in his pickup truck in a

generally northeasterly direction out of Wichita Falls, but nobody queried seemed to have heard of a dairy in that direction. Finally, after a couple of hours or more of searching, we found the dairy, from there located the lady's house and soon the aircraft, right where I had left it, watched over by a couple of long-eared jackrabbits and a few prairie dogs. The mechanic quickly located the trouble. Bolts fastening one of the cylinder heads, "cans" as they were known, had worked loose, losing compression from that cylinder. I had landed quickly enough to prevent any serious damage. We returned to town. He took me to the glass plant to catch up with Roy who, after checking in at the hotel, had gotten a ride to the plant.

The mechanic picked me up the next morning at the Kemp Hotel, drove quickly to the stranded aircraft, since we now knew where it was parked. He tightened the bolts, checked over the rest of the cylinders, I started it up—it ran smoothly, perfectly—and I was soon off on my improvised runway, landing at Wichita Falls Airport (then a sod field) with no further incidents.

I left the next day, returning to Muncie, leaving "Black Cat" Love to return to Muncie when his job in Wichita Falls was finished, I suspect somewhat relieved to be going by train.

The Wichita Falls field is now known as AFB/Wichita Falls Memorial Airport with multiple paved runways, one 13,100 feet long. Harter Urban, Isabel's brother, served there in the Air Force during World War II as a corporal clerk-typist. He was still on active duty there when John Fisher and I visited our glass plant after I had retired from active military duty. Cutting through some military red tap, we were able to arrange for him to have supper with us "off the post."

The Model A Waco NC13038, replacement for my stolen plane, which I flew successfully on my second attempt to California and return September 29–October 15, 1932. This is the same plane in my "Lost Plane" adventure and forced landing in "PPP," "Florida Air Race" and "Forced Landings."

A "Hot Seat"

September 1932

ANOTHER memorable experience in an unpleasant sort of way occurred in that same plane on September 3rd during a trip to New York. From Muncie I landed at the airport at Bellefonte, Pennsylvania, to refuel. It was the airport used then by the early Air Mail pilots as a refueling stop. During the refueling, I ate a sandwich and drank a Coke in a little restaurant adjoining the hangar. I had left in place my seat pack parachute, which we wore in those days more for show than for any really anticipated use, and the canopy open so the cockpit wouldn't get too hot under its "solarium" top.

After lunch, I paid my bill, got into the airplane, strapped the parachute on and took off for my final destination. In about fifteen minutes my seat began to feel very uncomfortable, itching and burning. I soon discovered that in the process of refueling the gas tank located in the mid-section of the upper wing, fuel had overflowed and onto my parachute. It was completely saturated with high test gasoline. Suffering, a really "hot seat," I slipped out of my parachute harness, dropped my trousers which by then were equally saturated, and finished the 2-1/2 hour flight to Glen Curtiss Airport, New York, half standing up in the cramped confines of my "celluloid solarium." Soap and water and soothing lotions did little good, and skin from my backside peeled off for days after. I stopped in Bellefonte on my return to Muncie. My log book does not record what I told that refueller my opinion was of his competence for the job.

Second California Attempt

October 1932—Successful

IT WAS IN October of that year that, undaunted by my first unsuccessful attempt, I completed a trip to California in my new Waco A, purchased with the insurance money from the stolen, wrecked plane. It was powered similarly by a 170 HP, 7 cylinder radial Jacobs engine.

This time I made it, but not without interesting and challenging experiences. Leaving Muncie on September 29, 1932, stops for refueling were made at St. Louis and Springfield, Missouri; then overnights in Oklahoma City, and Yuma, Arizona, California, on the Mexico border. The temperature at Yuma was about 120F. Here I had my first experience with a crude but welcomed sort of air conditioning—water dripping on to a fiber glass screen with an electric fan behind it. Before reaching Yuma I had refueled at Big Springs, Texas; El Paso and Tucson. Lots of wild, wide-open spaces, usually following railroads, and by dead reckoning. I arrived in San Diego October 2nd, three days out of Muncie, total flying time logged, 21 hours and 15 minutes.

After a pleasant visit with Diggie, Bob and Little Patsy, I flew to Los Angeles to meet a Ball Brothers sales representative, first name Vern, last name I've forgotten. He was a great salesman. His avocation was "perpetual motion." He was certain he and a young inventor had it solved. Unfortunately for science, Vern died before he found the answer. Returning to San Diego, I left for Muncie on the 11th, retracing my outward flight except for the stops at Wichita Falls and Okmulgee for plant visits.

Lest recalling these somewhat adventurous flights too matter-of-factly as being routine and without incident, let me record just one memorable incident. It occurred over the wide-open desert country between El Paso and Midland. The engine cowling somehow came loose and worked its way forward until it rubbed against the back side of the revolving propeller blades. Unable to reach the cowling from my covered cockpit to pull it back and without a suitable place to land, I continued flying to the nearest airport which was Midland. After what seemed an eternity speculating about how deep the groove was being cut into the base of the blades, with a sigh of relief I landed on a most-welcome, then unpaved, combined military-civilian airfield. It was presided over by a pleasant, accommodating and efficient Army Air Corps Tech Sergeant. He helped me remove the cowling and arranged to ship it back to Muncie. The cowl rubbing on the prop blades had cut about an inch groove equally on each blade, so there was no prop vibration and not deep enough to cause failure from the centrifugal force of 2,000 RPMs. We determined the cuts were not deep enough to weaken the blades dangerously and that I could proceed safely on to Muncie, which I did and where my trip ended with no further incident on the 15th of October.

Florida Bound and Three Forced Landings

January 1933

If engine fails while flying, land as soon as possible

Dudley P. Fudpucker

A TOUR IN which I participated along with others from Muncie was in January 1933. It was sponsored by Colonel Henry Doherty of Teapot Dome ill-fame. This was at the height or the depth of the Depression, whichever way one looked at it. The purpose was both to promote aviation and to advertise his Biltmore Hotel at Coral Gables, Florida. Because of the Depression, it was almost empty of guests. Flying my Waco "A," I left Muncie fairly early on the 4th, planning to refuel at Murfreesboro, Tennessee's, excellent airport about 300 miles south of Muncie. In those days, good airports were few and far between. With a full tank of gasoline, I figured I had enough for at least four hours of flying. Remember that in those days there were no radio communications and weather reports and forecasts were almost non-existent.

Somewhere between Muncie and Murfreesboro, probably around Cincinnati, I picked up strong headwinds, but it was difficult to estimate my ground speed on my sparsely detailed map. I realized from what checkpoints were available I could guess my speed had dropped from about 110 MPH, on which I based my calculations, to somewhere between 60 and 70 miles per hour ground speed. I passed Nashville far off to my right with some apprehension about sufficient gasoline, figuring that it would be about as close to continue to Murfreesboro as it would be to divert to Nashville. The further I went, the stronger the headwinds became. Throttling back to conserve gas decreased my ground speed, so that likely at the end of the flight I was barely doing 50 MPH ground speed. The fuel indicator located on the bottom of the upper wing tank kept going lower and lower and finally rested solidly on its bottom. At last, the Murfreesboro airport came in sight and just as I thought I had the field safely made, the engine quit cold. Without enough altitude left to clear the fence, I landed parallel with the fence but on the wrong side with an empty fuel tank. A pickup truck soon arrived to see what had happened since I had been observed on the approach but had disappeared from view before my anticipated landing. The truck driver, learning my problem, returned to operations across the field, and came back with a five-gallon can of fuel. Now with adequate fuel, I took off in a clear space alongside the fence, landed safely on the other side, refueled and proceeded on my way. That was the first, last and only time in 62 years of flying that I have ever run out of gas.

Continuing the flight from Murfreesboro, I stopped at Macon, Georgia, and then Waycross, to wait for fog to clear sufficiently to get into Jacksonville, then on to Daytona in time to enter a handicap race to Miami, based on aircraft manufacturer's published speeds.

We did more-or-less contour flying in those days at just above treetop level on the theory that we made better speed at lower altitudes. This was probably true if there were any headwinds. My Jacobs engine "swallowed a valve" approaching the then-small community of Pompano—another forced landing— my second so far this trip. The only open space available happened to be a pepper field straight ahead. Luckily, the rows exactly fit the span of my landing gear resulting in no damage whatsoever in the landing. The engine, however, was pretty well totalled by the broken valve stem going through the piston head and thrashing around inside the crank case, causing a considerable amount of internal damage.

I took a taxi into Miami, where arrangements were made with a fixed based operator to take a truck to Pompano, disassemble the aircraft, bring it to Miami, replace the damaged engine with a new one from the factory, then reassemble the airplane. All this required a layover of about two weeks in Miami—not too hard to take considering January weather in Indiana.

The incident was recorded, I believe, in the *Miami Herald* under this memorable alliteration headline, "Pilot Poops Out in Pepper Patch at Pompano."

To continue this series of "incidents," since my aircraft was out of business, Walter Davis, a World War I pilot whom I knew quite well from Richmond, Indiana, had a bad cold and didn't feel like flying. He persuaded me, without a check out, to fly his high wing monoplane Warner powered Davis aircraft in an air parade. Doherty had requested the "fly-about" to advertise his hotel. Since we were his guests, we felt obligated to get all the airplanes in the air that we could for this event. With some reluctance, I agreed to fly

Walter's plane without even a cockpit checkout. He simply told me to turn on the fuel, turn the switch which was connected with the starter, and after the engine had run a few minutes to warm up, just line up and take off. Simple enough, which I did. About ten or twelve minutes in flight, and directly over the hotel, for the third time this trip, my engine quit, forcing me to make an unexpected landing on the golf course directly in front of the hotel. Thinking that I had landed purposely as a matter of convenience and not necessity, Colonel Doherty thought this was a great advertising stunt, demonstrating the practicality of flying, and thanked me for it.

Reporting to Walter that his airplane was parked on number one fairway in front of the hotel with an unexplained engine failure, he thought it was a great joke when, by questioning me, he determined that I had turned on the valve to the reserve tank which was almost empty, mistaking it for the valve to the main tank which was full. Somewhat sheepishly I returned to the airplane, turned on the correct valve and took off from the fairway for the Miami Airport. Three forced landings in two days of flying!

My recollection is that the Miami International Airport at that time consisted of only one partially paved runway, the remainder was sod, and there was no such thing as a control tower.

With my airplane back in service, we departed Miami on January 22, preceded by a fifteen-minute test hop to check the new engine and to make small rigging adjustments necessary after the aircraft had been reassembled. Several of us stopped at Jacksonville to refuel, then flew on to Macon. My cousin Frank made an unfortunate landing in his Waco Cabin at Macon, which I watched. It resulted in some serious damage to the aircraft and to a cargo of Florida citrus fruits he was taking home. Fortunately, there was no injury to Frank. There was a deep depression in the middle of the airport which Frank failed to negotiate. He left his plane for repairs and flew back with me to

Atlanta for overnight and to Muncie the next day. I refueled again at Murfreesboro, this time with ample fuel on board and thence to Muncie. This concluded a great trip with experiences which could in no way be duplicated in this day of high-tech and closely controlled flying. Three forced landings, but those were the good old days, by some standards, and forced landings were almost standard procedure!

Forced Landings Continued

Jacobs Engine Distributor

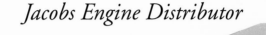

I SEEMED to specialize in forced landings.

With four previously recorded, and three more from my Florida venture, I had already successfully negotiated seven "Forced Landings" On May 23, 1933, my logbook again records a forced landing in this same aircraft with its new Jacobs 170 HP radial engine.

Returning from Chicago, the engine again "swallowed a valve," resulting in a forced landing on a farm near Bunker Hill, Indiana. The location of this farm I now identify as being a part of Grissom Air Force Base near Kokomo. I claim, therefore, to be the first pilot to land there. I was just in time for supper and was invited in to enjoy a wonderful chicken dinner prepared by the wife of the young farmer. They were recently married, were graduates of Purdue's School of Agriculture and just acquired their farm. I did not identify myself at the time, but later sent them a case of Ball jars in payment for my landing and the fine supper which I ate waiting for Clyde Shockley to pick me up and take me home. I used to hear from my gracious hosts occasionally, but have not for a long time so suppose they have passed on.

These incidents and others with Jacobs engines earned me the title of "Jacobs Engine Distributor," since I had done a pretty good job of distributing Jacobs engine parts all over the country.

"Ed Wheel-Off"

July 1933

IN 1933, on July 6th, for some reason not explained in my logbook, I flew my cousin Frank's Waco F-2 N11487, instead of my own, with Claude Kinzie, Purchasing Agent for Ball Brothers Glass Manufacturing Company, to Evansville. We drove to Salem, Kentucky, to look at a flourspar mine my uncle, George A. Ball, had purchased as a source of the material which was used in manufacturing opal glass innerliners for zinc fruit jar caps.

Edmund F. Ball

Taking off from Evansville, the keeper nut on the bottom of the spline on the right shock absorber came off, resulting in the whole wheel assembly dropping down into the slip stream, and rotating half sideways. The assembly was held from falling completely off only by the brake cable. I was immediately aware of the situation but could not advise Kinzie in the open cockpit front seat what had happened. There was no means of communications except sign language between pilot and passenger.

Throughout the two-hour flight to Muncie, I considered how best to land. Since it would be on grass, the crippled wheel, when it touched down would, I thought, dig into the ground and act as sort of a pivot on which the aircraft would rotate to the right. I planned therefore to land on the left wheel a bit crosswind, to hold the right wing up as long as possible, reducing speed to a minimum before the right wheel touched ground. This resulted in a very easy, safe landing with no damage to the aircraft or passengers. I think the spectators, news reporters, photographers, and emergency equipment assembled at the scene were somewhat disappointed.

In response to a newspaper reporter's questions as to whether I was aware of the problem, I was quoted in the paper as saying, "Yes, I've been thinking about it for two hours."

Evansville spectators, watching my departure, had seen this mishap after take-off and, without radio, were not sure I was aware of the problem. They had wisely telephoned Muncie to alert me, if possible, before landing.

The most exciting thing to me as I approached Muncie, since we had no radios in those days, was Pete Williams piloting another aircraft flying along side of me with the words painted in large, white letters on the side of his airplane, "Ed, wheel off." I signaled back to Pete that I understood. This, of course, informed my passenger, as well, of our situation. Claude was a stoic passenger, evidencing no major alarm throughout the landing. I think he flew again with me on a trip to southern Indiana to check delivery of some machinery he had ordered for the Ball Company. This second time, the flight was uneventful.

A Lost Airplane

July 1933

THIS WAS an experience which I might prefer to forget, except that it's indicative of some of the hazards of flying in those early days. It occurred on December 2, 1933. Frank Hanley, another pilot riding with me as passenger, and I were invited to Nashville, Tennessee, for some aviation meeting—perhaps it had something to do with the opening of the city's new airport. Several aircraft owners had been invited to participate. We got a late start in the afternoon, which I figured, without much concern, would put us into Nashville at about sunset or perhaps a little after. I had been assured that the field was well-lighted and that there should be no problem finding it.

My plane was equipped with a couple of parachute flares which could be shot out and theoretically stay lit long enough to pick out a suitable emergency field on which to land. Arriving in the Nashville area somewhat later than I'd expected, approaching darkness, I circled the area several times where I thought I had been told their "lighted" field was located. I was unable to find it. Deciding I'd better land while there was some light left, and before I ran out of fuel, I fired one of my parachute flares to help locate a suitable place to land. Its light mostly blinded me at first, but before it flared out I spotted what appeared to be an open field in the shadowy light. It looked long enough without obstacles, like cows and stumps, in it although there appeared to be a hedge row across the middle which I would need to clear. I planned to touch down in the first half of the field, then, with power, purposely bounce it over the hedge and come to a stop on the other side, a maneuver which I luckily accomplished. In this remote area, it was only after some considerable time and trouble that we found a farmer with a pickup truck willing to drive us to town and to our hotel. The next day, with search cars from the airport, it took us several hours to find our airplane parked on an isolated field west of Nashville where I was told there were no suitable places to land. They were telling me!?

After inquiry at several farmhouses in the neighborhood, we finally located the plane. I was alarmed to discover the "hedge" I had bounced over was a twelve-foot deep drainage ditch bordered by bushes and tall weeds. Frank said he wasn't sure whether it was my Masonic ring or his Rosary beads, or maybe the combination, that saved us.

Clearing weeds and an overcooked dove which had apparently been roosting in the underbrush out of my carburetor intake, I fired up and took off safely to the airport located on the far east side of Nashville, instead of the west side where I had been looking in vain. I noted that the lights for the "lighted" field consisted of two kerosene flair pots, one at each end of the runway!

A Trip to New Haven with Unexpected Experiences

"Any Port in a Storm," Fall 1934

I INCLUDE in my *Ramblings,* two individuals, perhaps not so well known in aviation circles as others, who were involved with me on a few notable experiences. One was Les Milligan and the other Phil Hatch.

Les was Muncie's self-acknowledged *bon vivant* and perennial bachelor. His sister, Lutie, was also remembered as an interesting participant in numerous Muncie activities, antics and events.

Les had served in the military briefly, I believe, at the end of World War I, just long enough for him to qualify as a veteran. He was a partner in the Harry Wolfe Insurance Agency and worked at it just hard enough to keep his dues paid at the Muncie Club and the Delaware Country Club, and provide himself with enough extra for his personal living.

He was one of the original investors in Muncie Aviation Corporation, owning one share of stock, purchased for $100. This, of course, made him eligible to participate in numerous activities.

He was my passenger flying with me in August 1931 in my Waco F to some aviation event in Galesburg, Illinois. Although it turned out that I was a bit premature, on the way home I estimated that I was flying my 100th hour solo. On impulse, and without warning my passenger, I made a neat shandelle or a loop, I've forgotten which. At the top of the maneuver, Les looked back to see if I had fallen out or had some way suddenly lost my sanity. After landing and explaining the reason for the maneuver, Les became more forgiving following a triple Scotch on the rocks at the Muncie Club at my expense.

Phil Hatch's mother was my Aunt Frances (Mrs. George A.) Ball's sister. The Hatch family occasionally visited in Muncie. In that way I had known Phil casually for some time. He also went to Yale a class behind me in the Sheffield Scientific School. I had gone to Yale Academic School (liberal arts). Occasionally, we saw each other while at New Haven, but that's about all.

After graduation, Phil and a couple of other adventuresome classmates signed up for Army Air Corps flight training and went to San Antonio, Texas, and were stationed at Randolph and Kelly Fields. In due course, Phil earned his wings, not without incident (note accompanying photograph), and graduated as Second Lieutenant in the United States Army Air Corp Reserves. For a couple of years, he flew as co-pilot on one of the early airlines, I'm not sure which, probably Allegheny or Eastern. He remained in the Army Reserve Corps and attained the rank of Captain before World War II.

I mention Phil here not only because of his aviation interest, but also because he later became a business associate and a close personal friend. Perhaps it was because of his flying that influenced my decision to make that significant visit to the Silver Fox Flying Service School back in 1929 to see what it took to become a pilot. Since I lacked 20/20 vision without glasses, I could not then qualify for military flying.

Our Uncle George persuaded Phil to forsake a career in aviation and come to work for Ball Brothers Manufacturing Company, first in the zinc and paper division under William Ball. He was ordered to active duty early in the war. After returning from active duty during the war, Phil was assigned to the commercial glass container division's sales department, directed by Fred Petty, and then Fred Reiman after Fred Petty's untimely death in 1949.

Phil was assigned to Wright-Patterson Field in Dayton, Ohio, at the outset of World War II in the Maintenance Command. He rose to the rank of full Colonel at the termination of his active duty, which also terminated his career as a pilot.

Before the war, Phil flew occasionally with me and one memorable flight also involved Les Milligan which is perhaps worth recording in these *Rambling Recollections.*

Neither Phil nor I had returned to Yale after graduation, mine in 1928 and Phil in 1929. Occasionally, we discussed the idea of going back sometime to a football game. It was October, 1934. Albie Booth was making quite a name for himself as an agile, elusive back setting records for yards gained in spite of his diminutive stature—about 5'8" tall and 150 pounds encased in his full football equipment.

On some impulse, I suggested to Phil that we ought to go back to New Haven and see Albie Booth play. I was able to get tickets for the Yale-Army game in which Booth was expected to play and to give Army literally a run for their money.

By that time, I had accumulated some 900 hours flying my beautiful blue Waco cabin plane to such distant places as Traverse City, Michigan; Chicago; Sheboygan; Cleveland; Syracuse; Akron, Ohio; and even Washington, D.C. I felt fairly confident as a pilot and perhaps was a bit over-confident.

I suggested to Phil that we fly to New Haven for the game and I think Phil suggested we invite Les Milligan to go with us and use one of my extra tickets.

We loaded up trusty NC14012 and headed for New Haven. There must have been some weather *en route,* for my logbook shows a three-hour-and-fifty minute flight to Allentown, Pennsylvania, to refuel and then on to New Haven, another hour and a half.

The weather was turning marginal at destination. We took a taxi from the airport and signed in at the old Taft Hotel in New Haven, three of us in one room. Saturday came cold and rainy with occasional snow squalls. I don't think Les ever left the hotel. It was a terrible game. Army was ahead a touchdown or two, but Albie Booth had not yet played. He would certainly save the day. He began warming up on the sidelines to the cheers of "Bulldog, Bulldog, Bow Wow Wow" and "Eli Yale." Time was called and Albie ran out onto the field. Much applause! The quarterback called his number. Eleven huge Army players, I think maybe including the coach and water boy, descended upon little Albie. When the pile up was uncovered, Albie failed to rise. A stretcher was brought out on the field and that was the end of Albie for the afternoon. The game was a debacle. We returned to the hotel room, ate a somber supper, washed down with sufficient libations to drown our disappointment and to toast Albie's speedy and full recovery after his brief appearance in the Army game.

By a strange coincidence, my future brother-in-law, John A. Beall, who earned his nickname "Tiger" playing football at West Point, retired with the rank of Major General, played in that game at tackle. I chided him about what they did to little Albie. His response was, "I only did what the Coach told me to do. Get Albie!" That night before going to bed, Les put a full tumbler of straight Scotch whiskey outside our window on the sill. Responding to Phil's and my questioning as to why, he said that was the way he always began a day—a tumbler of ice cold Scotch!

Sunday was no exception. That's the way he faced the world on that cold, gray morning in New Haven—a full tumbler of "liquid sunshine."

We perhaps should have stayed in bed. Scattered to broken cumulus clouds were galloping by from the west and headed out towards the ocean at 1,000-1,500 feet and at 35 to 40 knots. I thought, rather optimistically, that I might sneak through the hills of western Connecticut, find the Hudson River valley and fly up it all the way to Albany and then head westward through the Mohawk Valley to Ithaca, Rochester and, finally, Buffalo, Phil's hometown.

It didn't work. I got through the western Connecticut hills, to the Hudson River Valley, but Albany was socked in tight with heavy snow squalls. No way could I even get across the Hudson River, nor any further north. Suddenly and gratefully beneath me, in a break in the clouds and snow squalls, I spotted a beautiful paved runway of an airport not shown on my maps. I circled and landed with visibility and ceiling rapidly deteriorating. After taxiing back on the runway, onto what appeared to be a parking area, with a sign of relief, I cut the engine. The weather continued to deteriorate. As we prepared to disembark, a police car drove up with headlights on and beacons flashing. My immediate reaction was, "Now what have I done wrong? Is the field closed? What flight regulations had I broken?" I had visions of my plane being confiscated, a fine levied, maybe even a jail sentence and my license revoked or suspended. There was no explanation from the uniformed driver as we were driven, with our bags and baggage, back to the terminal—only that the Mayor wanted to see us. Wow! I must really be in trouble! What had I done? What crimes committed? And, incidentally, where were we?

There was quite a crowd assembled in the small terminal's lobby. We were introduced to the Mayor, several city dignitaries, newspaper reporters and we still didn't have a clue as to why. Finally, it was explained. We had landed on the just-dedicated new airport at Troy, New York. Numerous airplanes had been expected to fly in for the occasion. Because of the inclement weather, we were the only plane that had arrived all afternoon. After some ceremonial greetings, questions by the reporters and a few photographs, we were driven into town in the Mayor's car with a police escort, given free lodgings at the leading hotel and a sumptuous banquet, at which we were the only honored guests. Afterwards, we were taken to a moving picture theater where we were seated in a box at the side of the auditorium. We could not see the movie screen from that angle, but from it were introduced to the audience as the intrepid flyers who had braved bad weather to help dedicate the city's new airport! We were heroes!

The next morning, feeling that we had worn out our welcome in Troy, we took off hopefully for Buffalo. After a ten-minute flight through snow squalls and low ceilings, I was able to get across the Hudson River and land at the Albany airport with ceilings and visibility minimal. We took a taxi to town, signed in at the leading hotel to wait out the weather. Some way I never understood clearly, Phil managed to hitch a ride into Buffalo that night, leaving a note under my door to pick him up in Buffalo when, and if the weather ever cleared. Les, after his usual morning eye-opener, and I met in the lobby of the hotel next day, twiddled our thumbs and read newspapers. About noon, the weather seemed to be improving a bit; we went out to the airport, cranked up our airplane and flew beneath the clouds, as I had originally planned, westward down the Mohawk Valley to Buffalo. There we refueled, picked up Phil and, with a routine refueling stop in Cleveland, made it on into Muncie.

I'm not sure that either Phil or Les ever flew with me again—nor did I have the courage to invite them—nor have I ever returned to Troy!

The airport is now known as the Troy–Rensselear County Airport, boasting one small asphalt runway, 18-36, 2,675 by 50 feet, but it looked big and beautiful that afternoon in October 1934!

Philip W. Hatch was a nephew of George and Frances Ball. After graduating from Yale, 1929, Phil enlisted in United States Army Air Corp and was assigned to Kelly Field, San Antonio, for flight training. Married Bonny McDonald of Muncie. They had one son, Steven W. Hatch, to whom I am indebted for these photographs.
Courtesy of Mrs. Hatch and Steve W. Hatch

Courtesy of Mrs. Hatch and Steve W. Hatch
Colonel Philip W. Hatch, Maintenance Command Department, Wright-Patterson, Dayton, Ohio, World War II 1944.

Courtesy of Mrs. Hatch and Steve W. Hatch
Unplanned conclusion of a training flight at Kelly, 1930.

As a "Corporate Pilot"

1937

I GUESS I can rightly claim that I was Ball Brothers Manufacturing Company's first corporate pilot, Frank Ball would be second, and John Fisher would then be the third. John and I were followed by Bill Greene, the company's first full-time, professional pilot, and shortly thereafter by Hank Heiner. Both flew for the company for close to a quarter of a century and compiled over 40,000 hours of accident-free flying.

I used my plane rather extensively to visit outside plants, to occasionally transport company personnel, call on customers and, sometimes, take customers on trips. The company now employees eight full-time, professional pilots flying jet aircraft.

I'm reminded of one unusual incident when it served a critical purpose in an early company-union relationship which would no longer be possible.

It was back in the mid-1930s when a great tidal wave of unionization, swept the industrial world following Congress' passing of President Roosevelt's Labor Relations Act requiring companies to negotiate with unions "in good faith." It was a bonanza for the cause of unionization which previously had been essentially trade unions for skilled craftsmen only. This provided an open invitation for the organization of unskilled workers, the so-called "Miscellaneous" group, and the creation of such massive organizations as John L. Lewis' Congress of Industrial Organizations (CIO).

Labor leaders and organizers leapt on industries like ants to spilled honey. In due time, our plants were fully organized by the Glass Bottle Blowers Association, an old line trade union still led by leadership trained in the Samuel Gompers image. Their philosophy and policy was to meet with the "owners," as they were referred to in those days, or the "management," to negotiate for the solution of mutual problems, and not as adversaries. The procedure was quite formalized by tradition. At the outset of the meeting, a representative of management was traditionally elected Chairman and a representative of the union was elected Vice Chairman. They sat side-by-side at a head table with a podium between. Each of the parties elected or appointed secretaries, one management, one union, and at the end of each session and the conclusion of the negotiations, the two secretaries compared notes, reconciled them and would jointly prepare the minutes to which they would both certify as being correct.

Ball Brothers had no Labor Relations Department *per se* at that time, only an Employment Office. By default, I was elected Chairman, then scarcely out of college and with superiors who felt that the wave of unionization would subside and soon disappear. They treated the negotiations accordingly. Bill Campbell, Vice President of the Glass Bottle Blowers Association, an experienced labor leader of the old school, served as Vice Chairman of the conferees and I, the complete novice, as the Chairman. Although our negotiations were tough, and sometimes bitter, Bill coached me through them and I was always grateful to him for that. We had our share of disagreements and even strikes in those days, but these "old school" leaders still endeavored to keep negotiations civil and conducted in a rather gentlemanly manner. Efforts were made to prevent vilification and there were few invectives permitted. If they appeared to be getting out of hand, which they did a time or two, Bill would whisper to me, "Bang the gavel. Tell them they're out of order and sit down." I did and they did, sometimes much to my surprise!

The incident I have in mind is related to aviation, flying and my joint role as a corporate pilot.

We were obviously coming to the conclusion of our negotiations and appeared to be reaching an agreement after several days of conferences. We broke for supper at about six o'clock and Campbell wanted to get the matter resolved as much as I did. I suggested we meet after supper and wind it up. Bill expressed a desire to do so, but said that he had to leave almost immediately to catch a train to St. Louis in order to make connections to Tulsa where he would have to get a car and drive to our Okmulgee plant where he was scheduled to meet that afternoon at two o'clock.

I said to Bill, "If you will stay over and wind this up, I'll fly you to Okmulgee in time for your two o'clock meeting." Much to my surprise, he agreed, but he said he needed to take Gish Johnson, his young assistant, a retired policeman from East St. Louis, along with him. Gish was less than enthusiastic about the idea. I remember Bill saying, "Gish, what's the matter? What are you worried about? Lots better people than you have been killed in an airplane."

We met again after supper, wound up our negotiations about midnight. I met them at the airport early the next morning, as agreed, and flew them to Okmulgee, landing them there in plenty of time for their two o'clock appointment. My recollection is that those negotiations also were finally successfully concluded. So much for negotiations to solve mutual problems instead of aggressively fighting as antagonists over who gets the biggest piece of the pie, and as a "corporate pilot."

A Special Trip to Texas and Old Mexico

March 1936

I RECORD this next special trip in Waco Model C NC14012 because it was an unusual flight and included several significant events.

I had become well acquainted with Ken Frazier and his French wife, Madeline. He was a salesman for the Southern Alkali Company in Corpus Christi which manufactured and sold soda ash, an important ingredient in manufacturing glass, to Ball Brothers for plants in Wichita Falls, briefly to Three Rivers, Texas and Okmulgee, Oklahoma. He was attractive, about my age and liked to fish and hunt, as did I. His wife, Madeline, was charming. We remained close friends for many years. The more time Madeline spent in this country, the more pronounced her French accent seemed to become.

At Corpus Christi, Ken showed me an ideal plant location on the turning basin in the channel to the Gulf. Here would be available soda ash next door, limestone, also an important ingredient in glass-making, and silica sand from quarries not too far away. The most significant feature was that the minerals went with the land. Gas, one of the major costs in manufacturing glass, was right here. We would own our own fuel supply! It could have been purchased and a plant built for $350,000. On my return I took the proposition to my uncles, F. C. and G. A., but must not have been a very good salesman, for they turned down my proposal.

I still have the Cost Department's computations that the Wichita Falls plant furnace could be repaired for about that amount of money. Since the organization was all in place there, and we didn't have the people to manage another plant and it was so far from our markets, the decision was made in favor of repairing Wichita Falls. This plant was closed down after World War II and production moved to Okmulgee.

The value of the Corpus Christi property today would be worth many times the entire net worth of Ball Brothers Manufacturing Company at that time.

With all due respect to them and their great accomplishments, both of my uncles, F. C. and G. A., were well over 70 at the time. Could the lurking memory of this disappointment have had something to do with, when it was my turn to make the rules, deciding that it was age 65 for mandatory retirement from active management, and age 70 retirement from the Board?

I've often speculated on what might have been the results had that piece of land been acquired, and even what if I had purchased it as a speculation myself. It could have been a colossal failure—or a spectacular success!

This particular trip began on March 3, 1936, as most of them did, from Muncie, with a strong headwind from the west. Three hours and five minutes to a refuel at St. Louis and a long four hours and five minutes flight on to Okmulgee. Then a plant visit there, next day to Wichita Falls to visit that plant. It was going down for furnace repairs. Paris, Texas, next day for refueling and then to Dallas for two days.

I might have picked up Ken Frazier there, but I believe I met him in Corpus Christi on the 7th.

I spent a couple of days at Corpus looking over the land site and speculating on its possibilities. On the 9th, we took off for Laredo, refueled and hopped the Rio Grande, a five minute flight to Nuevo Laredo to clear Mexican Customs. Airplanes flying into Mexico in those days were more curiosities than suspects of heinous crimes. A matter of perhaps five dollars U.S. would expedite the bureaucratic paper work.

Don Martin's Reservoir was our destination. Ken had made all the arrangements. A comfortable lodge on the shore of the lake, a nearby landing strip. A chartered boat and guide would be ready. A fish on every cast. We were ready!

At Mexican Customs in Nuevo Laredo, a friendly customs officer greeted us: "Oh, *si señor*, Don Martin Reservoir sixty miles straight west from Laredo, very good landing strip, thirty minutes, no problem, good luck fishing, *adios,*" he said.

An hour and fifteen minutes later, I was still looking for a lodge and a landing strip on the shore of the Reservoir. Finally I decided to land and inquire. A cultivated field with straight plowed rows looked usable—no stumps or large rocks. We landed and were soon surrounded by curious natives who seemed to appear from behind every cactus plant, but none spoke English or understood our questions. Ken's solution to a language problem was simply to talk louder. Finally, a little girl about twelve years old timidly came forward. "*Si, señors. I habla un poco Inglase.*" Yes, we could leave the plane here. It would be safe. Yes, she knew of Don Martin Lodge and could get a message to them to come and get us. Word travels mysteriously and fast. In not too long a time, a pick-up truck arrived to take us to our destination. Comfortable cabanas with a commissary adjacent for meals, fishing tackle and supplies—not plush, but most adequate.

Next day, we fished with some success, many bass, but fairly small, eight to ten inches. We kept a few to eat and a few for a guide and his family.

"*Mañana* we find place where are many big fish." Tomorrow came and we took off after a hearty breakfast in Juan's (our guide) "tin" rowboat powered by 2-1/2 HP motor. By 10:00 A.M., the wind was rising; thirty minutes later it was a gale. Waves in the shallow water were choppy to rough and breaking over the bow of our boat. Juan wisely sought shelter behind an island and put ashore. "You stay. I come back bigger boat—take you back—big storm coming." The last we saw of Juan was his boat disappearing around the point at the end of the island, bow high out of the water at about a 45 degree angle with Juan in the stern coaxing onward his valiant little outboard and facing directly into the wind.

Ken and I walked around the island in opposite directions to explore. I encountered four Mexicans, driven ashore by the wind as we had been, also exploring the island. One, a customs official of some sort, spoke English and we continued our exploring together. He discovered a small cache where a fisherman had left an iron skillet, some lard and a bit of corn meal. My new friend asked, "You eat Mexican hoe cake?" I said I didn't think so. He replied reassuringly, "Okay, you eat it tonight!"

I suppose it was a good hour or more later Ken and I met back at our landing site and I happened to look out from a small hill over the lake. I spotted a strange object splashing and struggling through some small dead trees and bushes off shore a couple of hundred yards or so out. We quickly decided it was a man in distress. Ken ran for the water. Ken thought I was deserting him, but I ran up the beach to pick up a couple of pillow-type life preservers Juan had left with us. I also picked up a stick big enough to put between them to make a sort of a float and struck out to meet Ken and our rescuee. Indeed, it was Juan, almost drowned, but still holding his hat on his head with one hand, splashing along with the other. When we got him ashore, we found he was still wearing his heavy coveralls with one pocket filled with tools—screw drivers, pliers, wrenches. How he had kept his head above water with all these encumbrances, we could never understand. He was hyperthermic and shivering as if he had the ague. He refused to let us take off his heavy coveralls, but we did put him close to the fire we had started and plied him with as much hot water as we could pour down him. He finally began to recover and told us a bit of what happened. As he rounded the point and into the teeth of the gale, his boat, with the bow high out of the water, flipped over backwards and sank. He had been in the water for almost an hour. The wind and waves kept him off shore until he drifted around the point where luckily we saw him.

In the meantime, I had told Ken of my conversation with my Mexican fellow castaway, overnight on the island and Mexican hoe cakes. Ken said, "Not for me!" We took some burning branches from our fire up the hill behind where the wind would catch it and started a brush fire. Soon it seemed half the island was engulfed in a raging fire with lots of smoke.

Maybe half an hour later, a large motor launch arrived, manned by the Sheriff, our Lodge Manager and an assistant. We were shortly safely ashore on the mainland, but with the guide's boat at the bottom of the lake awaiting rescue at a later date.

We decided we'd had enough fishing at Don Martin's Reservoir and would leave the next day. When we returned to our make-shift airport, our plane was there but with one very flat tire! With no services available, we borrowed an automobile jack from the Lodge manager's pickup truck and a hand tire pump. Laboriously we jacked it up and, taking turns at the pump, got the tire nearly inflated, gingerly lowered the jack, listened for tell-tale hisses from a possible leak, and hearing none, said goodbye to our assembled friends and took off. We cleared customs out of Mexico at Nuevo Laredo and across the Rio Grande for United States customs at Laredo. A young customs officer, new on the job, checked us through with some concern as to procedure, since he had cleared all sorts of transients travelling by automobile, pickup truck, horseback, mule back, wagons, ox carts, and on foot, but he had never cleared an airplane.

Our tire seemed to be holding, so we took off for Dallas, landing there with one very soft tire, but without damage. Inspection and repairs revealed a fairly large thorn stuck in the tire, which fortunately had self-sealed making a slow leak, instead of a disaster, if it had blown out.

In Dallas we reunited with our much relieved wives, Isabel and Madeline, and thence to Muncie with a memorable adventure safely behind us.

How I Earned My Wings as a Service Pilot

A Long Story

FRANK E. BALL, while at Princeton, had joined the ROTC and wound up getting a commission in the Coast Guard Artillery Reserve which seemed a reasonably good assignment in case of war. I hadn't joined the rather small group of ROTCs at Yale, but decided to remedy that situation by joining with several friends in 1929, doing the same thing as a sort of mid-winter activity at Muncie. I signed up as a Private in the Infantry Reserve and in due course received my 2nd Lieutenant's commission. A two weeks summer tour of active duty at Fort Knox, Kentucky, resulted in my promotion to the rank of 1st Lieutenant, Infantry Reserve.

For all intents and purposes, I expected that would be the end of my military career.

I tried for the National Guard Air Reserve, but because I didn't have 20/20 vision without glasses, my request was declined.

I'd almost forgotten about my commission until 24 June 1941 when I received a red-bordered letter of greetings from the President of the United States ordering me to active duty with a couple options as to where I wished to be stationed. One of them, I recall, with some financial incentives was the Philippines. A few of my contemporaries accepted that assignment and history records what happened there when MacArthur was driven out of the Philippines—Corregidor, the Death March of prisoners of war, tortures, horrible deaths, and MacArthur's stirring words, "I shall return."

I chose the Air Service, then known as the Army Air Corps, for my assignment, and because it was the closest home, I selected Middletown Air Depot, Middletown, Pennsylvania. There I thought I might be able to earn flying status. According to the order, my active duty was for only one year.

I was wrong on both counts! I didn't make flying status until much later. It was four years, with two of them overseas, before I returned to civilian life.

A restored AT-6 in flight similar to the one in which I flew for my military flight rating.

From Fifth Army Headquarters to VI Corps and a Service Pilot Rating

PERHAPS it is appropriate to include in these *Ramblings* how the circumstances developed to the point that I finally got my rating.

I was ordered overseas as part of the Headquarters cadre which General Mark W. Clark had temporarily assembled, designated II Corps. Most of this cadre became the nucleus for the Fifth Army Headquarters which was eventually activated in Oujda, Morocco, North Africa in January 1943.

Although being sent overseas and transferred to several different units and assignments, I continued to pursue my objective of getting a pilot's rating. Often there was no response to my request, and sometimes it was simply rejected as impossible. No one seemed to know how it could be done. Maybe it could be arranged in the States, but certainly not overseas.

The story begins in North Africa, Fifth Army Headquarters, Oujda, Algiers.

I was Senior Aide to General Clark in Oujda, Algiers, when the Fifth Army was officially organized, which gave me some privileges. On February 14, 1944, still in pursuit of flight status, I, with some difficulty, arranged to get my physical examination at LaSenia airport for a pilot's rating, and passed it. For what good seemed very doubtful.

Following a ten-day's tour at the Field Officers Training School near Chanzy, Morocco, on May 19th I returned briefly to Fifth Army Headquarters in Oujda. I learned I was being assigned to "Bigot," the code name for an operation as yet unidentified. I would be transferred to Headquarters, I Armored Corps and XII Air Support Command at Mostaganem and reported there to a Colonel Hickey who was in nominal command of the yet-undesignated Air Support unit. These two "shadow" headquarters turned out to be the nucleus for General George

Patton's Seventh Army Headquarters preparing for the invasion of Sicily under the code name "Husky." I was being transferred from a Fifth Army Training Command to a combat unit.

Colonel Steve Mack, a graduate of West Point and Air Force flight officer also being transferred from 5th Army Headquarters, and I reported together. We told Colonel Hickey we were being assigned there as observers. He replied, "Observers, hell, we're short of officers and you're going to work."

We were eventually assigned as Air Support Officers to the 45th Division which was scheduled for the assault and would land on the shores of Sicily on July 10, 1944, D-Day, under command of General Troy Middleton. We were Air Support Officers but without radios or any means of communications. Useless!

From the D-Day landing at Gela, a few days later, I was transferred back to Headquarters XII Air Support Command and then to II Corps under General Omar Bradley as his Air Support Officer, replacing a casualty.

At the end of the thirty-two-day Sicilian Campaign, on October 19, I left II Corps Headquarters and returned to XII Air Support Headquarters in Palermo. Since no return trip ticket came with my orders from Fifth Army, I had pretty well decided that this Air Support or Air Liaison job was going to be mine for the duration.

Sitting around as all of us were as sort of "unemployed" for the time being waiting our next assignment, I was told by General House, Commanding General of XII Air Support Command, that I would be sent back to North Africa and assigned to VI Corps as its Air Liaison Officer.

How it ever found me, I never knew, but—wonder of wonders—almost simultaneously with this information I received orders to report to the North African Training Command for a flight test to determine whether I would qualify for a military pilot's rating. With my medical examination in hand, that was no problem. I learned later my request had carried the endorsement of General Mark Clark, which I'm sure was helpful.

But there I was in Sicily, and in my hands I held what I had sought for in vain for many months, but I was now faced with a terrible dilemma. Except for its being in North Africa, there wasn't the slightest clue as to where the Training Command was located, what kind of aircraft was available for this test, whether there would be an opportunity to practice, and who would give the test. Furthermore, I was on notice that very soon I would be ordered to my new assignment with VI Corps which had recently arrived from the States for "Avalanche," the code name for landing on the mainland of Italy. I was now a "veteran" having been in actual combat with the enemy, and under fire.

After collecting the few materials I thought needed by an Air Liaison or Air Support Officer, and my personal belongings, I hitched a ride in a C-47 plane at Palermo's very inadequate airport headed for Bizerte. At Bizerte, on a hunch, I looked up my brother-in-law, Bob Morris[1], at Landing Craft Headquarters. He then held the rank of Commander and was in charge of all landing craft training. We would be participants in the same forthcoming campaign. We enjoyed a fine visit and agreed to meet "somewhere" later. (That would be in Naples in January 1944 when, of all incongruous things, we put on our best uniforms and went together to the Opera in the midst of final planning for Operation "Shingle," the code name for the landing at Anzio on the 22nd). I left Bizerte for LaSenia with bag and baggage and hitch-hiked from there to Port Aux Poules where I finally found VI Corps Headquarters and reported for duty.

With nothing to do but wait around after a few introductions to my new comrades-in-arms, and with this elusive order to report for flight test in my hot little hands, I got permission from Chief of Staff, Colonel Don Galloway, to continue my search for NATC.

At the LaSenia Airport, somebody thought NATC was at Telergama. I hitched a flight there with Colonel Engstrom. He was ferrying a B-25 to Casablanca and would land at Telergama. Yes, they knew that NATC was moving there, but had not yet arrived; it probably was still in Casablanca. With nothing better to do, I continued on to Casablanca. There I finally located NATC on a satellite field on the outskirts of the city.

But—they were moving and no one was available to give me a flight check. After all this, was I to be thwarted? Luck was finally on my side. I ran into

Captain Robert M. Morris, USN, and Major Edmund F. Ball at Naples, Italy, briefly and casually meeting during the planning days for operation "Shingle", the invasion of the mainland of Italy.

Colonel B. B. Taylor, whom I had known at Fifth Army Headquarters in Oujda, and told him my long, sad story of trying for a rating and my current predicament. He persuaded Colonel Engstrom, the pilot of the plane in which I had hitched rides from LaSenia, to be my orientation check pilot! We commandeered a jeep and, with butterflies in my stomach, returned to the airport.

My test would be in an AT-6, an advanced training aircraft, powered by the biggest engine I'd ever seen, a Wright Whirlwind 550 HP engine, but it looked to me to be at least a 1,200 HP. Many of these planes have been purchased and carefully restored. Several were on display at Oshkosh in 1992.

The good colonel climbed into the front seat, put me into the back seat (the pilot's), told me to strap on a parachute, close the hood, and with a few preliminary instructions, started the engine and with

some reassuring comments like "This is a real stable aircraft, easy to fly. Don't worry about it." Nevertheless, I couldn't help worrying that after all this time working to get this opportunity and now that it had finally arrived, would I blow it?

With no more preliminaries, we taxied out, he gave me the signal to take off, and after climbing up to around 4,500 feet, through our intercom communication system told me to do some figure S's, a couple of 360's and then simulated two or three forced landings by pulling back the throttle as if the engine had failed. This is one place where my numerous experience in forced landings came in handy. I had no difficulty at all selecting the most appropriate field and making a proper approach had a real forced landing been necessary. He would then tell me to give it the gun and go around, of course without landing. Finally, after about three hours he was satisfied. We

A review of a French Air Force detachment at Marrakech Airport, February 23, 1943. Left to right: Colonel Charles Saltzman, General Norgues (French), Major Edmund F. Ball, and Lieutenant General Mark W. Clark.

Courtesy of Edmund F. Ball, from Staff Officer with the Fifth Army.

Major Edmund F. Ball (right) proudly wearing wings of a "Service Pilot" earned August 29, 1943, Casablanca, Morocco. Photo April 1945

An AT-6 (below) in flight.

Ball Aerospace Collection, School of Aeronautics and Astronautics, Purdue University

returned to headquarters and he informed Colonel Taylor that he thought I was ready. Lieutenant Colonel Ruebbel, a qualified Flight Instructor, would complete my flight test the next day and, hopefully, approve me for an Air Force Service Pilots rating. I was delighted and grateful.

I spent a restless night at NATC headquarters amidst boxes, crates, foot lockers, bags, file cabinets in the process of moving.

On the memorable morning of August 29, 1943, Lieutenant Colonel Ruebbel in AT-6 509 conducted my official flight test. After several take-offs and landings and a reasonable number of maneuvers in the air, 360 degree turns, and figure eights, he gave me the approval and signed my certification. After all those months of disappointments, frustrations, I now had my Air Force Rating as a Service Pilot. But there was nothing to fly and my assignment as an Air Support Officer with ground units did not include or need an aircraft.

It would be after two more D-Day landings, Salerno and Anzio, and my rotation return to the United States before I actually flew a military aircraft and was finally placed on flying status.

But my mission was accomplished; my long quest achieved!

I returned to LaSenia still using the emergency order that had transported me from Sicily to LaSenia, thence to Port aux Poules and Headquarters VI Corps, ready for our impending landing at Salerno.

I now had my coveted pilot's rating but no aircraft to fly nor opportunities to do so. I was still just a Ground Air Support Officer assigned to the Infantry.

But most importantly, I had finally achieved my objective. I had earned my military pilot's wings!

That's how it all came about.

Returning from my two years' stint overseas, I was first sent to Air Force Redistribution Center at MacDill Field, Florida, where I was checked out on a Twin Beech 18 with a few brief orientation flights. I was soon assigned to Headquarters III Tactical Air Command at Barksdale Field, Louisiana. I was assigned, almost as my personal airplane, a Twin Beech, to transport personnel on inspection trips and training sessions in other locations under the command of III TAC. I also was assigned a smaller Stinson single-engine plane for shorter trips. I thoroughly enjoyed this assignment. Isabel and I, with son Frank and baby Marilyn, had satisfactory quarters on the Post, access to the Officers Club, the Post Exchange, and many other perquisites. But it didn't last.

I was sent back to Washington for a three-week course on procurement contracts, negotiations and disposal of surplus property, then reassigned to Central Procurement District, Air Technical Service Command, Detroit, Michigan, at the Ford Motor Company plant, River Rouge, Dearborn. There I was under command of Colonel Perk Heart a grand and understanding World War I balloon observer.

For me, my war was ended. I was the only flying officer in the Headquarters, so occasionally, when I could get an aircraft and someone had orders for transportation, I served as a sort of aerial chauffeur.

My next "permanent post" would be back in Muncie, 1707 Riverside, and the Ball Brothers Manufacturing Company.

Morris-isms

[1]MY SISTER, Adelia Ball, and the then Lieutenant Senior Grade Robert M. Morris, were married January 20, 1932. A graduate of the United States Naval Academy, Bob's entire career was that of a professional naval officer, retiring with the rank of Rear Admiral.

His "Morris-isms" were well known among his friends in the Navy as well as civilian friends and family. For posterity, I record a few of them herewith:

We do our best and suddenly there is a rainbow in the sky.

Life is too short to be little.

On children: Love them first, then try to understand them.

Tell them they are wonderful until they are.

On rejection of an invitation: Take credit for the thought.

On effort: Genius is attention to significant detail.

On looking for a job: The experience of interviewing, in itself, is a valuable education.

On living in New York City: If you can live in Manhattan, you can live anywhere.

On war: Some of the best military men are civilians; they want to end the war quickly and get back to civilian jobs.

On people: The guy in the boiler room is just as important to the results as the guy at the helm.

On recognition: Never believe your own publicity—either the good or the bad.

On dancing: Bend your knees.

On anger: You never know the burden the other fellow carries.

On love (his favorite was from the Sound of Music): Love isn't love 'til you give it away.

On losing him: Together doesn't always mean sitting at the same table or always under the same roof.

On money: There are some things you cannot not afford.

On achievements: We are in the building business.

Another from South Pacific: You've got to have a dream to make a dream come true.

His salted fish parable: When the Navy gives you a ship, you are also given a barrel of salted fish. On any ship you will have a number of close calls. This is expected. It's all part of the game. After each one, all you have to do is reach in the barrel, grab a fish, and throw it over the side. Then it will be all right. But some day, you'll reach into the barrel and there won't be any fish left.

His advice to a junior officer on receiving a critical fitness report: I wouldn't worry too much about this if I were you. Just write back that if all these things were true, you would have wrecked your ship sometime during the past six months. But what is important, is that you learn something from these things. Any bad situation with someone else is like a bad martini—ask yourself if it was his gin or your vermouth.

The above one-liners courtesy of Admiral Morris' daughters Patricia (Mrs. James A. Ganter), Barbara (Mrs. James A. Goodbody), and Ann (Mrs. Christopher Stack), and Captain (Ret USN) William B. Hayler.

Errors Lead to Errors and to Trouble

June 1979

Piper–Aztec N5246Y

Out of sequence chronologically, I include this experience in these *Ramblings,* with some embarrassment, only as an example of what not to do and how a series of bad decisions, resulting mostly from a case of "get there-itis," can result in real trouble. I'm not very proud of it and, for obvious reasons, omit some names, dates and places.

By 1979, I had accumulated over 10,000 hours of flying. Virginia had joined me as co-pilot when we were married in 1952. I should have known better than to have done what I did. We learn by the mistakes which we make and yet manage to survive.

The story begins when my diving "Buddy" and I had arranged to go scuba diving in Old Mexico. Virginia and I agreed to pick him up at the Los Angeles-Ontario Airport, then fly south of the border. I had cautioned him about weights for baggage, estimated time *en route,* and when we needed to depart.

"Buddy" asked me if he couldn't bring his two young daughters who were just starting their vacation from school. Since my plane was a four-place Aztec, I advised that he might, if all three of them could sit on the back seat. He said they certainly could with no problem.

Error Number One—I said "Okay" but neglected to ask their weights and how much baggage they would bring. "Buddy" arrived at the Fixed Base Operator which I had designated, about three hours late due to his daughters having overslept and he having gotten lost on the way. Their combined baggage would fill the back of a large pickup truck. His camera and flash attachments, which he carried in his lap, alone must have weighed close to fifty pounds.

Error Number Two—I packed them all in with baggage piled up to the ceiling with barely enough room for Virginia and me to crawl into the pilot's and co-pilot's seats. I had wanted to get an especially early departure, no later than mid-morning, but by this time it was early afternoon. I had filed for 9,000 *en route* to Mexicali, on the border, where I would land, refuel and then cross the border and land on the Mexico side to clear customs. With all that weight, I never reached the 9,000 foot level before it was time to descend. Our overweight also slowed our ground speed requiring a half hour longer *en route* than I had planned.

It took quite a while, much longer than I anticipated, to clear customs, file my flight plan to destination, and, of course, the girls were hungry and had to fill up with their first taste of food south of the border before we left.

We departed for our destination with less than three hours before sunset.

Error Number Three—I should have overnighted there or someplace *en route*, but "get there-itis" got me. I took off with full tanks of fuel, luggage, well-fed passengers, aware of the "south of the border" requirement that all flights except instrument, which I had not filed, were to be concluded at or before sunset.

I did not try for a higher altitude for a more scenic ride, but flew closer to the ground, simply to save time. After two and a half hours' flying with the sun rapidly setting, there was an excellent airport below us at a town sixty or so miles north of our destination. It would be only twenty or thirty minutes more of flying to destination, so I elected to proceed into the twilight.

It was not quite dark when I arrived at destination, enough light to see the windsock and, dimly, the runway. My approach would be from out over the water, avoiding the hills and mountains I knew were to the west. I landed gently with use of our landing lights, came safely to a stop near the end of the runway, and turned to taxi back to park the aircraft.

Disaster struck! A culmination of all my previous errors.

Close to the edge of the runway on my turn, my right wheel landing gear seemed someway to have collapsed. We came to a sudden halt with right engine props obviously in hard contact with the ground and the aircraft canted alarmingly downward to the right. Cutting switches and closing fuel valves to prevent any possible dangers of fire, we disembarked. In the darkness, I had run a bit off the runway. My right wheel had dropped into an unlighted ditch that I learned the next day had recently been dug, ironically, to bury the cable for boundary landing lights.

Although the cant of the aircraft was not so bad as to damage the wing or flap, obviously both blades of the propeller were bent.

"Buddy" somehow found a telephone, called the hotel where we were expected, and summoned a taxi. It eventually arrived; we retrieved our luggage from the crippled aircraft and left for the hotel. It was the end of an eventful but disastrous day. We ate a late supper and went to bed.

My concerns, however, thwarted sleep. First of all, how could I get my stranded aircraft out of that ditch without any equipment, and, most importantly, what could be done about my bent propeller blades here five hundred miles and perhaps $2,000 to $3,000 away from the nearest repair shop. Not a pleasant prospect.

The next morning, I took a taxi back to the airport to face the Commandant with my predicament. Fortunately, he spoke enough English for me to explain my problem, corralled five or six husky, young Mexican boys who were hanging around the building. Distributing them strategically along the under side of the right wing as human jacks, with much shouting, gestures, groaning, grunting and laughter, raised it up high enough to get the wheel out of the ditch and the aircraft onto the runway. Pushing it up to the terminal parking area was also no problem. But what about my poor bent prop, and my unauthorized landing after sunset? Would I be fined? My aircraft confiscated? My license suspended? All sorts of terrible thoughts ran through my mind.

In retrospect, perhaps the Commandant himself was as concerned that I might cause him trouble for having left an unmarked, unlighted open ditch so close to an active runway. But I was so overwhelmed with my own concerns that I overlooked what might possibly be equally worrying him. At any rate, he told me there was a retired Mexico Airlines mechanic who lived somewhere on the edge of town and he might be of some help. With many gestures and what seemed to be angry exchanges of words with the taxi driver, the Commandant indicated that the driver would take me to this mechanic's home and see if he could help me. In due course, we found it. With some apprehension, I knocked on the door, and tried by gestures and a few Spanish words to explain my problem. He indicated I should return about 2:00 in the afternoon (I presumed after lunch and a siesta), and that he would go to the airport and see what he could do.

I returned to the mechanic's house promptly at 2:00 and somewhat to my surprise he was ready to go dressed in mechanic's coveralls carrying two large C-clamps, a Stilson wrench and two 2" x 4" pieces of wood about three feet long each. I was baffled by his equipment and not too assured how it might solve my problem. In response to my obvious concerns, he kept repeating to me, "OK, I think I fix. OK, I fix."

Arriving at the airport and after looking over the situation, he went to work immediately, again assuring me, "OK, I fix. OK, I fix."

With me holding the lumber in place, he carefully put the pieces of 2" x 4" on each side of the worst bent prop blade, and tightened his C-clamps using his Stilson wrench for leverage. Methodically, a small turn at a time, he tightened the clamps. I couldn't see much happening at first but could hear some creaking and cracking of the metal, protesting the pressure. From time to time he would loosen the clamps, remove the 2" x 4's", sight down the blade with a straight-edge, then move them to a slightly different position on the blade, and repeat the process. Gradually I could see the blade beginning to straighten. Again and again, he would take the 2 x 4's off and sight along each propeller blade with a straight edge to judge progress and compare it with the undamaged left prop.

He must have worked, painstakingly, perhaps an hour and a half on each blade. Watching how the blades began to resume their original state, my confidence slowly improved.

Finally, he was satisfied that both blades were straightened and, amazingly, except for a few minor scratches and nicks which he smoothed out with a file, they looked pretty good.

Reassuringly now he kept saying, "It's OK. It's OK. Now it's OK to fly."

I started up the engine, cautiously at first, increased the throttle and to my pleasant surprise, there was no vibration, indicating that the props were not out of balance or improperly restraightened. I tried full throttle, feathered the blades and re-feathered them, low RPM, full forward, full throttle with no apparent vibration. I shut the engine down and indicated that I wished to test it in flight, and requested that he come along with me. He kept reassuring me, "No problem. No problem. Is OK. Is OK. Sure I fly with you." He crawled into the co-pilot's seat and, again going through all the ground tests I could think of, took off and climbed to 3,500-4,000 feet. Then I proceeded with all the tests I could think of in the air—turns and banks, different attitudes of the aircraft, slow speed, high speed, full throttle down to almost idle, changing pitch, all with no apparent problems.

He indicated that he had done some flying himself and he was pleased when I let him take over control from the co-pilot's seat. He flew over some places he wanted to see from the air, did some turns and banks and, after perhaps a half hour or more of testing, I was satisfied that the aircraft was now flyable and returned to the airport and landed. I was pleased, relieved, and elated.

He did a little bit of figuring as to time it had taken and somewhat to my surprise, came up with a rather modest bill. I think it might have been $50 or $60. I voluntarily upped it a bit realizing how lucky I was not to have to call in some high priced mechanic from the States with specialized tools and equipment which likely would have cost me at least $1,000.

I took my mechanic friend back home with profuse thanks and returned to the hotel, relieved that the results of my errors and bad judgement had been remedied so inexpensively.

"Buddy," daughters and I went scuba diving for the several days we had planned and when time came for departure, I assured them and Virginia, who remained somewhat apprehensive, that there should be no problem in flying back to the United States. This proved to be the case. However, when I telephoned Muncie and told mechanics there what had been done, and that I had noticed an indication of a small leakage of hydraulic fluid at the hub, they thought I should not fly the plane back to Muncie. Caution prevailed and we took a commercial airline home, a decision I readily made after the several examples of bad judgement that had caused the problem. I was in no mood to take any further chances. A mechanic was dispatched from Muncie who determined that there was a small hydraulic leak through the "O" ring seal around the prop control mechanism which might possibly cause it to fail. A new prop with variable pitch control hub assembly was installed before the plane was returned to Muncie.

As a token of appreciation to the Commandant for his assistance since he wasn't at the airport when we left, I slipped an envelope under the glass covering his desk containing a hundred dollar bill simply with one word on the envelope, "Thanks." Thus ended an experience which I would preferred not to have had, and as soon forgotten. I include it in these *Rambling Recollections* as an example of what not to do and how one case of bad judgment can lead to others and eventually to trouble.

Virginia and I returned to this same airport many years later. By then it was thoroughly modern, long paved runways, fully lighted, control tower, modern terminal, customs and fuel available, served by several airlines from and to the United States and elsewhere.

The site bore no resemblance to remind me of my "Errors and Troubles" experience, only the name of the town, now with several modern hotels, golf courses, tennis courts and swimming pools. The Commandant had long since retired.

CHAPTER IV

THE PIONEERS

*Indiana's Prestigious Pioneer Pilots
I Have Known*

T HESE WORLD WAR I vintage pilots were a bit older than I, but I knew most of them and flew with them on several occasions. They were a very special breed. Most of them have "gone west," but memory of their accomplishments lingers on in the annals of aviation history.

Lawrence "Cap" Aretz

LAWRENCE "CAP" ARETZ from Lafayette was a captain in the National Guard. He learned to fly in 1917 and became an instructor. He was Clyde Shockley's instructor and sold Clyde his first airplane, a Curtiss Jenny (JN14). Its cranky and dangerous characteristics all too often suddenly ended violently the career of many young pilots of World War I vintage. It well deserved its reputation and the title that "Jenny Was No Lady."

When I knew him, "Cap" operated the Aretz Airport at West Lafayette, still operated by his son.

Most of the information here has been provided by his daughter, Mrs. Carol Thieme of Lafayette. It not only provides interesting information concerning "Cap" himself, but also of events related to the development of aviation in its early years in Indiana. The following is from her article entitled:

*Aretz Flying Service
Founded 1946
by Carol Thieme*

IN 1912 at a Chicago Fair, Cap Aretz watched two daredevil stunt flyers perform in Curtiss "Pushers." From that day on he was in love with the sky.

He worked until 1917 at the Northwestern Cadillac Company in St. Paul, Minnesota, selling automobiles. He says, "I was a pretty fair salesman, but the war came along, so I enlisted."

In 1917 the slim, dark, handsome, young flyer with the thin mustache enrolled at the Army's aerial repair school at Chanute Field. During those early months, he learned the fundamentals of flight, aerial engineering, mechanics and common sense which have combined to make him one of the safest flyers of his time.

"I was mustered out in 1919 after knowing people like Doolittle and Rickenbacker." 'Cap' and a service companion, Major Wilbur Fagley interested several Kokomo businessmen in opening a commercial airport. So the Kokomo Flying Service was formed in 1919. The men bought wings and tails and engines and bodies and wired together a rickety fleet of 'Jennies.' The Kokomo flyers used their skill and daring to put planes in the public eye by visiting big city airports, community picnics and county fairs. It would have been fun and profitable if the Kokomo

Flying Service had survived but tragedy in 1921 turned the career of 'Cap' Aretz. One night a sizzling light bulb probably touched one of the wings. The painted and lacquered canvas smoldered and burst into flames. The planes and equipment vanished in the column of black smoke which rose and melted into the wind.

But Aretz and Fagley remained with the Indiana National Guard to teach flying and maintain the aircraft of the 113th Observation Squadron at Kokomo. In 1926 the squadron was moved to Stout Field, Indianapolis. In 1927 Aretz took a leave of absence from the Guard to join the Standard Oil Company flying the company's famous Ford Tri-Motor. He met many airport managers and observed their operations.

Then early in 1928, on a charter flight to Florida, he met Dr. A. C. Arnett of Lafayette who remarked that his city was ready to go 'big time' in aviation. The money was there but a man was needed to run the show. The businessmen were Charles Shambaugh, pioneer automobile designer and dealer, and Dr. A. C. Arnett, physician, amateur pilot and president of the Lafayette Chamber of Commerce.

Dr. Arnett, Shambaugh and 'Cap' Aretz put their heads together and came up with the Shambaugh Airport.

Mention of Dr. A. C. Arnett calls to my mind a tragic event involving his son and bride on their honeymoon. Dick and his bride were well-known by many of us connected with Indiana aviation. He, as I recall it, had just graduated from Purdue and joined with "Cap" Aretz in operating the Lafayette airport and its fixed based sales and training service. Flying a Waco cabin at night over the rough, desolate Wyoming territory, they struck the peak of Laramie Mountain, just a few feet below its top. The wreckage was not discovered for several days during which hope persisted that they might have survived the crash, but this was not to be. It was determined that a misreading or misadjustment of the altimeter was the cause. Another two or three hundred feet altitude would have safely cleared the highest terrain. I knew Dick and his bride-to-be before they were married, and shared their loss with their many other friends. Their father entered personally into the search and never gave up hope for

their survival until the wreckage was finally discovered.

Mrs. Thieme continues: The airport opened in 1928 in a field south of Lafayette which today is the Tecumseh Addition. Four Waco planes were housed at the airport. The field was grass and oats. A three-plane hangar was built and the flying school established. A spectacular air show, free planes rides, stunt flights and aerial broadcasting heralded the opening of the airport. A Standard Oil sponsored Ford Tri-Motor was flown in from Chicago. In the summer of 1929 an air show at Shambaugh airport drew 10,000 spectators for stunt flying and a pilot named Eddie Rickenbacker participated.

The Shambaugh Airport thrived from 1928 to 1934 when Aretz took over the job of manager at Purdue University's brand new airport. The Shambaugh venture was dropped.

The field at Purdue was the first university-owned airport in the world and began operating with fifteen planes and a glider. It became a testing ground for aviation equipment and theory and a classroom for a thousand young pilot trainees. 'Cap' also worked with such aviation idols as Amelia Earhart and Wiley Post.

In 1937 Aretz flew medicine and emergency supplies in a four-a-day round trips from Indianapolis to a flood disaster area at Louisville.

Many Aretz-trained CPT flyers joined British and Canadian air forces and fought in the fiery Battle of Britain in 1940.

In June 1942 the Purdue field was closed to the public when wartime and a Naval pilot training program began. Aretz sold his interest in the Purdue airport and Grove Webster, a CAA official from New York, became manager. Aretz remained as head of the airport's maintenance division until the end of the war.

After V-J Day in 1946, Aretz bought eighty-seven acres northeast of Lafayette on Indiana Highway 25 where the Aretz Flying Service was born and still exists.

It prospered under the expert guidance of 'Cap' Aretz and later by his son, Don Aretz, and now by Don's widow, Ruth. Ruth continues emphasizing the teaching of air safety. Certainly there was no better teacher than 'Cap' Aretz. In over forty years of the toughest kind of flying, 'Cap' was never involved in a serious crash. Much of that safety record could have been luck. But it is most likely that his own set of 'Golden Rules' of flying had a major part in his safety record.

The following are excerpts from columnist Bob Kriebel's articles appearing in the *Lafayette Journal & Courier,* furnished by Mrs. Thieme. They contain a considerable amount of interesting information about aviation history in Kokomo and Lafayette and are only recorded here in the briefest detail.

> June 1957: His ("Cap's") rules were: Human errors such as poor calculations, judgement and mental lapses cause most plane disasters. The engines may be to blame once in a while, but they and the plane are built to do just so much and no more. You cannot take a chance with a plane that you might take with a car such as speed, size of load and flying conditions.
> He also stated what it takes to make a good pilot. "They have got to have three things—a little bird in 'em—good judgment—and common sense."

Shortly after the turn of the century, Howard County residents had their first glimpse of an airplane. It was a boxlike contraption which landed there in 1909, its barnstorming pilot selling rides for fifty cents to a dollar, depending on the length of the ride. Ten years later, at the end of World War I, the Kokomo Chamber of Commerce was asked to make available a temporary landing field so the United States Air Service could stimulate recruitment. Space was needed for two airplanes to land, but only one, flown by a Major Wilbur M. Fagley, arrived. He came back two weeks later and met several prominent businessmen, including Elwood Haynes of early automobile manufacturing fame. The first field opened in August 1919 was named the Haynes Aviation Field.

In April 1926, Clyde Shockley leased forty acres of land to operate as a commercial air field and Continental Airways began Kokomo's first commercial passenger service from the field.

Later, another well-known flyer, Mike Murphy, took over the field and operated it until 1937 when John Ruzicka acquired it and named it the Ruzicka Airport.

In a series of Bob Kriebel's columns in the *Lafayette Journal & Courier,* written in 1990 under the heading "Old Lafayette," many items of interest concerning aviation developments in Tippecanoe County and Lafayette are related.

He records that its aviation history began about seven years after the Wright brothers' first flight at Kitty Hawk in 1903.

In May 1911, the Lafayette newspaper announced that, in cooperation with the Purdue Alumni Association, a "Greater Lafayette" first air show was sponsored. The airport's location was on the Stuart farm west of Lafayette, now the site of the Purdue football stadium. It would feature such aviators as J. A. D. McCurdy, flying a Curtiss-Wright bi-plane with a sixty horsepower, eight cylinder engine. Lincoln Beachey, a well-known pioneer aviator, would accompany McCurdy, and an enormous crowd, estimated at 17,000 persons, came to view the events. There are no air shows reported after 1911.

In 1918, during World War I, a "Lt. Roberts" ran out of fuel and glided to a landing in a gravel pit south of the Purdue campus. He refueled and took off safely out of the gravel pit, but attempting to land at Stuart Field, somehow lost control, crash landed with little or no damage to himself. It was reported as Tippecanoe's first "airplane crash."

World War I stimulated interest in aviation at Lafayette as well as at other airports throughout the state. Many publicized fund-raising events and offered training of pilots.

A Lafayette citizen by the name of Henry G. Boonstra emerged in the early 1920s as a sort of "folk hero" for Lafayette residents. He had learned to fly in 1917, and volunteered for service in the United States Air Corps when the United States entered World War I. He distinguished himself as a fighter pilot over the battlefields of Europe and also as a trainer of pilots at various air fields in the United States. After the war, he barnstormed a number of communities in the

Midwest and entered the United States Mail Service in 1921. In December 1922, he a flew a DeHaviland Bi-Plane from Salt Lake City bound for Rock Springs, Wyoming, encountered a heavy blizzard and never reached Rock Springs. For three days, a search was made over the route and the empty wreckage of his plane was finally discovered near Coalville, Utah, only about fifteen miles out of Salt Lake City. The next day Boonstra turned up safe and sound, having miraculously survived a 10,000 foot plunge, limped away from his wrecked plane and walked through howling winds and deep snow for nearly thirty-six hours to the safety of a ranch house where there was no telephone to report his survival. All vehicle travel was blocked for several days. Similar experiences were not unique in those early days of air mail flying and many, unfortunately, without so happy an ending. Kriebel reports that "Cap" Aretz knew Boonstra during World War I when he was stationed at Chanute Field, Illinois.

Aretz had become an Army Air Corps flight instructor in 1917, but continued numerous barn-storming expeditions to earn money before joining the Indiana National Guard as instructor with the rank of Captain.

During his over fifty years as a flight instructor, he "graduated" over 4,000 students. Aretz came to Lafayette to manage the field. He teamed up with Charley Shambaugh who had opened Lafayette's first real airport on eighty acres southeast of town in 1928.

After a disastrous fire in 1921, his career at Kokomo ended and he became an instructor for the Indiana National Guard at Stout Field in Indianapolis. He took leave from the Guard to join the Standard Oil Company, flying one of its Ford Tri-Motor planes on public relations trips until 1928, when he met Dr. A. C. Arnett on a charter flight to Florida. Arnett employed him to become manager of the Shambaugh Airport which opened in 1928 offering instruction, transportation and services.

Among Aretz' early flying pupils was Michael C. Murphy, a Lafayette boy, who some day would earn our nation's highest aviation award for "outstanding contributions to American aviation." Operations on the Shambaugh Airport led to the opening of the Purdue Airport offering courses related to aviation, the forerunner of Purdue University's School of Aviation and Avionics.

In the fall of 1934, under the leadership of "Cap" Aretz, Purdue University opened the nation's first college-owned airport, complete with beacon, runway lights, paved runways and hangars. The University immediately took up training of pilots and students in other related disciplines and aeronautics research.

In 1939, Aretz began training Purdue students under authority of the

Courtesy of Purdue University Special Collection
"Cap" Aretz and Amelia Earhart as President Elliott gives smiling approval of the School of Aviation.

Courtesy of Purdue University Special Collections
"Cap" Aretz with Amelia Earhart at Purdue's School of Aviation, 1933, when he leased the University's airport to teach flying.

for the pre-planned "crash landing." Post and Aretz had been friends since barnstorming days in 1922.

Aretz was credited with many emergency mercy flights during the unprecedented floods of 1937.

In 1938 Grove Webster was employed by the new Civil Aeronautics Authority to create a civilian pilot training program, including Purdue University. He submitted a plan in 1942 for the creation of a non-profit corporation to be known as the Purdue Aeronautics Corporation, responsible for the operation of the field, and was named general manager, taking over from Aretz.

Amelia Earhart had a brief tour of duty at Purdue University as a "flying professor." With help from Purdue Research Foundation, she took delivery of her Lockheed Electra experimental plane, stating that it was her ambition to "produce practical results for the future of commercial flying and for the women who may want to fly tomorrow's planes." This was the plane in which she flew on the world's flight with navigator Fred Newman to disappear without a trace near Howland Islands en route from New Guinea.

Her connection with Purdue University was of short duration, but left a profound and lasting effect at the school, emphasizing as she did the importance of women in aviation. She was followed by Jill McCormick as instructor. Jill co-piloted in one of the Powder Puff Derbies with Margaret Ball Petty, recorded in *Rambling Recollections of Flying & Flyers, Volume II.*

Civil Aeronautics Administration and became a part of the nation's program to train 2,000 flyers in anticipation of World War II.

Wiley Post, pilot of the famous Winnie May, "crash landed" at the Purdue airport in the midst of his coast-to-coast speed record flight attempt, resulting from a supercharger failure at 36,000 foot altitude. To reduce drag and increase its speed capabilities, the landing gear had been purposely dropped, accounting

Milo G. Burcham

1903-1944

MILO G. BURCHAM was a popular, good natured, and meticulous pilot who, on many occasions, used Muncie Airport as his home base before World War II. He perfected many of his spectacular aerobatics demonstrations there, and often used, with Clyde Shockley's help, Muncie Aviation Corporation's tools, facilities and technical know-how.

At times he flew as pilot in various aircraft on charter, cross-country flights to Chicago, New York and elsewhere, to augment his income. He was equally competent and meticulous, simply flying commercially and instructing, as he was as an aerobatics expert and test pilot.

Burcham, one of East Central Indiana's most distinguished pilots, was born in Henry County, close to the birthplace of Wilbur Wright. He was nationally known for his accomplishments as a skilled aerobatics pilot, and internationally during World War II as Chief Test Pilot for Lockheed Aircraft Corporation in England.

His family moved from Henry County, Indiana, to Whittier, California, when he was quite young and it was there that he learned to fly and decided that he wanted to make aviation his career. He became interested in world records for inverted flying and in competition with an Italian pilot, Falcone, he made an inverted flight from San Diego to Los Angeles in 1933. Falcone increased the record in a flight from St. Louis to Chicago of three hours and six minutes. Milo then broke Falconi's record by more than an hour, a feat which has never been exceeded.

He went from inverted flying to stunt flying and was a perfectionist in every maneuver he attempted, carefully working out each detail in advance.

Maneuvers which might appear to be daring and reckless actually were carefully and scientifically planned.

While his plane was based at Muncie Airport, he developed a "lost wheel" demonstration which was quite spectacular. In the midst of some maneuver, from the cockpit he could release a pin holding the wheel on its axle with a spring device behind it that would push the wheel off the axle, resulting in its falling dramatically, and apparently accidentally, from whatever altitude, four or five hundred feet above the

Courtesy of First United Bank, Sulphur Springs Office
Milo G. Burcham, 1903–1944. One of East Central Indiana's foremost pilots. A master of aerobatics, a transport pilot and test pilot who lost his life much too early in the line of duty testing a Navy advanced Model P-80.

Milo G. Burcham flying a Lockheed 12 prepares to leave for New York with Gladys Rose, wife of Fred D. Rose, president of the Merchants Trust and Savings Company and mother of Andrew W. Rose and Margaret Marsh, in 1937.
Courtesy of Andrew W. Rose

Courtesy of William E. Moffitt
Milo G. Burcham as a young pilot with his Boeing 100 which he used in his "lost wheel" act and inverted flying.

Courtesy of First United Bank, Sulphur Springs Office
A Lockheed P-80 such as Milo was testing at the time of his tragic accident in 1944.

ground, culminating in a gigantic bounce followed by a series of shorter ones which were always spectacular crowd pleasers. There was a smaller wheel, invisible to spectators, mounted in back of the ejected wheel. He then would make what appeared to be a dangerous and difficult landing on one wheel, very simple and safe after he had practiced it a few times.

Another stunt was picking off flags between poles held by assistants and picking up handkerchiefs from the ground with a wing tip.

He was invited to participate in air meets in France and won many international aerial acrobatic titles.

In 1937 he went to work for Lockheed Aircraft and volunteered for high altitude flying research. At the outbreak of World War II, he was ordered home from England, where he had been serving as Chief

Pilot for Lockheed's Liverpool Division. He was needed to work with and test-fly Lockheed's P-38 and its famous Shooting Star, a P-80.

It was in the process of testing an advanced model P-80 that he lost his life. The plane left the runway, and barely cleared a row of houses. Spectators, including his family, realized something was dreadfully wrong. The plane sank below the rim of an abandoned stone quarry dead ahead and struck the further rim. Milo was killed instantly.

The Navy paid tribute to his memory, flying two V-shaped formations of Lightnings over the services at Forest Lawn with more than 1,000 persons in attendance.

Milo was another of those early native Hoosier pilots who left their vapor trails on the pages of aviation history.

Colonel H. Weir Cook

I KNEW Colonel H. Weir Cook of Indianapolis quite well through his participation in numerous events promoting aviation. He was a World War I ace and flew in the National Guard in the period between the world wars. He participated in several Indiana air tours and appeared at numerous aviation events, usually demonstrating Curtiss-Wright Aircraft Company planes. Occasionally, he was successful in selling the plane in which he was flying. A popular model was a small, two-place, open cockpit monoplane with engine mounted above and to the rear of the cockpit. One of Cook's eye-catching acts was to

Courtesy of Harry C. Block, Jr.
Colonel Weir Cook, pilot in both World War I and World War II. One of Indiana's most historic figures in the history of Indiana aviation.

fly slowly over an airfield, or sometimes at a low altitude above streets of small towns, controlling the plane with the stick between his knees, paddling with a paddle as if he was in a canoe. It was a crowd pleaser as well as a demonstration of the aircraft's ease of handling.

He was reactivated as a command pilot in the Pacific during World War II and lost his life on a military mission.

H. (for Harvey) Weir Cook is one of the historic figures in the story of aviation in Indiana. A native of Wilkinson, Indiana, Cook grew up with a love of flight combined with a strong sense of patriotism which he later translated into a career as both a military aviator and as an executive in the aviation business. As a youth, Cook grew up in Wilkinson and Anderson where he attended public schools before entering DePauw University and Washington and Jefferson University.

Cook's introduction to the importance of military aviation began shortly after World War I broke out in Europe in 1914. Determined to make a contribution to the Allied war effort, Cook withdrew from Washington and Jefferson University to go to France in 1916 as a member of the Ambulance Corps. Following America's entry in the war in 1917, however, Cook enlisted as a private in the aviation section of the Army Signal Corps. He was sent to Tours, France, for flight instruction and, upon completion of his training, he joined Captain Eddie Rickenbacker's famous 94th "Hat in the Ring" squadron of the First Pursuit Group. During this time, Cook became a flying "ace" and was awarded the Distinguished Service Cross with Oak Leaves after being credited with the destruction of seven German planes during "dog fight" encounters over the skies of France.

As a flying ace in World War I, Cook experienced one of the most dangerous periods in the history of wartime aviation. As a rule, American fliers were not as well-trained as their German foes and often flew less advanced machines. Of the approximately 260 pilots who served during this period, only about 65 survived their combat experiences. In 1917, the average life expectancy for an American pilot was 30 days. For his part, Cook had his share of brushes with death, once squaring off in the skies over France against Herman Goering, later the head of Hitler's Luft-waffe.

Cook's bravery in battle was later recounted by one of his military colleagues, General Joseph T. McNarney, who remembered: "There was the day near Crepion, France, when (Cook's) gun jammed just as he was heading alone into three German planes. How he got it fixed, I don't know, but he did in time to destroy one of the surprised Germans. The other two turned tail in the face of his flying skill and deadly marksmanship."

After World War I, Cook had the occasion to discuss his experiences in the conflict with many members of the United States Congress. Cook was surprised, however, about the lack of interest which many national political leaders displayed about the importance of aviation and the necessity to create a postwar world where peace would prevail. Cook was convinced that aviation would become an important part of military strategy and tactics, including naval operations. He set about to convince as many people as possible that advancements in aviation science should not be neglected during peacetime. His enthusiasm for advocating the military uses of aviation often created

tensions between himself and the military brass at the time.

During the 1920s, Cook continued his career as an aviator. He became one of the first Air Mail pilots in the United States, flying a route between Salt Lake City, Utah, and Cheyenne, Wyoming. In this position, he also promoted the cause of airplane safety and many people credit his efforts in this area, along with other concerned pilots, with the establishment of the Civil Aeronautics Authority, the forerunner of the Federal Aviation Administration.

While flying his Air Mail route in the western United States, Cook met his future wife, Katherine Kintz Cook. The couple had three children, Harvey Weir Cook, Jr; Susannah; and Peter Parr Cook. In 1934, Cook was primarily responsible for having Indianapolis placed on the mail route between New York and St. Louis.

Cook recorded numerous other achievements in his aviation career during the 1920s and 1930s. In 1926, for example, he became the first aviator in the United States to fly medical supplies (provided by Eli Lilly and Company) into a hurricane-devastated

Courtesy of Harry C. Block, Jr.
Cook with his "Hat in the Ring" World War I fighter plane.

Courtesy of Harry C. Block, Jr.
Colonel Wier Cook, World War I Ace.

The outbreak of World War II in Europe led Cook to re-enter military service in 1941 as a lieutenant colonel in the Army Air Corps. Shortly after his re-entry into military service, Cook took an assignment at Wright Field near Dayton, Ohio, where he received his orders to go to the Pacific Theater. Although technically past the legal age of active military service, Cook eagerly sought the opportunity to fight for his country once again. As he explained to Brigadier General James Doolittle in 1942: "Several of my old friends in the service tell me that I am too old to fly with a group, but I am sure [that] this is an erroneous assumption because I actually want to do this, and I honestly think [that] it would have a good effect on the morale of the unit to have an old-timer flying with them. Furthermore, in case I should be shot down, the youngsters in the group would probably conclude that it was too bad [that] the old boy was shot down but that was to be expected to happen to a man of his age, so you readily see [that] regardless of what might happen to me if I were a Group Commander, there would have been a favorable reaction under any condition."

section of Miami, Florida. In 1928, Cook resigned his Army commission in order to accept a position as vice president and general manager of the Curtiss Flying Service in Indianapolis. While in civilian life, he continued to promote the importance of aviation safety and organized a group of young men, known as the "Flying Cadets." He personally taught them how to operate an aircraft.

One of the most important phases of Cook's career during the interwar years involved his work as director and vice chairman of the American Legion's National Aeronautics Commission. In this capacity, he was instrumental in developing the Legion's model airplane program for boys. He also promoted airline expansion programs for cities and towns throughout the United States. He became involved in a personal crusade to commemorate the significance of the Wright brothers' contribution to the origin of manned flight in the United States.

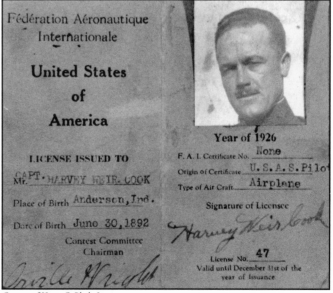

Courtesy of Harry C. Block, Jr.
Lieutenant Weir Cook, 1926, United States Air Service Pilot's License.

Cook carried his share of the flying responsibility of his unit—and more. He took part in the rescue of his contemporary, Eddie Rickenbacker, after the famed aviator had been adrift in the Pacific and feared lost at sea.

Perhaps Cook had an intimation of what lay ahead for him when he wrote that letter to Jimmy Doolittle in 1942. On March 24, 1943, Colonel Cook died when his plane crashed into the side of a mountain in New Caledonia Island in the Pacific. At the time of his death, Cook was the commanding officer of several island bases in the Pacific. He was checking out the safety of a newly arrived aircraft when the accident occurred. Following Cook's death, Roscoe Turner, a fellow Indiana pilot, remembered his friend with the following words: "Colonel Cook met his death as he would have wished to have met it—in the cockpit of a fighter plane serving his country in World War II. The record of Colonel Cook's service to God and country is one of unselfish devotion. He served tirelessly, faithfully, and with no expectation of personal reward. He helped America develop her wings. Behind roaring motors, up where the clouds float, he blazed the trail of America's conquest of the skyway. He was the type of American whom we all idolize—a fighter, a pioneer, a leader." In March 1944, the year after Cook's death, the civic leaders of Indianapolis renamed the Indianapolis Municipal Airport in his memory. For the next three decades, visitors to Weir Cook Field (now Indianapolis International Airport) would be reminded of the life of this Hoosier pilot and his contribution to aviation.

Courtesy of Roland "Tack" S. Nail

Fifty Years Ago (1943)

COLONEL H. WEIR COOK, Indiana's first ace in World War I, was killed in the South Pacific Theater where he was in command of a group of airfields. He was believed to be the first ace of World War I to die in the present conflict. Only a few weeks earlier he had directed rescue efforts for his former commanding officer, Captain Edward V. Rickenbacker. (The Indianapolis municipal airport was named in Cook's honor.)

Colonel Clarence "Cap" F. Cornish

COLONEL CLARENCE "CAP" F. CORNISH was another of Indiana's illustrious early aviators, important in Indiana's aviation history, whom I have known for many years. "Cap" was born in Canada but his parents moved to Fort Wayne in October 1900 when he was two years old. He flew during both World War I and World War II.

At the outset of World War I, at the age of eighteen, he and three friends tried to enlist in the Navy as radio operators, but he was too light—under 120 pounds—so he enlisted in the Cavalry on April 27, 1917. Later, with the encouragement of his Commanding Officer, who felt he might make a better pilot than cavalry man, he transferred to the Aviation Section of the Army Signal Corps for pilot training. Cornish made his first flight on May 6, 1918, and soloed three weeks later (May 27th).

His final examination was a "shoot down" with his instructor using a camera gun, which he did so convincingly that he was made an instructor himself. One of his prize students later became the well-known airplane manufacturer, Eddie Stinson.

Cornish was appointed by Governor Henry Gates as the first director of the Indiana State Aviation Commission. He advocated building a new airport for Fort Wayne and selected the location for what is now called Baer Field. His biography was published in *OX-5 News,* Volume 32, Number 2, April 1990:

COLONEL Clarence F. Cornish, or "Cap" as he is affectionately known by his many old friends and acquaintances, began his aviation career as an Aviation Cadet in the Air Corps branch of the United States Signal Corps at Millington, Tennessee, where he soloed a Curtiss Jenny JN4D on May 27, 1918. Upon completion of his training, he became a pursuit pilot and aerial gunnery instructor.

When World War I ended, he returned to Fort Wayne, Indiana, where he opened the first radio business store and flew on weekends for the Air Corps Reserve. He also operated as a barnstormer and flight instructor, flying a Curtiss Oriole and Curtiss Robins, Waco 10's, powered with OX-5 engines and later flew the Ryan airplane owned by the *Fort Wayne News Sentinel.*

"Cap" became widely known throughout Indiana and other midwestern states. He was extremely active in promoting aviation and flying safety throughout the midwest. He sponsored and participated in the original Indiana State Air Tour in the early 1930's, promoting civil aviation everywhere he went.

Courtesy of Clarence F. Cornish
Colonel Clarence F. Cornish, another of Indiana's illustrious and accomplished aviators who contributed importantly to Indiana's aviation history.

He was named airport manager of Paul F. Baer Field in Fort Wayne, Indiana, where he operated one of the first CAA approved flight schools. This field was later renamed Smith Field. Fort Wayne's present commercial field, named Baer Field, was constructed in 1941 for the United States Army to use as a training base for World War II pilots. "Cap" Cornish was chosen to select the site and was its sponsor. This is a good example of his foresight and wisdom in planning airports as it is now one of the four major commercial airports in the State of Indiana. He was also instrumental in selecting the site of Bunker Hill Air Force Base near Peru, Indiana, where one of the President's National Emergency Flying Offices is stationed. Its name was changed to Grissom Field following the tragic death of the Purdue graduate astronaut.

"Cap's" personal efforts in establishing safety programs while serving as State Director of Aeronautics, 1945–1953, are still regarded as very important facets in the development of civil aviation activities in the State of Indiana.

He served as Chief of the Air Traffic Control Section of the Army Air Force Staff in Washington, D. C., during World War II, and as alternate Army member of the Inter-Departmental Air Traffic Control Board. The objective of both organizations was the promotion of safety by all users of air space within the continental limits of the United States. The results of this early action are evident to this day.

His sixty-eight years of active participation in aviation history was recognized by the OX-5 Aviation

Courtesy of Clarence F. Cornish
"Cap" Cornish (above) at Indianapolis Metropolitan Airport about to fly the Cessna 142 on his 94th birthday in 1992.
Cornish (left) as aviation cadet and instructor in the Air Corps branch of United States Signal Corp at Millington, Tennessee, where he soloed May 27, 1918, in a Curtiss "Jenny", a JN4D.

Courtesy of Clarence F. Cornish

"Edmund F. Ball (right) with "Cap" Cornish celebrating the seventy-fifth anniversary of his first solo flight at the Indianapolis Metropolitan Airport on May 6, 1993.

Pioneers in 1986, when he was elected to the OX-5 Aviation Pioneers Hall of Fame. We proudly salute Cap Cornish.

Cornish flew several different types of early planes in addition to those reported in the OX-5 biography. One of his favorites was a Thomas-Moines Scout which was the last one he flew in World War I at Arcadia, Florida.

He was released from the Army in 1919, got a job as a copy reader for the Fort Wayne newspaper, resumed his early interest in radios and flew whenever he had an opportunity. He flew a Curtiss Oriole, barnstormed and participated in air shows flying the old World War I workhorse, Curtiss "Jenny." He remained in the Air Corps Reserve and kept current flying out of Schoen Field, Fort Benjamin Harrison, Indiana. In July of 1941, he was recalled to active duty and retired with rank of full Colonel.

Cornish was a born birdman. He flew the old Rotary LeRohen engines which rotated around a fixed shaft, burned gasoline mixed with castor oil, which made many pilots sick, but not Cornish. He flew at night, got lost, landed in fogs, and one time had a lady parachutist caught in his airplane's wing strut. He was able to shake her loose at a safe altitude for her chute to open properly. He survived them all.

"Cap" has kept his flying status current all these years and flies on each flight anniversary (74 years) the most recent at this writing, 1992, at the age of 94. He belongs to the "Early Birds," the "Quiet Birdmen," the OX-5 Aviation Pioneers, the U.F.O.s (United Flying Octogenarians) and many others. Keep it up "Cap" at least to 100!

I was recently an invited guest on May 6, 1993, at the Indianapolis Metropolitan Airport when the indomitable "Cap" Cornish celebrated the seventy-fifth anniversary of his first solo flight by taking family and numerous friends for short sight-seeing hops over Indianapolis. He is looking forward to next year to do the same celebrating his 95th birthday.

Walter C. Davis

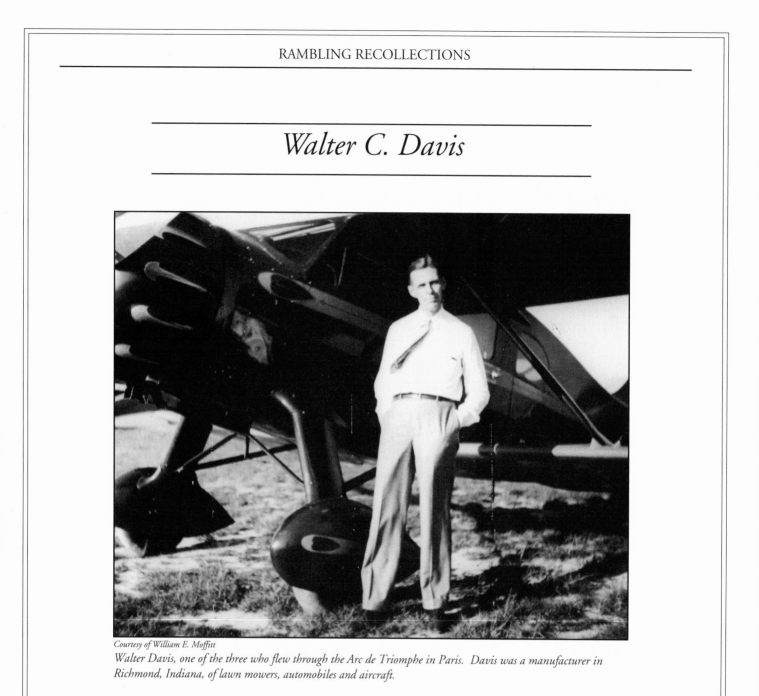

Courtesy of William E. Moffitt
Walter Davis, one of the three who flew through the Arc de Triomphe in Paris. Davis was a manufacturer in Richmond, Indiana, of lawn mowers, automobiles and aircraft.

WALTER C. DAVIS, manufacturer of lawn mowers, aircraft and automobiles located in Richmond, Indiana, was born in Winchester, Indiana, March 31, 1893. He moved to Richmond with his parents when he was eleven years old. From that age until his death in 1952, his entire life was dedicated to aviation.

I became quite well-acquainted with Walter. He flew with me on several occasions on air tours and to aviation-related meetings after he had let his license expire. Along with my cousin Frank, we were charter members of the Sportsman Pilot Association and AOPA (Aircraft Owners and Pilots Association).

Walter began flying well before World War I and was sent overseas with the rank of First Lieutenant—Flight Instructor. In contrast with his contemporaries, he bragged that he never flew in combat and was not an "Ace." As an experienced pilot, he was assigned mainly to instruction. He is credited with being one of three pilots who flew, in defiance of orders, at low level down the Champs Elysses in Paris and through the Arc de Triomphe with about eight inches to spare

Courtesy of Quiet Birdmen, from the archives of Q-B Beam.
Casey Jones, one of the three pilots who flew through the Arc de Triomphe in violation of all orders in World War I.

at each wing tip. Captain "Casey" Jones, a World War I ace, Walter told me, was one of the others and I had forgotten the name of the third pilot, until Jeanette Short from Lexington Kentucky, fellow member of the Sportsman Pilot Association, thought it was "Rasty" Wright. All three were threatened with a court martial if their names were discovered, but their identity was never revealed until long after the close of the war and they were well out of the range of any military court martial.

Davis' interest in aviation dated back to his boyhood days when he visited the aircraft plant of the Wright brothers in Dayton, Ohio, at the age of about eleven. This visit triggered his long interest in aviation. At the age of eighteen, he acquired a glider that had been wrecked, rebuilt it and attempted to fly it on a deserted race track just outside of Richmond. He tied a hundred foot rope to a motorcycle driven by a high school classmate to lift it off the ground, since there were no hills or cliffs in that vicinity to launch with gravity providing the power. Shortly after reaching flying speed, the motorcycle was forced to turn with the race track, the embryo glider pilot was unable to turn resulting in a crash of both aircraft and motorcycle, but,

fortunately, without physical harm to either pilot or cyclist. The glider itself was terminated, but Walter's interest in aviation was not.

Shortly after the United States entered World War I, Davis enlisted in the Signal Office Reserve Corps to which, at that time, aviation operations were assigned. He applied for and received flying instruction at the Wilbur Wright Field in Dayton and was commissioned a First Lieutenant (Flying Officer) in December 1917. In January 1918, he was sent to France with the American Expeditionary Force as a pursuit instructor and was named commanding officer of the Third Aviation Center, Issoudun, France. By the end of that year, he was promoted to captain. Carl A. Spaatz, later commanding general of the United States air forces in France, was one of his students.

Captain Davis was severely injured in a crash caused by a sudden maneuver avoiding a collision with another aircraft. It resulted in his wearing a plaster cast for eighteen months, but it did not prevent him from flying and instructing.

While overseas, he wrote graphic letters to his parents back in Richmond about the beauties of flying above the clouds, glorious sights from the air far above the ground, the thrill of acrobatics in the cold, clear air at 20,000 feet.

He was cited by General Pershing for conspicuous and meritorious service in 1918.

He returned to civilian life in 1919 and rejoined his father at the Davis Motor Company, which had originally made buggies and wagons. It had been briefly converted to automobile manufacturing, only to be forced out of business by combinations of companies to create General Motors, Ford Motor Company, Chrysler and others. The company continued to make an occasional automobile and, under Walter's guidance, began the manufacture of aircraft. Later came lawn mowers. Walter had great fun identifying himself as being a manufacturer of automobiles for experience, aircraft for fun, and lawn mowers to make money.

Walter was a great storyteller. He loved to tell incidents, usually about something that occurred to him, with many interruptions by his own contagious, hearty laughter. I recall one story about his loading a lawn mower into the front cockpit of his plane to take on a sales trip for a demonstration, which took much longer flying time than he had anticipated. His compass seemed to be very erratic and took him far off course. Finally, he realized that the compass, instead of pointing to magnetic north was pointing to the lawn mower in the front seat.

In 1928, to get into the aircraft manufacturing business, Davis acquired a small aircraft manufacturing firm in Portsmouth, Ohio, called the Vulcan Aircraft Company. In 1929, the operation was moved to Richmond, Indiana, and its name changed to the Davis Aircraft Corporation.

The Davis aircraft was a trim, efficient, two-seater "parasol" monoplane that won numerous awards at air shows and air races. Dealerships were set up in such distant places as the Philippine Islands, Hawaii, Mexico and Argentina. The aircraft were noted for speed, economy and ease of flying, but the timing was bad. The Wall Street crash in 1929 and ensuing Depression brought an end to sales. Simultaneously, a fire destroyed the plant in 1930. By 1933, the company ceased to exist. A few planes were produced over the years until 1937, when Walter again joined his father in business manufacturing lawn mowers very successfully, but he never lost his interest in and love for aviation.

Davis flew thousands of miles annually. He held a transport pilot's license. At one time, he was assistant manager at the Pratt and Whitney airplane engine plant in Kansas City, Missouri; he was secretary of the Manufacturers Aircraft Association, and was affiliated with the Society of Automotive Engineers, the National Aeronautics Association of the United States, the Federation of Aeronautique Internationale and the Society of Early Birds, an organization of pilots prior to or during World War I. He was a graduate of Richmond High School, attended Earlham College and graduated from the University of Pennsylvania.

Walter died at the relatively young age of 59, but during his life span, he had experienced the development and growth of aviation from primitive aircraft to a high degree of sophistication in two World Wars.

Walter was survived by his widow, three sons and one grandchild at the time of his death in July 1952.

Walter was one of the most interesting persons it was ever my privilege to know, and his significant contributions to aviation are largely unrecognized. I salute his memory as one of the great pioneer aviators.

Courtesy of Dr. Herbert E. Ware
Photograph of Davis Aircraft.

Herbert O. Fisher

Civilian Test Pilot

HERBERT O. FISHER was one of Indiana's most distinguished pilots during World War II and enjoyed a distinguished career which spanned the interwar years and also the period after World War II. I knew him quite well when he was the Secretary of the Aviation Division of the Indianapolis Chamber of Commerce. Herb began his career with the Chamber as an office boy, learned to fly at the old Hoosier Airport in 1927, and joined the 309th Observation Squadron of the United States Army Air Corps at Schoen Field, Fort Benjamin Harrison. He soon advanced from office boy to Secretary of the Aviation Division and shortly thereafter was assigned the job of selecting the site for the Indianapolis International Airport.

During the interwar period, Herb handled press and public relations for Transcontinental Air Transport (now TWA) when it started transcontinental passenger service using Ford Tri-Motor aircraft. He also assisted Embry-Riddle and American Airlines when they began mail and passenger service out of Indianapolis. During the 1930s, he worked extensively on the selection and improvement of 35 airports in Indiana as part of the Works Project Administration (WPA).

Herb also became president of the American Society for the Promotion of Aviation. He organized numerous Indiana Air Tours and sponsored an air marketing program painting direction signs on rooftops in over 300 locations throughout the state. Mention of this program reminds me of the

time I undertook to have one of Fisher's direction signs painted on the roof of the Ball Brothers office. We were supplied directions, kind and color of paint and an example indicating size and type of letters. All were clearly depicted using the fictitious name of AIRVILLE with a large arrow pointing to the airport. I gave it to the company's painter foreman, who

Courtesy of Curtiss-Wright Corporation and Roland "Tack" S. Nail

Herbert O. Fisher, one of Indiana's most distinguished and important persons in the history of Indiana and United States World War II aviation. An early promoter of aviation and civilian test pilot. He received numerous awards for his many achievements including the Air Force Medal presented to him by President Roosevelt and he was named a "Doolittle Fellow." He held a Doctoral degree in Aeronautical Science.

Courtesy of Curtiss-Wright Corporation and Roland "Tack" S. Nail
Herb Fisher with a P-47 propeller driven Thunderbird with experimentally contoured propeller. He tested trans-sonic and sweep-back propellers in a power dive from 38,000 feet. He reached a velocity of 600 MPH.

accepted the challenge as a welcome relief from the routine of painting warehouses and factory roofs. A few days later, he invited me to inspect his work, with obvious pride. I couldn't believe it. He had duplicated the instructions exactly! There was "AIRVILLE," complete with an arrow pointing north to Muncie airport! He was crestfallen when I pointed out the error, and I'm not sure that he ever got around to making the correction.

Herb's aviation career got a start in 1937 when he joined the airplane division of Curtiss-Wright Corporation in Buffalo, New York, as emergency test pilot. He soon became Chief Production Test Pilot and then the Chief Test Pilot for all types of aircraft and modifications during his twenty years with that company. While working for Curtiss-Wright, he conducted literally thousands of test flights on

propellers, jet transports, and fighter type aircrafts.

In World War II, Herb was sent to the China-Burma-India Theater where, as a civilian test pilot, he conducted many tests on C-46s and P-40s. As a result, he was credited with saving hundreds of pilots and passenger lives during his thirteen-month tour. He had the responsibility of assisting pilots, engineering and flight operations of the Air Transport, Troop Carrier, and Fighter Commands in the technique of flying and maintenance of C-46 transports and P-40 fighters. As a civilian, he flew 96 missions, including 10 combat missions, many when "The Hump" was officially closed over the Himalayans so that he purposely could encounter severe icing and other phenomena to learn how it might affect the C-46.

One of his most remarkable and spectacular tests was to see what happened if all four engines of a B-17 were suddenly thrown into reverse pitch while in flight. The predictable result was that the aircraft simply fell out of the sky at an alarming rate of descent, something like 15,000 feet per minute. The truly remarkable thing, the purpose of the test, was to

Courtesy of Roland "Tack" S. Nail
Herb Fisher on left with three other military pilots, Cox, Straub, and Carpenter, 1929.

see if and how a recovery could be made. After a fall of about 14,000 feet, Herb was able to re-establish control of the aircraft and land it safely. The test was to determine, in the event of an involuntary human error or mechanical malfunction, whether it was possible to regain control of the aircraft and survive. It could be done.

Herb also led the field in numerous other spectacular tests. He directed and flew tests of many Grumman F8-1 Bearcats using Curtiss reversing propellers and dive brakes for dive bombing from 25,000 feet, reaching rates of descent of 30,000 to 35,000 feet per minute.

Courtesy of Curtiss-Wright Corporation and Roland "Tack" S. Nail
Herb Fisher making a first flight in a Japanese Zero at Curtiss Aircraft Plant, Buffalo, September 10, 1943. Herb's analysis of captured enemy aircraft, their strengths and weaknesses, contributed greatly to Allied pilots' success in combat.

Another was a dive from 38,000 feet in a P-47 propeller-driven Thunderbird, during which its velocity reached 600 miles-per-hour, testing transsonic and sweep-back type propellers. During the war, he flew captured enemy aircraft to analyze their strengths and weaknesses. He served on numerous committees as a technical advisor and on the boards of related organizations. For his achievements, he was awarded the Air Force Medal by President Franklin D. Roosevelt, the first civilian to receive the honor.

After World War II, he returned to Curtiss-Wright, where he continued testing and researching many tests on many types of civilian and military aircraft. In 1953, he resigned from Curtiss-Wright and spent the next 22 years as an executive of the Aviation Department of the Port Authority of New York and New Jersey. In this position, he had the opportunity to fly and evaluate every commercial and business jet, both foreign and domestic, prior to their receiving permission to land at the New York airports, in order to assess possible noise problems related to take-offs and landings. Fisher was one of the four members of the Technical Committee of the National Air Transport Coordinating Committee (NATCC), the first organization of this type in the United States to study and set safe take-off and landing procedures to help reduce jet noise over the hundreds of communities in the entire New York, Long Island and New Jersey areas.

Herb Fisher received many aviation honors during his lifetime. Among his many awards were The General Doolittle Fellow (presented by Senator Barry Goldwater), a Doctorate of Aeronautical Sciences from Embry-Riddle Aeronautical University, and the OX-5 Hall of Fame, to which Larry Hirschinger and I have also been inducted.

Fisher was also presented Command Pilot Wings and the rank of Full Colonel by the Commander-in-Chief of the Chinese Air Force, Taipei, Taiwan, in recognition of his professional assistance to the Chinese government.

In his sixty years of flying under a variety of unusual circumstances and conditions, he accumulated almost 20,000 hours of flying without an accident or a violation. Herb died from natural causes in 1990.

Colonel Michael C. Murphy

MICHAEL C. MURPHY, the "Flying Irishman" was one of "Cap" Aretz's distinguished students. He grew up on a farm west of Indianapolis and watched airplanes flying overhead with wonder and envy. It was inevitable that some day he would fly and own his own aircraft. Mike began flying in 1927 as an apprentice mechanic and student pilot under the watchful eye of Aretz at Lafayette. After earning his license, he purchased a used World War I training plane, an OX-5 Canuck, rebuilt it and went barnstorming to earn enough money to pay for his commercial transport license and his airplane. His money-raising technique, like most of his contemporary barnstormers, was to search for a small town in an essentially rural area, circle around it, do a few stunts to attract attention, and then land in a convenient pasture close to town. Soon a crowd would gather.

His preferred procedure then would be to try to attract the attention of an attractive young lady and offer her, with a friend, a free ride. When they returned safely and usually excited and enthusiastic, others were persuaded to give this new adventure a try. Usually, by the end of the day, he would return to his base at Kokomo with sufficient money to tide him over for a week or so when he would repeat the procedure. He put on spectacular shows at various county and state fairs, at each improving his reputation as a superior stunt flyer.

He participated in many Indiana Air Tours and shows. I flew my plane in several in which Mike was a featured participant. I remember one particularly, flying all the way to New York, in which Mike did aerobatics at every step. I stood in awe of his spectacular stunts and, with others, admired the "Flying Irishman" as a pilot and as an individual.

He developed several spectacular feats that I well remember. One was a precision landing and take off from a small platform on the back of a fast-moving truck. In this event, he flew a Cub airplane landing on a truck traveling at about forty miles-per-hour. Another spectacular stunt was to land a plane with specially built landing gear upside down. I believe that he is the only pilot ever to have accomplished this feat.

Courtesy of Mrs. Michael Murphy
Mike Murphy

Courtesy of Marathon Oil Company
At aerobatic shows across the country, Mike thrilled audiences by landing on top of a moving automobile.

Courtesy of Marathon Oil Company
A popular attraction at aerobatic shows was Mike's landing a plane upside down.

Courtesy of Marathon Oil Company
Mike Murphy's career spanned nearly forty-five years.

My recollection is that he used a Waco F-2 with a souped up Pratt and Whitney or Wright engine for stunts requiring higher performance.

Mike went to Findlay, Ohio, in 1937 and founded an air show troupe advertising Marathon Oil products featuring night shows, banner towing and stunting. He did test flying for Curtiss aircraft and was employed by the Canadian government as aircraft acceptance pilot for United States aircraft just before World War II.

During Mike's career he earned many honors. He was three times National Aerobatics Champion and retired the Freddy Lund Trophy for his aerobatics skills. He was two times International Aerobatics Champion. He was the first world judge on the world competition events and president of the FAI rules committee. He was inducted into the Curtiss Hall of Fame at Hammondsport, New York.

He entered the military service early in World War II and was assigned to Cargo Glider Operations of the Air Force Transport Training Command. No one was better qualified than Mike for glider training, with his long experience with dead stick landings and powerless flights during this professional stunting career.

He was called up by General H. H. "Hap" Arnold, Commander of the United States Army Air Corps, to take on the job of training glider pilots for the military operations, even before any gliders were actually available. As a Lieutenant Colonel, he was ordered to England to prepare for D-Day and a night glider landing operation across the Channel into Normandy. He crash landed, as did so many others, broke both legs and was rescued. For all of this he received, from General Hoyt Vandenberg, Chief of Staff of the Air Corps at that time, the Legion of Merit. In addition, he earned the Purple Heart and the Air Medal with clusters, and, in 1945, the Edward S. Evans trophy for his glider skills.

Upon returning from military service in 1945, he rejoined Marathon and was promptly assigned by President J. C. Donnell the responsibility for building its "aviation division," pretty much from the ground up. When he retired twenty-six years later, he left a legend for high standards of performance for his accomplishments as a teacher and leader. By that time, the Marathon fleet consisted of eighteen aircraft flown by thirty-one pilots. The fleet included two Beechcraft Hawker Model 125 jet aircraft, a Grumman Gulfstream, seven King Aires, four Twin Bonanzas, one Beech Baron and three Musketeers, the latter used for pipeline patrol. At one time, the company owned twenty-nine airplanes, but eventually, with more efficient equipment, it was possible to do the aerial work with a much fewer number of aircraft.

Back in civilian life after the war, he was awarded one of the only two honor awards ever given by the Federal Administrative

Association. He was named Corporate Pilot of the Year in 1970 and received meritorious awards from NBAA in 1971. He held the record for operating the safest business flying operation in the world for over fifteen years. He was inducted into the Ohio Hall of Fame in Cleveland in 1977, and the OX-5 Hall of Fame in San Diego.

Mike's advice for success as a manager, which is well worth heeding, was "pick the right people for the right job, pay them well, treat them fairly, and you've got it made!" Mike was a contemporary of such Indiana pilots as Herb Fisher, "Cap" Aretz, Clyde Shockley, Weir Cook, Walter Davis, and Milo Burcham, and deservedly is on the roles of highest honors among Indiana pilots.

I'm deeply indebted for the above information to Mike's widow, Mrs. "Cissie" Murphy, and to the *Marathon World, Marathon Messenger* and *Flight, a Journal of Executive Aviation,* both issued in 1971 at the time of Mike's retirement.

Courtesy of Mrs. Michael Murphy
Mike Murphy in the early "barn storming" days.

Colonel Roscoe Turner

ANOTHER distinguished pilot was "Colonel" Roscoe Turner, originally from Mississippi, with his waxed moustache, powder blue uniforms, Sam Brown belt, leather riding boots and, at times, with his pet lion cub named Gilmore that flew with him on occasions advertising gasoline. Roscoe was a showman but a hell of a good pilot as well. Among others, he successfully flew the Gee Bee, a huge twelve hundred horsepower Pratt and Whitney engine stabilized by a couple of stubby wings, tiny tail assembly and a fuselage just big enough to squeeze in a pilot's seat. Roscoe broke all kinds of records for closed course and cross country races, chilled and thrilled spectators and other pilots. I knew Roscoe fairly well in later years.

Most of the material herewith are excerpts from *Colonel Roscoe Turner—Knight Errant of the Air* by Roy Rutherford, and from newspaper articles.

Roscoe Turner was born near a small town in Mississippi just before the turn of the century, in 1895, to a farming family of six children.

His adventuresome spirit was evidenced quite early. He tried to build a kite big enough to lift him off the ground. It didn't work! He told his father he wanted to be a railroad engineer and a race car driver, but his father thought they were too dangerous careers to consider.

Although he excelled in mathematics, history and geography, he didn't finish school. He ran away from his home at the age of sixteen because of a disagreement with his father, worked at various jobs including driving a truck, licensed to do so by learning the names of all the streets in the city of Memphis where he worked.

He improved his mechanical skills working as an automobile mechanic, which served him well later in life as he became involved with piston-driven aircraft engines.

He tried to enlist in the aviation section of the Signal Corps at the outbreak of World War I, but he was not accepted since he did not have a college education.

He finally made it into aviation by enlisting as an ambulance driver in the Signal Corps where, in due course, he was commissioned a Second Lieutenant and sent to France and Germany for pilot training. The war ended before he was ready for combat flying.

It's interesting to note that his first venture into space from the earth was by balloon.

Edmund F. Ball, Fred Lockwood, and Roscoe Turner, circa 1938.

The Western Reserve Historical Society, Cleveland, Ohio
Colonel Turner after winning Thompson Trophy Race.

After returning to the United States after the war, he remained in the service long enough to fly airplanes in the New York area but, at the age of twenty-three, he was mustered out. Then, with borrowed money, he managed to buy half interest in an airplane, went on air tours through the south, earning enough money to pay for the plane doing acrobatics and putting on air shows under the title of Roscoe Turner's Flying Circus. He advertised such stunts as a burning airplane falling out of the sky, simulated by trailing smoke from canisters on the wings. There would also be wing-walking, a swing of death, a parachute jump, aerial acrobatics including loops, spins, wing overs, whip stalls and rolls. Depending on how much the area could afford, he was paid $500 to $1,000 for each show.

With his earnings, he bought the first passenger plane built by Sikorsky in America. It carried eight passengers. He tried all sorts of things to interest passengers—held a ladies tea party aloft, flew distinguished people about the country, and just about anything to make a little money. He went to California in 1928 and broke into the movie business with disastrous results. Another pilot wrecked his plane doing a stunt and insurance collected was only about one-third of the cost. That was the end of that venture.

He started an airline to Reno, Nevada, called the "Alimony Express," carrying many movie stars, managers and directors including Will Rogers for his first ride. He taught Bebe Daniels to fly and made the acquaintance of the newspaper publisher, William Randolph Hearst. He flew him and guests to New York City and to Hearst's famous ranch, San Simeon.

He adopted his famous pale blue uniform, waxed his moustache to points, and acquired his famous lion cub named Gilmore after the oil company which had employed him to advertise their products.

He developed a popular kid's show broadcast from his airplane, telling as he flew about shooting down, single-handed, squadrons of evil smugglers and capturing thieves with millions of stolen dollars and returning them to their rightful owner.

He loved speed. He remained insatiable, never satisfied in his quest for spectacular aircraft performances and always where speed was the principal objective. Racing airplanes became his principal interest and he is remembered, rightly I believe, as being the greatest of all competing race pilots. He was a great showman, both lucky and unlucky.

He established a speed record in 1929 carrying passengers from New York to Los Angeles in twenty hours and twenty minutes. That was the year he became particularly interested in aviation racing. He placed third in the non-stop Los Angeles to Cleveland flight and third in the Thompson Trophy closed-circuit at Cleveland. In 1932, he came in first in the Thompson Trophy, closed-circuit, race but accepted as fact when told he had cut a pylon which disqualified him. He accepted the ruling, congratulated the declared winner, even though they determined later that he had not actually cut the pylon.

Turner was the only three-time winner of the Thompson Trophy.

At the urging of the Indianapolis Chamber of Commerce and the City Council, they persuaded Turner to locate on the newly-developed Indianapolis

The Western Reserve Historical Society, Cleveland, Ohio
Colonel Turner, winner of Thompson Trophy Race 1932.

airport using his name as a big attraction. He provided transportation to company executives in Indianapolis, principally Stokley-VanCamp and Schwitzer Corporation. With is own money, he started an airline service to Chicago but it failed.

He married the former Madonna Miller from Sheridan, Indiana, and she became president and treasurer of the Turner Aeronautical Corporation which was housed in the principal hangar on the Indianapolis airport. In reaching the decision to locate in Indianapolis, Colonel Weir Cook, a long-time friend of his, was quite instrumental in the final decision.

I recall he had one of his famous Bee Gee racing aircraft, the only survivor of fatal crashes, suspended from the top girders of the building as if it was in flight. It was a remarkably fast plane but flying it

Muncie Aviation Corporation
Colonel Roscoe Turner and Clyde Shockley with Mayor Rollin H. Bunch in front of Stagger-Wing Beechcraft circa 1938.

The Western Reserve Historical Society, Cleveland, Ohio
Colonel Turner with his lion cub, Gilmore, advertising Gilmore Oil products. He and Gilmore flew together many times. When he got older and bigger, he was given to a zoo where Turner visited him often, brought him bits of meat and retained a friendly recognition from Gilmore throughout his lifetime.

Courtesy of Edmund F. Ball
Photograph of a restored Gee Bee taken by Edmund F. Ball at Oshkosh Air Show 1992.

required the skills of a master pilot. Turner was that master. He described it from a pilot's point of view, with his famous, deep-throated laugh, as "having 1,200 horses sitting in your lap and a feather sticking out your tail."

After Turner's retirement from racing, he started a business named Turner Aviation. He continued to fly at every opportunity, but gradually decreased his time in the air. He sold an interest in his business to the Gates Rubber Company, changing the name of his operations to Turner-Gates. The Turner name was eventually dropped and became Combs-Gates and, the latest, AMR-Gates.

Behind all his showmanship, I felt he was actually somewhat of a reticent person, concealing his shyness with his flamboyant uniforms and blustering bravado. Towards the end of his life, he became quite religious.

Roscoe Turner, undoubtedly one of the all-time great pilots, died at Indianapolis from cancer June 24, 1970, at the age of 74—certainly, one of the giants in the annals of aviation.

Orin Welch

ORIN WELCH was one of Indiana's early aviation entrepreneurs. He probably flew with Muncie's first commercial pilot, Ernie Basham, in the mid 1920s. There seems to be no records of when or where he learned to fly in 1923, but Harry White, who soloed me, could well have been his instructor.

Harry White flew for Welch's Anderson Aircraft Company (AAC) before coming Muncie to take charge of Wall Field in 1927.

My first log book records several flights all the way to Anderson and return when Welch was operating its airfield. One of them records a thirty-minute flight. I must have gotten lost somewhere on the way.

I remember Welch quite well as a competent, respected operator of the field, which was located on the southwest side of Anderson at the junction of old Pendleton Pike and Highway 9. Its one grass runway ran generally north to south. My recollection is that it paralleled a long, open drainage ditch, which was sort of a mental hazard. Visiting aircraft parked along the west side of the grass runway. It was from Welch's Anderson Airport that Isabel Urban took off for New York in a Ford Tri-Motor in 1934, somewhat to my concern. We were married in 1936.

I lost track of Welch after he left Anderson. His operations are outlined in the accompanying copy of Indiana Aeronautical Chart, published during Governor Robert Orr's administration.

I did not recall that Welch was lost flying the Hump in China during World War II and that his remains had never been recovered.

A truly great pioneer in Indiana's history of aviation.

ORIN WELCH: INDIANA AVIATOR

This year's cover pays tribute to Orin Welch and some of his contributions to Indiana's aviation history. Born in 1906, Orin grew up in the early years of flight, becoming a pilot himself by the age of 17. Orin became highly skilled in the areas of aircraft design and construction even though he had no formal engineering education.

In 1927, Orin and his family acquired operation of the Anderson Aircraft Company (AAC). It was there that Orin completed work on the "MISS ANDERSON" airplane. It was mainly used for flight instruction and promotional purposes.

In late August 1927, The Orin Welch Aircraft Company bought out the AAC. The success of the company led to the dedication of the Welch Airfield in Anderson in 1929. A hangar fire in November of the same year destroyed several Welch airplanes and equipment. The losses were never really recovered.

Orin moved his company to Portland, Indiana for a short time, and then to South Bend. It was here that mass production began on the Welch monoplane. Between 1936 and 1940, approximately 60 of these planes were manufactured. By this time Welch engines and tires had been developed and were being used on many of these monoplanes.

During World War II, Orin was a pilot for Pan American Airways Ferry Command. He later was trained for flights over China, Burma, and the India Theatre (C.B.I.). In 1943, Orin Welch disappeared on a mission for the China National Aviation Corporation (C.N.A.C.) while flying the Hump. His remains were never found.

INDIANA AERONAUTICAL CHART

FREQUENT PROMINENT VISITORS

James H. Doolittle

JAMES H. DOOLITTLE, then a Lieutenant, promoted to Captain and finally Major in the United States Army Air Force, participated in several local events. On leave, and to earn a living, he headed up Shell Oil Company's aviation gasoline division. He beat out other bidders for Muncie Aviation Corporation's fuel business in 1932 by promising to give the airport a windsock and to replace it from time to time as needed. I saw him frequently during World War II in England, Africa and Italy, some time after he had led the "Doolittle Raiders" on the first aircraft carrier attack on Japan in B-25 bombers launched from the *U.S. Hornet* on April 19, 1942. By then, he was a Lieutenant General commanding the 7th Air Force in the Mediterranean-European theater. I never had the courage to remind him of the windsock deal with MAC.

The then-Lieutenant Colonel James H. Doolittle, following Japan's attack on Pearl Harbor December 7, 1941, had been ordered to explore the possibilities for a raid on Japan from an aircraft carrier. Theoretically, the planes would have sufficient fuel to continue flying to friendly airfields on the Chinese mainland.

Doolittle confirmed by experimentation with short runways and careful calculation that B-25s, carrying a ton of bombs and enough fuel could reach the Chinese mainland. His volunteer pilots practiced

Photo courtesy of the National Archives and Record Administration 208-PU-52LL-2
Lieutenant General James H. Doolittle, leader of the Tokyo Raiders in 1940.

flying off small airfields. For the sake of security, they were not told what their mission was until they were at sea on board the newly commissioned aircraft carrier, *U.S. Hornet*. The *Hornet*, with sixteen B-25 bombers and crews on board, sailed from San Francisco on April 2, 1942, escorted by another aircraft carrier, Enterprise.

On the morning of April 18th, they sighted a Japanese picket boat, which was unceremoniously sunk, but there was fear that it had sighted the Hornet and might have radioed a warning to Tokyo. Decision was made to take off immediately, upsetting Doolittle's plan to bomb Japan by night and reach China mainland by dawn.

The weather got worse, with gale force winds blowing—both a curse and a blessing. The wind would shorten the take-off run, but the pitching deck was frightening to land trained pilots, and the strong head winds made it marginal whether they would have enough fuel remaining to fly to China after completing their mission to drop token bombs on Tokyo, Yokohama, Osaka, and Nagoya.

Doolittle was the first to take off at 8:00 A.M. on April 18. The last of the sixteen aircraft took off successfully exactly one hour later on the eight hundred mile journey to Tokyo.

The raid was not of great importance as to destruction of military targets, but it was an immense morale booster for the United States after the Pearl Harbor bombing, and it was a warning to Japan that they were in for a real war.

The raiders suffered no damage over Japan, but problems reaching mainland China were extremely difficult. One aircraft, recognizing its fuel shortage,

diverted safely to Russia, where the crew was interned. Others reached the mainland, only to run out of fuel before making an airport. Eleven crews bailed out of their aircraft and four, including Doolittle's, crash landed.

The accompanying photograph is of Doolittle's take-off.

Delaware County's aviation enthusiasts, and, in fact, those throughout the state of Indiana who had come to know the ebullient Jimmy well as the representative of Shell Gasoline company, were thrilled to learn about "Doolittle and his Raiders" token retaliation for the sneak attack on Pearl Harbor.

Smithsonian Institution photo number A45882-B

Jimmy Doolittle and his Tokyo Bombing crew after bailing out out their B-25 bomber over friendly Chinese territory. (Left to right) Staff Sergeant F. A. Broemer, Bombadier, Seattle; Staff Sergeant Paul J. Leonard, Engineer-Gunner, Denver; First Lieutenant R. E. Cole, Co-pilot, Dayton, Ohio; General Doolittle, Pilot; First Lieutenant H. A. Potter, Navigator, Pierre, South Dakota. Sergeant Leonard, General Doolittle's personal flight engineer was later killed in North Africa. Chinese, (left to right) General Ho, Director of the Branch of Government of Western Chekiang Provence; Mr. Henry H. Shen, Manager of the Bank; Mr. Chao Foo Ki, Secretary of the Branch Government of Western Chekiang Province. Doolittle was promoted to Brigadier General and returned to the United States for reassignment.

United States Air Force Museum,
Wright–Patterson Air Force Base, Ohio
Lieutenant Colonel Doolittle
and his B-25 crew before
take-off to Tokyo.

United States Air Force Museum, Wright–Patterson Air Force Base, Ohio
Doolittle's in first plane taking off on 800 mile journey to Tokyo.

Photo courtesy of the National Archives and Record Administration 208-PU-52LL-9

This is the impressive way Doolittle (left) was attired when I would see him first around Eisenhower and Clark's headquarters in London, and later, in North Africa and Italy. I, then a lowly Major, never had the courage to approach him with an "I remember you when. . ." you were a gasoline salesman and got our Muncie Aviation's business by promising a wind sock.

Brigadier General Doolittle (below), accompanied by his wife, was presented the Congressional Medal of Honor by President Roosevelt, witnessed by General H. H. "Hap" Arnold, then Chief of the Army Air Force, and General George G. Marshall, Commanding General of United States Ground Forces and of the Joint Chiefs of Staff.

United States Air Force Museum, Wright–Patterson Air Force Base, Ohio

United States Air Force Museum, Wright–Patterson Air Force Base, Ohio

133

Jimmy Haizlip

JIMMY HAIZLIP, who visited Muncie on several occasions when based in St. Louis, began flying in 1917. He was considered at the time as being one of the most experienced pilots in the world. Muncie newspapers reported his visit to Muncie on February 24, 1933. At that time he was as well, if not better, known than his contemporary, Jimmy Doolittle, later, Lieutenant General James H. Doolittle, who led the surprise bombing on Japan, the first from an aircraft carrier at sea. He later commanded the 7th Air Force in Europe.

Haizlip spoke at the Muncie Exchange Club's luncheon meeting and then to a group of fliers in the evening at the Roberts Hotel. He praised the Muncie Airport and said he considered it potentially one of the best airports in the Midwest. He also had high praise for Clyde Shockley, General Manager. He said, "Whenever one thinks of aviation in Indiana, one thinks of Clyde Shockley."

Haizlip held the transcontinental speed record from Los Angeles to New York in the "amazing time" of ten hours and nineteen minutes at an average speed of 240 MPH. He spoke modestly of his other records and accomplishments of stressing safety, comfort and convenience of flying, and predicted there would be improvements for aircraft to increase their speed, such as streamlining cowlings around the engine and retracting landing gears. He anticipated a happy future for aviation when travel by air would be as commonplace as travel by automobiles. His wife was also a famous flier and held several women's records. She was taught by her husband, who was very proud of her and her flying. He said, "She's one of the best

and can beat a lot of male pilots in handling an aircraft. When she jumps into a plane, she makes it do tricks, and if there were more women interested in aviation and able to fly well, the industry would see a bit of a boost." He continued to say it was only a question of time until more women would turn to the air.

Haizlip trained pilots with the French Army during World War I. Towards the end of the war was requested to come back to the United States to help train American fliers. Because of his personality, his cheery smile and his unaffected manners, he won hosts of friends and was an excellent ambassador for aviation.

Smithsonian Institution photo number 87-5715

Jimmy Haizlip visited Muncie on several occasions when he and Jimmy Doolittle headed Shell Oil's Aircraft Fuel Division in the late 1920s and 1930s prior to World War II.

Art Davis

ART DAVIS (no relation to Walter C. Davis of Richmond, Indiana) put on great acrobatic shows in his souped-up open cockpit Waco. He also participated in several air races in his aircraft class.

I first met Art Davis at the Miami Air Show in 1933 after my forced landing in the pepper patch at Pompano. We happened to be standing together watching when Frank E. Ball miscalculated his landing at Macon, Georgia. Together, we ran to assist Frank, fortunately not hurt, thanks to his seat belt, and helped unload and dispose of his cargo of citrus fruit intended for Muncie.

Art was an occasional visitor at the Muncie Airport, and a friend of Clyde Shockley's.

OTHERS WORTHY OF MENTION

THERE WAS John Ruzicka, who operated the Ruzicka Airport at Kokomo and then relocated in Wabash. John flew small artillery target spotting aircraft in the Italian campaign during World War II. I heard of him flying off a strip near one of the Headquarters of VI Corps where I was stationed, but never actually saw him. John is mentioned earlier in "Cap" Aretz's biography.

There were Don Orbaugh, "Bo" Grundy, "Pinky" Grimes and many others. Bob Shank, mentioned earlier in these recollections, the first official United States Government Air Mail Pilot, founded and operated the Shank Airport near the Indianapolis Speedway for many years until real estate values became so high that he was forced to sell.

"Cap" Aretz makes reference to Henry Boonstra, also an early Air Mail pilot, in his biography.

Another pilot of distinction whom I did not know, but is appropriate to mention, is Willa C. Brown, born in Indianapolis, now of Chicago, the first African-American woman to hold a commercial pilot's license and the first African-American woman to run for Congress.

Prior to World War II, she helped train some of the men who made up the famous all-black 99th Pursuit Squadron, which trained at Tuskegee Institute. She was also the first black woman to become a member of the Civil Air Patrol, and, with her then husband, Lieutenant Cornelius Coffey, established the Coffey School of Aeronautics, the first formal flying school owned and operated by African-Americans.

She ran for Congress on three occasions and for Chicago alderman in one election.

R. H. Pelham Photo

CHAPTER V

THOSE
HALCYON YEARS
—PROMOTING AVIATION—

Air Tours

1930–1940

THERE WERE numerous "air tours" planned promoting aviation in those early days. I participated along with other Muncie flyers in several of these events.

On Saturday, November 27, 1937, a caravan of planes from Michigan, Illinois, Wisconsin and Indiana stopped at Muncie Airport *en route* to Miami. Pilots and passengers attended a dinner at the Roberts Hotel, stayed overnight and prepared for an early departure the next morning. Among the visiting pilots were Mr. and Mrs. Clarence McElroy from Winomac. Clarence had a harrowing experience resulting from a forced landing in Mexico about which he wrote a book. His wife, at that time, was the only woman in Indiana to hold a Commercial Pilot's License.

Derby Frye, a Muncie Aviation Corporation salesman and later very successful in the aviation insurance industry, was to lead the contingent out of Muncie. Derby flew a plane for business, pleasure and fun. John and Janice Fisher remember him landing in a small pasture on their farm on Burlington Drive "just for fun" and to "say hello." Participating also would be Andrew W. Rose, an executive at Warner Gear, also Secretary of Muncie Aviation Corporation, and aviation columnist for the *Muncie Press.* He would fly to Louisville in an Aeronca to join the tour as far as Nashville and return to Muncie from there.

Also with the Muncie contingent were Earl Merry from Dunkirk and George McClure of Marion, who hangared their planes in Muncie. Andy later joined the Naval Air Force in World War II and served as a flight instructor at Bunker Hill Naval Airport, now known as Grissom Air Force Base.

Muncie Aviation Corporation at that time was the Indiana distributor for Aeroncas, made in Cincinnati.

Muncie Aero Club held a meeting at Lake Wawasee in Summer, 1934. Fifteen planes had been flown to the airport at the lake. Edmund F. Ball's plane is the third from the right, his first plane after the "celluloid solarium," blue and white Waco Cabin plane NC14012.

Muncie Aero Club held a meeting at Lake Wawasee. Fifteen planes had been flown to the airport at the lake. Edmund F. Ball's plane, third from right; his first cabin plane after the "celluloid solarium."

State Aviation Meeting

A STATE aviation meeting was held in Muncie on Wednesday, November 18, 1937, to discuss a variety of aviation subjects, under the auspices of the Indiana Aircraft Trades Association. Clarence Cornish was president and Lawrence Aretz was vice president of the Association. Aretz was assistant manager at the time of Purdue University Airport in Lafayette. Herbert O. Fisher was secretary of the Association and Walker W. Winslow of Indianapolis was Chairman of the Board.

The meeting was held in the classroom at Muncie Airport with dinner following at the Roberts Hotel.

Frank Hanley was toastmaster and Walter Davis, aircraft manufacturer and World War I pilot and instructor from Richmond, was the speaker.

As President of Muncie Aviation Corporation, Edmund F. Ball was in charge of local arrangements, assisted by Andy Rose, Secretary, and Derby Frye, manager of the Cub Distributing Company, division of Muncie Aviation Corporation. The subject of the meeting was "Better Service and Continued Development of High Standards and Safety."

Tours Promoting Aviation were Annual Events

Ninth Annual Air Tour, 1937

THE NINTH annual State Air Tour arrived at Muncie on June 19th, 1937. At a banquet in the Roberts Hotel on Saturday evening, the end of the tour, trophies for participants were presented.

The committee in charge of arrangements for the meeting were Clyde Shockley, Andy Rose and myself.

Fifty pilots and passengers, along with a hundred guests, attended.

Frank Hanley, President of the Pilots Association of Muncie and member of the Aviation Commission served as Toastmaster at the banquet. He introduced Bob Parkinson, City Controller, representing the city administration and Mayor Rollin Bunch. He addressed the group as "fellow fliers," saying that they didn't really know what flying was until they took a flier into politics. He complimented Frank Hanley and Abbott Johnson for the work they had done in promoting aviation in Muncie.

Other fliers introduced were myself, Arthur Ball and Andy Rose of Muncie; Mike Murphy, Herb Fisher, Nish Dienhart, Clarence Cornish, and Elvan Tarkington, all of whom became prominent in Indiana and several in the national history of aviation. J. H. Townsend, representative of the Ohio Oil Company which furnished the gasoline for the tour, was also introduced.

Winslow, veteran sportsman pilot from Indianapolis, served as chairman of the Association. He spoke at the conclusion of the banquet that evening.

Walker Winslow particularly complimented all the pilots for good judgment, especially when heavy fog coming off Lake Michigan on Thursday afternoon delayed the pilots' departure. Some landed in Muncie so late they came directly to the banquet from the airport still dressed in their wrinkled flying clothes and greasy coveralls. There was even a bride and groom on the tour who would leave Muncie for Cleveland the next day on their honeymoon. Winslow also complimented the fifty pilots and their passengers for their excellent airmanship throughout the tour, demonstrating good judgment and sportsmanship at all times.

The Walker Winslow Cup for student or amateur fliers went to Ted Thompson of Indianapolis for good judgment when he requested his passengers to find other means of transportation to the next stop when he felt that his plane would be overloaded and unsafe to try to take off out of the small airport in which he had landed. Without their added weight, he flew safely out of the small field and picked his passengers up at the next stop.

Lawrence "Cap" Aretz, identified as of Indianapolis (I think he was actually from Lafayette), received the Lincoln Life Insurance Company trophy for displaying all-around best flying judgment, observation of regulations and sportsmanship. Runner-up was "Red" McVey of Fort Wayne and third was Ivan Hillyard of Evansville. Honorable mention was Elvan Tarkington of Indianapolis.

Numerous other prizes were given, such as for the youngest pilot, for the pilot who came the furthest, and other qualifications.

Before leaving Muncie, Walker Winslow placed a wreath on Frank E. Ball's mausoleum in Beech Grove Cemetery; and departing, a formation of aircraft flew overhead, paying tribute to Frank for what he had contributed to aviation in his few short years as a pilot.

Tenth Annual Air Tour, 1938

THE TENTH annual State Air Tour sponsored by the Indiana Aircraft Trade Association stopped at the Muncie Airport on October 14, 1938.

Mike Murphy, well-known stunt flier from Kokomo who kept his plane hangared at Muncie, again entertained the visitors and local aviation enthusiasts with some spectacular acrobatic flying.

Planes began to land at the airport around 3:00 in the afternoon and about an hour later took off towards Indianapolis, where the tour terminated.

With the fliers was Oswald Ryan of Anderson, then head of the Civil Aeronautics Authority in Washington.

There were eighteen planes in the caravan. Lee Eikenberry, Cub salesman representing the Muncie flying group, was with them, as well as myself, then a director of Indiana Aircraft Trade Association. Frank E. Hanley and other Muncie men interested in aviation were among the local persons welcoming the visitors.

Winter Special Events

IN THOSE early fun years there were all sorts of activities organized to promote aviation. There were air shows, air races, air tours, anything to draw a crowd and perhaps pick up a few bucks hauling passengers, or some free gasoline, or maybe a few modest dollars as prizes for winning some sort of contest.

For example, on January 5, 1939, the 6th "Flying Alligator Club Frolics" were held in Orlando. Clyde Shockley and his wife, Ruth, flew in, as did Andy Rose. It was reputed to be the largest assembly of privately owned aircraft in history. Three hundred forty-seven planes were in attendance, greeted by Mayor S. Y. Way and Ed Nelson, "Grand Scaly Alligator."

Back in the "Olden Golden Days" of aviation in the late 1920s and 1930s, most flying came to a standstill during the winter months. We put our planes in hangars, jacked up on blocks to keep the tires from going flat, drained the oil and put the battery into storage until the spring thaw.

But a few hardy souls kept some of them flying. Clyde Shockley was one, as a professional, and Walker Winslow, of Indianapolis, an early sportsman pilot, was another.

Clyde would organize winter air tours using frozen lakes in northern Indiana as big airports with plenty of room for everybody. There would be bonfires along the frozen shorelines, hot dogs, hamburgers, hot coffee and chocolate served. There were opportunities to go tobogganing, ice skating, and ice boating, even skiing, but there wasn't much of that done in those days.

On Lake Maxinkuckee, Culver was a favorite site, as was the north shore of Wawasee, and the old Spink Arms Hotel when the ice was thick enough.

An overnight, or sometimes even a few hours out in the cold wind on the ice, would lead to cold engines, congealed oil and there was no way that those first, primitive, compressed air starters would turn over an engine lubricated with oil congealed like frozen molasses.

It took ingenuity. Some drained the oil from the engine's crank case and put it in metal containers near the bonfires on the shore or, for overnight, took it inside someplace beside a radiator or electric heater to keep it warm. That usually worked, if vaporized gasoline fed into the cylinders didn't condense on the cold plugs, forming drops of moisture which drowned out the spark. Some used a blow torch flame directly

Courtesy of Andrew W. Rose
Clyde Shockley, organizer of special Winter Events.

onto the cylinders, the plugs and crank case, but that took a lot of standing on cold ice, sometimes in a cold, driving wind, and there was always danger of starting a fire.

With Clyde's help, I rigged up sort of a canvas hood over my radial engine. It was like a large tire cover that fit loosely around the engine, including the air intake and, of course, the crank case which was in the center of the radial engine. Pieces of stove pipe assembled in an "S" shaped configuration, resting on an empty oil drum, with the flame of a blow torch, made a pretty good preheater. Depending mostly on wind and temperature, it would take perhaps twenty to thirty minutes to heat up the oil in the crank case and the spark plugs and the cylinder heads sufficiently to make an easy start. If it was necessary to "prop" by hand, as many of them did in those days, the wheels had to be properly chocked, and a non-skid footing

was arranged for whoever was going to pull the prop through. When the engine caught, we'd throttle it down to idling, get out of the cockpit, clean up and stow away any of our warming equipment, round up our passengers, if any, and our baggage, and take off for home.

When we got home, we would all agree that it had been a fun day and we would do it again. Maybe winter wasn't all that bad after all! Walker Winslow had an ice boat on Lake Maxinkuckee. He took me for a ride which almost both scared and froze me to death. I wondered why he was dressed in a heavy flying suit with helmet, goggles and gloves. I soon found out. I wore my helmet and goggles, but had no heavy clothing and only light-weight gloves. We took off like something we knew nothing about in those days—a jet turning on its after burner. As probably everybody knows, an ice boat has three runners—two

Muncie Aviation Corporation
On the ice at Maxinkuckee

Muncie Aviation Corporation
On the ice at Maxinkuckee

But it was all fun!

In the June 1992 edition of the *Culver Alumnus* magazine appeared an article entitled "From the Ground Up" authored by Robert B. D. Hartman, secretary of the Central Committee of the Culver Educational Foundation's Board of Trustees.

He writes about the early days of Culver's aviation program and how it started only seventeen years after Orville and Wilbur Wright's first flight at Kitty Hawk, North Carolina.

General L. R. Gignillat, whom I happened to know, was Culver's distinguished Superintendent.

Shortly after World War I, Culver acquired five Curtiss N-9 Float Planes and hired three Naval Reserve Officers to promote aviation, teach, and keep the aircraft properly maintained. Apparently only one aircraft was ever assembled from the crates in which they were delivered. Access to the aircraft was by piggyback, on someone's shoulders, wading from shore. The cost for a student for thirty hours of flight training was $1,400.

main ones on the pilot's side, and the third on the opposite side where the passenger sits with the runner resting on the ice. That is, until the boat gets underway and then it becomes airborne. All this I didn't know. As we began to pick up speed and Winslow held it up to the wind, the third runner, with me on it, became airborne. The wind tore at my helmet and goggles; chips of ice stung my face. I was afraid to take my hands off the seat arms for fear I would fall off. I could scarcely breathe because the wind simply took my breath away. Finally he reached the far shore of the lake and came about, returning to our starting point to pick up another victim.

Shivering and with teeth chattering, partly from cold and/or being scared to death, I painfully pried my hands loose from their clenched grip around the seat structure, struggled uncertainly to my feet, politely thanked Winslow while at the same time declining a second ride to allow someone else the opportunity. I timidly asked how fast he thought we had been going and he matter-of-factly said, "Oh, 90, maybe 100 miles-per-hour." That was ten or twenty miles faster than my plane flew!

Courtesy of Andrew W. Rose
Winter sports flying. Andy Rose with Aeronca K on skies, Muncie Airport, circa February 1939.

Flight training for cadets was sporadic during the early 1920s and finally terminated when the Academy opened for school in the fall of 1925.

It was impossible to keep Culver and Lake Maxinkuckee entirely void of aviation activities. "Drop in" pilots were frequent, landing on nearby open fields in spite of efforts to discourage such disturbances to the Academy's routine.

"Colonel" Roscoe Turner, whose brief biography is included in these *Ramblings,* operated the Turner Flight Service on the Indianapolis airport. He was always an eye-catching "drop in," dressed in his powder blue uniform, Sam Brown belt and riding boots.

An Indianapolis citizen by the name of Norman Perry leased eighty acres east of town, and opened an airport in 1929. It was superseded by a joint City-Academy municipal airport further east of town with the help of WPA funds and labor augmented by additional funds from the Culver Educational Foundation. The field was completed in 1940, and listed on aviation maps as being suitable for emergency landings only.

I participated in several aviation winter rendezvous. I'm certain that I participated in the one at Maxinkuckee in March 1936, referred to as being the largest gathering ever of aircraft in the winter. It was sponsored by the Aeronca Aircraft Company.

Of special interest to me is the photograph run with the article, in which the Waco cabin plane shown at the extreme left is the one owned by my cousin. Frank E. Ball is the tall, slender person just to right of center of the picture wearing a hat and a long, dark overcoat.

This is the plane in which Frank lost his life when a faultily designed fitting on the wing strut failed and crashed near Findlay, Ohio, later that year on May 28.

It's difficult to identify, but I believe my cabin plane is the one parked just beyond the plane next to Frank's, which I think was Walker Winslow's Curtiss Travel Air cabin.

Every pilot in those days knew of the legendary Reuben Fleet, class of 1906 at Culver, mentioned in the article. He was named by President Wilson to head up the first Air Mail Service and was founder of the Consolidated Aircraft Company.

I knew Cass Hough, Culver class of 1920, as one of the early members of the Sportsman Pilots Association, of which I was a charter member. Cass was not an official test pilot during World War II, but solved the problem being experienced with Lockheed P-38s becoming uncontrollable in high speed descents. Cass, from 43,000 feet, purposely went into a dive, attaining a speed of 525 miles-per-hour at 35,000 feet in the longest terminal velocity dive ever attempted to that date. He managed to pull his plane out and determined the handling problem resulted from a vacuum building up around the elevators, causing them to become ineffective at high rates of speed.

His greatest contribution to aviation during the War was the development of auxiliary fuel tanks beneath the fuselage, significantly extending the range of fighter planes.

In 1974, Hough was named "Elder Statesman of Aviation" by the National Aeronautics Association. He died in 1990.

My cousin, William Ball, who had a summer home on Maxinkuckee, owned a twin Beechcraft Model 18. Dick Whitney, whose experiences are related elsewhere in these Ramblings, was William's long time pilot. Occasionally he would land at the Culver field, although it was a pretty tight fit for that type of aircraft.

I'm sure that the Piper aircraft referred to in the article used as training planes by Culver School of Aviation were purchased from Muncie Aviation Corporation. It held the Piper distributor for Indiana at that time.

Culver Military Academy believes that it is the only high school in the country ever to have owned both its own aviation ground school and airport.

Culver Academy Archives
An air rally, Lake Maxinkuckee, early 1936. Frank's plane left foreground. Frank E., the tall person, black overcoat and hat, near right center. Edmund F. Ball's plane probably the third in line behind Walker Winslow's Curtiss Cabin plane next to Frank's.

Six Inches Would Have Made
a Big Difference

WHEN I CAME home after World War II and acquired a surplus Cessna C-78, as recorded elsewhere in this book, we occasionally flew to Traverse City in the winter and landed on the ice on Lake Leelanau, spent the night in our cottages there, skated, tobogganed, skied and enjoyed the usual winter sports. I guess I was too complacent, finally, because that's when trouble usually seems to come, when it's least expected, and it did.

At the conclusion of one of our winter trips to Michigan, I was taking-off frozen Lake Leelanau for Traverse City in my C-78. John Fisher, Jack Coyle, I think Dave Meeks and perhaps Ray Applegate—I'm not certain, but all Muncie pilots—were my passengers. It had been fun, a fine day, no problem starting the engine. I taxied away from shore for a clear place more or less into the wind to take-off. Then the unexpected happened. We were just gathering speed and lifting off when an errant gust of wind caught the plane a bit from the left and slid the wheels sideways; the right one struck a frozen hummock of snow and ice. Heavily braced for stresses and shocks fore and aft, a blow from the side was not contemplated by the designers. The landing gear snapped and the wheel and shock assembly assumed an ungainly, crippled configuration, dangling loose, held only by its brake cable, and obviously useless. It could not be retracted. Maybe that was just as well. Another six inches above the ice surface, or to the left a bit, would easily have cleared the obstacle, but it didn't. With four other

pilots on board, I might have expected plenty of advice, but they were pretty stoic. It was strictly my problem.

As in Evansville several years before, I negotiated the same sort of emergency landing procedure: slightly cross wind, on the grass, not on the runway—no sparks—holding the crippled gear up as long as I possibly could so that it would make ground contact at as slow a speed as possible. I used full flaps on the approach and, as soon as the left wheel touched down, I cut the right engine ignition and retracted the flaps so the right wouldn't drag on the ground. The result was a very gentle landing, with only a quarter turn pivoting on the right gear, with no damage to the passengers and minimum damage to the aircraft.

The trailing edge of the right flap, which had not quite fully retracted, was bent a bit, the navigation light on the right wing tip was broken off, and the underpart of the right engine nacelle was dented.

The small amount of damage was fortunate, but I was certainly not happy about the incident. Whether because of that incident or not, I believe that was the last time we ever used a frozen lake as an airport. Certainly, it was my last time! Perhaps we matured a bit and our judgment and our ideas of fun became a bit more sophisticated. No more ice landings!

All sorts of things were done in those exciting earlier years of aviation. I participated in my share of them.

The Orlando to Miami Air Derby

Courtesy of David W. Meeks
January 9, 1934, Air Tour at Orlando, Florida, en route to Miami, in front of Frank Ball's Waco cabin plane. Left to right, David Meeks, Edmund F. Ball, Esther Brady, George Brady, Frank E. Ball, Isabel Urban (to become Mrs. E. F. Ball in 1936), Alta Leonard, Lucius B. "Lute" Leonard, Edmund F. Ball's roommate at Yale.

ON THE front page of the *Miami Daily News,* January 10, 1934, headlines, "Planes Winging Way to Miami for Air Meet."

It went on to say that scores of Army, Navy, and private ships would participate in races. It would provide, by far, the greatest air entertainment ever.

The lead paragraph states, "The first two entries in the Orlando to Miami Air Derby, a sidelight of the All American Air Races, arrived here today in a cabin monoplane. (It was actually a bi-plane.) They were *D.* F. Ball and D. *Weeks* of Muncie, Indiana, who left Orlando at 11:08 A.M. and were clocked here at 12:58 P.M. Their ship is one of ninety-four planes competing for the Florida year-round club prizes offered by Colonel Henry L. Doherty." This is the same Colonel Doherty who promoted the event in Miami in 1933 during which I experienced three forced landings reported earlier in this account.

A complete picture of Miami's growth as an aviation center and its future possibilities was given by Arthur E. Curtis, president of the Miami Aeronautical Association. Eugene Vedal, Chief of the United States Department of Aeronautics, and General C. B. Fulois, Chief of the United States Army Air Corps were in attendance, as well as and Colonel Clarence Young, former Chief of Army Aviation, then serving as

Director of the United States of America Department of Commerce Aeronautics Branch, who signed my original license in 1930.

Numerous other individuals prominent in the aviation industry served as officials and judges. Assisting other officials was Herbert O. Fisher, Secretary of the Indiana Trade Association, and Co-Director of the tour. On the same front page of that edition was another headline, "Six U. S. Planes Poised for Hop to Honolulu. They Were Scheduled to Leave at Noon from San Francisco on the 'Hazardous 2,150 Mile Flight'". It would be the longest and most hazardous formation flight ever attempted. Lieutenant Commander Kneffler McGinnis would be the Squadron Leader of the flight definitely set for 12:00, each plane loaded with between 700 and 1,000 gallons of gasoline, predicted to land at Pearl Harbor by noon, Pacific Standard Time Thursday, or even earlier if there was a tailwind. It would be an estimated twenty-four hour flight. I don't recall the results, I believe the flight was successful and established new records.

A Rigged Air Race

ON SUNDAY, September 30, 1934, with Dave Meeks as passenger, we flew to Columbus, Ohio, to participate in an Air Show, planning to make a short appearance, then proceed to Cincinnati and home to Muncie.

The show's promoters were short of enough airplanes to make a decent air race, so they persuaded me reluctantly to enter with the assurance that I would be the winner. I should lay behind and on the final lap, speed up and they would throttle back a bit and I would win! Which they did and I did!

Andy Rose, aviation writer for the Muncie Evening Press *in his column "The Observer," reported the event as follows:*

IF YOU had picked up a Columbus, Ohio newspaper last Monday morning and read that Cliff Ball had won the unlimited displacement, free-for-all race at the Charity Air Meet at Port Columbus the day before, it probably would not have been particularly significant. That's nice, but who's Cliff Ball?

Well, since you're all such good friends of ours, and we know you won't tell, we'll let you in on the secret. Last Sunday being a very fine day with little or nothing to stop them, Ed Ball and Dave Meeks "snuck" out to the airport and hastily headed for Columbus in Edmund's shiny blue Waco cabin.

There a large charity air pageant was in progress, being sponsored by the Kroger stores. All of the usual acrobatics and contests were being run off with fine precision to the great delight of the assembled multitude, when Larry Schmidlapp, commodore of the Cincinnati Cruisaire Club, slid up beside Ed and whispered in his ear that he had to fly in the feature race of the afternoon, which was to be run in just a few minutes.

Ed, of course, protested but shortly before the starters flag signalled the take-off, the announcer called for "Cliff" Ball of Muncie to go to his ship for the closed course free-for-all. The crowd thinking the announcer had said "Swift" Ball, rose as one and the ovation shook the very top of the A. I. U. tower. They expected to see some speed merchant blister the sky around Columbus' peaceful east side. Ed had been framed, double-crossed, and taken for a ride. He ran in what he thought was the opposite direction from his ship, but soon found himself tripping over the lower wing of the blue cream cabin. Stepping on his heels was Dave Meeks who scrambled on in the ship.

Thinking fast, Ed taxied down the field to takeoff for Muncie, but just as he kicked it around into the wind he found himself carefully flanked, with Larry Schmidlapp on one side and Gordon Mougey on the other. The starting flag whipped and four ships streaked down the field together. He had no choice, he was in the race.

Meeks, with most of the pink bleached out of his cheeks by now, busy cranking the stabilizer, opening and closing windows, and emptying the ash tray so that all the ashes blew back in his face. All the time Ed was slapping at his wrists to make him quit, and when they finally settled down they had missed the first turn and were going on the Bucyrus, with the other three entries shooting down the back stretch of the first lap.

Right then they got down to business and Dave got an Indiana map which was folded up inside his umbrella on the back seat. Dave recommended following the Pennsylvania Railroad in to Richmond and then taking No. 21 into Muncie. Ed tried not to listen and concentrated on the tails of those three ships up ahead. On the third lap he passed the back man pulled up behind Mougey. One more quick turn and he had overtaken the Cincinnati flash and was gaining steadily on Schmidlapp, then in first place. Dave got mad and climbed into the back seat and stretched out with a copy of Saturday night's Press to see if his name was in it.

While he was engrossed perusing the delightful words of that noted aviation columnist, Ed thundered down the home stretch getting every ounce of performance out of his speedy cabin and crossed the finish line less than a hundred yards ahead of Schmidlapp who was in second place.

When they landed the crowds were cheering for the winner to come up to the microphone. Not trusting them Buckeyes, Ed sat tight in the ship and made Dave go up and receive the prize. To his amazement it was a very handsome, large silver trophy, of very impressive proportions.

The boys had to go to Cincinnati that night to rest and recover from the excitement, but early Monday morning they slipped into Muncie bearing the rewards of their prowess. In the waiting room at the airport the "mug" is on display, and Ed is resting on his laurels.

From Goggles and Scarf to Cabin Aircraft

My first true cabin plane. Waco Model C NC14012, 210 HP Continental engine, rated speed 140 knots. Flown over, estimated 90,000 miles including Isabel's and my honeymoon to Texas January 1936.

ON MAY 5, 1934 I had graduated from open cockpit planes with helmet, goggles and silk scarf to a Waco A model side-by-side, two-seater with its "celluloid solariums" to a beautiful blue and white cabin plane, a Waco Model C NC14012 powered with a 210 HP Continental engine. Its cruise speed rated about 140 MPH, with comfortable seating for three passengers in addition to the pilot, and plenty of baggage capacity.

The only damage it ever suffered was caused by some overly curious woman who walked on one of the wings with high heeled shoes and punched a couple of holes in the fabric. I had parked it unattended in an open field at New Braunfel, Texas, to visit a silica sand quarry from which both Wichita Falls and Okmulgee glass plants were being supplied. The holes weren't serious and were easily patched.

I flew this great plane on many memorable flights for a total of 655 hours, covering an estimated 90,000 miles without a scratch. On September 7, 1939, I traded it in on the purchase of a Stagger-Wing Beechcraft, Model E17B, NC 18043, 4 to 5 place cabin powered by a 285 HP Jacobs engine, with a cruising speed about 150 MPH. It and its two successors are undoubtedly the most distinctive and exciting planes I have ever flown. But more about them later.

Aircraft of Distinction

Stagger-Wings

*Beechcraft NC18043, "E17B" Stagger-Wing, 4-5 place, 285 HP
Jacobs engine. Cruising speed 145 MPH. November 1, 1937–
June 27, 1938.*

CLYDE SHOCKLEY knew Walter Beech quite well and had flown him as his sort of private pilot on several occasions after Beech had given up his license and stopped flying because of health problems. As a result, Clyde was able to get a dealership, not a distributorship, for Beechcraft Aircraft in 1938. He was successful in selling several planes.

As had been the custom, I usually bought the demonstrator aircraft at the dealer's discount and then made it available to Muncie Aviation Corporation to use for demonstrations. Stagger-Wing Beechcraft NC18043 was the first of three stagger-wing Beeches it was my privilege to own and fly. In retrospect, it is probably one of the most beautiful and memorable aircraft ever built and that I have ever flown. The first one was painted a soft grey color with a pink stripe and was the focal point of attention every place I flew it. It was followed by two additional "Stagger-Wings," equally beautiful and equally exciting to fly—one red and the other a deep blue. It's a shame that we do not still own one. The Smithsonian Aerospace Museum in Washington displays a beautiful yellow "stagger-wing" Beech flying overhead as one enters the building. The few existing rebuilt "stagger-wings" still flying are all priced at from $50,000 to $100,000.

Edmund F. Ball (below) posing before a Stagger-Wing Beech, 1939.

A restored Stagger-Wing Beechcraft (above) at Oshkosh, 1992, similar, including color, to one I owned and flew.

R. H. Pelham Photo

Edmund F. Ball and Bill Moffitt in cockpit of Stagger-Wing Beech, circa 1939/40.

Cessna Aircraft

Twin Cessna NC1630–"F-50" 5-place Cabin 225 HP Jacobs engine. Cruising speed 145 MPH. Later in World War II designated a C-78. November 24, 1940–September 30, 1941, requisitioned by United States Army Air Corps as a transitional training plane, then designated a T-50. Lost at sea when ship transporting to North Africa was torpedoed.

MY NEXT landmark aircraft would take me from single- to multi-engine aircraft.

After considerable thought, discussions, and negotiations, Clyde decided to try Cessna, since our relationships with Beechcraft were not very secure after Walter Beech's death. The Wallace brothers, Dwight and Dwayne, had taken over the struggling Cessna Aircraft Company after Eldon Cessna's death and were converting it from the original distinctive monocock construction to a series of more successful, high wing, single-engine models. It was rumored they were coming out with a new light twin at a reasonable price, and which seemed to have a good future.

It was this prototype that would gain fame during World War II as a primary transitional training from single- to multi-engine aircraft. It earned the somewhat derogatory name of "The Bamboo Bomber."

Clyde and I went to Wichita, Kansas, in November 1940 to receive the aircraft we had purchased, neither of us as yet having twin-engine ratings. I had flown a demonstrator to Traverse City and back with Don Flowers, then Cessna's star salesman, later to become prominent in the aviation insurance business, and a long-time friend. (Later Don became a member of the Sportsman Pilots Association. We saw Don and his wife at several SPA rendezvous.) Clyde and I took a commercial airline flight to Wichita on November 24. We only had time before dark for a ten-minute check ride in our recently purchased NC1630, just off the production line and flight tested by Duane Wallace himself. It was powered by two Jacobs 225 HP engines. Next day, impossibly bad weather arrived. Clyde and I waited around for five long days before it got clear enough to take another brief check ride lasting about thirty minutes. The next day we took off for Muncie, neither of us with either twin-engine or instrument ratings. Nevertheless, with one stop *en route* to refuel, we arrived safely back in Muncie. At the very end of our journey, we had a thrill when one of the Jacobs engines got balky and we finished our flight with it idling.

I flew it locally in Muncie, on a couple of trips to Indianapolis and Fort Wayne and then on December 6 flew with an FAA inspector for my license—it might have been Dan Molton. He had never flown in the aircraft and I'm not even sure he had flown or was qualified at that time for multi-engines. We did a few gentle turns, a couple of "touch and go"s, and reduced power on one engine. He said I knew more about it than he did, and filled out the necessary forms for my multi-engine rating. That virtually brought an end to my flying single-engine aircraft.

(There is a note in my logbook that on April 14, 1940, Frank Edmund, our oldest son, and our only child at the time, would be two years old the next day, was given his first ride in an airplane.)

Acquisition of this aircraft occurred a little more than a year before I was called up for active duty on 9 July 1941, as a reserve officer. Our country was preparing for World War II. My first assignment was at the Middletown Air Depot in Pennsylvania. Not long after my departure, Clyde advised me that the United States government had confiscated, with some reimbursement, of course, our—almost new—N1604 Twin Cessna. It was off to war! Later we learned that it had been put on board a transport ship headed for North Africa, where it would have been used for transitional training and as a personnel transport aircraft, but it never arrived. The ship was torpedoed. My plane and its final hangar, the deck of that transport ship, rest somewhere on the bottom of the Atlantic Ocean.

The sometimes-maligned aircraft, nicknamed the "Bamboo Bomber," was really a great airplane, I thought. When the 225 HP Jacobs engines were upgraded to 300 HP Lycomings, it then had safe, single-engine performance, and became a useful member of Uncle Sam's fleet of aircraft. Never built for combat, it trained hundreds of pilots to fly twin engine aircraft and provided economic transportation for personnel.

It was rated as a five person aircraft, pilot and co-pilot forward, with a wide back seat for three passengers, with ample baggage space in the rear.

Several years later during a fishing trip in Alaska, I flew in a converted "Bamboo Bomber," known then as a T-50, equipped with pontoons. The rear seats and baggage compartment had been removed and replaced with bench type seats on each side of the fuselage making room for nine passengers. Now, it would carry eleven persons, including a pilot and co-pilot, plus all the baggage and paraphernalia, often for as many as ten transient fishermen. It groaned a bit on takeoff, but those bush pilots never flew more than two or three hundred feet above the ground anyway, so getting altitude was no concern.

After serving its purpose well as a transitional training plane and personnel transport during the War, many C-78s (Air Force identification), along with countless other aircraft and vehicles, all declared surplus, were put on the market at ridiculously low prices. Clyde visited one of the surplus airports, I believe located near Oklahoma City, and picked one out from the wide selection that he thought seemed to be in very good condition, bought it and flew it back to Muncie. It still had the original 225 HP Jacobs engines. We replaced the smaller engines with 300 HP Lycomings, increasing its speed by about ten miles per hour as well as improving its carrying capacity and its single-engine performance. Its license was number

51381; as a civilian, a T-50. I flew it for five years from October 1946 through September 1951, when it was sold.

With Isabel and family, I flew this plane on a great many trips, most of them to Traverse City and to Florida with the children when they were quite small. One time at Fort Lauderdale, when the children were small, an FAA inspector asked permission to look inside the plane, which I said, with a little concern, would be fine with me. We had only just arrived with Annie, our nurse, and three little children. I had not yet cleaned out the newspapers protecting the floor and the "potty" which the children had been using during the flight. The inspector took one look inside, turned around roaring with laughter and said something like, "I guess it's a pretty useful airplane." No other comment.

It really was a great plane, even though its passenger compartment was not the greatest. It was poorly insulated and the heating system was inadequate for winter flying. But it beat trains, automobiles and even most airlines, when travel time to air terminals was considered.

Cessna T-50, N51381 a World War II surplus aircraft, purchased in October, 1946 and refitted with two Lycoming 300HP engines. Flown until sold in 1951 and replaced by a V Tail Bonanza–B35 N5173C, also an aircraft of great significance in my flying saga.

Russ Morris, Robert "A." McDaniels, and Al Heath, 1936.

William E. Moffitt

CHAPTER VI

THE ENDURANCE FLYERS

A Very Special Event
and
A Special Brand of Pilot

IN 1939, Muncie became nationally famous for its Endurance Flyers. Kelvin Baxter and Robert "A" McDaniels took off with high hopes from Muncie Airport on September 10 at 9:30 A.M. in a small highwing monoplane, a Piper Cub powered by a 55 HP Franklin engine, christened "Miss Sun Tan," named after sponsor Singer's Bakery trade mark, "Sun Tan Bread." Their objective was to break the world record for light planes of 365 hours and 46 minutes set a few weeks before by the Moody brothers at Springfield, Illinois. In their flight, the Moody brothers had broken the previous record held by Russell Morris of Richmond, Indiana, of 120 hours and six minutes the previous October.

Mayor I. J. Wilson was on hand for the take-off to wish them well. Hundreds of spectators assembled to wish them luck. Mrs. Wilson had christened the plane by breaking a bottle of champagne over the propeller. The bottle didn't break on the first attempt which might have been an ill omen.

The young flyers would be in communication by radio with their ground crew through WLBC, whose radio announcer, Jim Fiddler, would then broadcast the flight's progress periodically at prearranged times. There were several other sponsors besides Singer's Bakery providing support, such as Franklin Engine, Piper, and other aviation-related products.

The plane was resupplied from a pickup truck carrying cans of fuel on schedules relayed through WLBC—water, food, whatever might be needed.

It was exciting to watch what became a routine event. The plane would dip low over the field dangling a twenty-foot rope with a hook at the end. The ground crew, under the leadership of "Red" Luker, standing in the bed of a speeding pickup truck, would attach a container which would swing dangerously back and forth as it was hoisted up into the plane's little cabin. Empty containers were dropped at low altitudes attached to small four foot parachutes so that they would not be damaged hitting the ground and could be used over and over.

The operation required precise piloting as well as driving the truck as it gathered speed to synchronize with the speed of the low-flying plane as it approached. Traveling at fifty to sixty miles-per-hour beneath the plane, with the crew standing up in the back to catch a dangling hook, attaching the container, and dodging it as it swung wildly, with the fence approaching at an alarming rate, required nerve and driving skills equal to the pilot's.

The plane had been in the air for 185 hours when an exhaust valve stuck in the engine causing a forced landing on an emergency field near New Castle.

No damage was done to plane or crew and another attempt was made in about a week.

On October 1, a second attempt was launched. A new engine supplied by Franklin had been installed and several changes had been made, resulting from experience gained in the first attempt, including the installation of a heater as autumn was approaching and nights were cold.

They took off from Muncie at 10:53 in the morning, with a large crowd of spectators on hand to witness. Between 4:30 and 6:00 that evening, the first refueling operation was accomplished and "Miss Sun Tan" was embarked on what would be a successful attempt to break the world's endurance record. They would not set foot on the ground until 6:38 P.M. on October 23rd.

Day and night, the little plane circled around east central Indiana. Day and night, its faithful ground crew provided its many services, four to six times every twenty-four hours. Muncie got accustomed to listening for the sound of the motor as it went to bed, and for its steady throb as it awakened in the morning.

For 535 hours and 45 minutes it stayed aloft. Thousands greeted the tired flyers as they returned to earth after more than three weeks aloft. The faithful engine was still purring perfectly.

R. H. Pelham Photo

Access to "sleeping accommodations" by stepping out of the plane on the landing gear, turning around, and crawing over the back of the seat.

R. H. Pelham Photo

Fuel cans lined up and ready for delivery to the plane.

R. H. Pelham Photo

The Endurance Flyers refueling truck and crew with "Red" Luker, crew chief.

R. H. Pelham Photo

It was exciting to watch the refueling process.

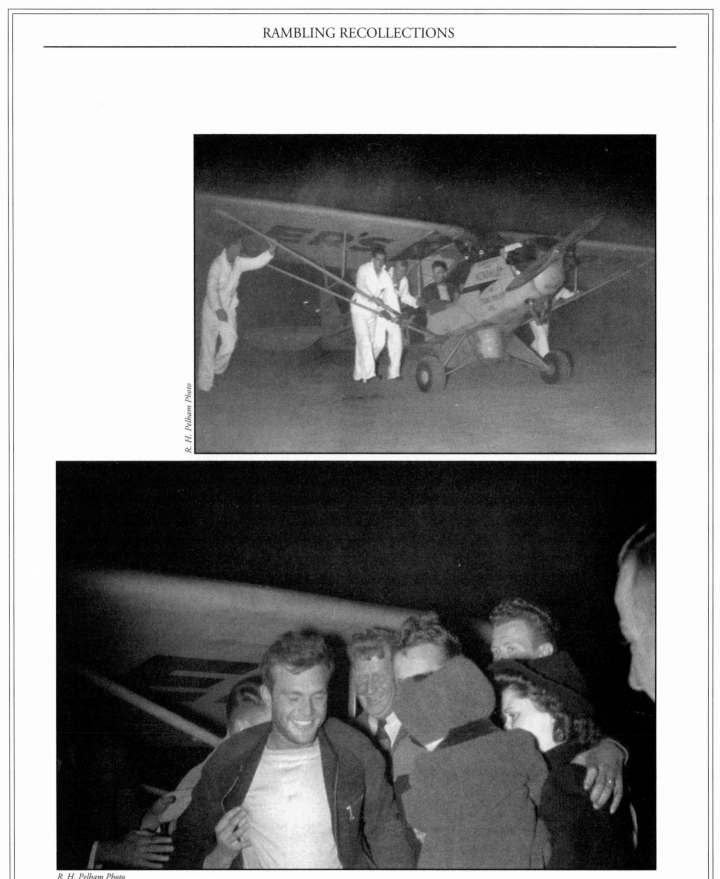

R. H. Pelham Photo

R. H. Pelham Photo
At the termination of the flight, 535 hours and 45 minutes, their legs were rendered so weak they had to be supported through the cheering crowd to the car waiting to whisk them away to the hotel for a shower, shave and rest.

R. H. Pelham Photo
The Endurance Flyers, Kelvin Baxter on left and Robert "A" McDaniels on the right being greeted and congratulated on their record-breaking venture by Mrs. Eleanor Roosevelt.

Bill Moffitt is reported to have taken the plane aloft after the tired fliers had left for bed to prove the engine was still functioning perfectly after over 500 hours of continuous flying.

They had been refueled for the last time at 3:49 the previous afternoon after which the pilots threw out the refueling cans and shouted down to the crew, "That's all. You're fired!"

The exhausted, heavily bearded flyers were greeted by the faithful ground crew and assisted from the plane. Dr. Karl T. Brown, Flight Service Examiner, pronounced them fit and well, even though their legs were weak and they could not stand without assistance.

Their flight had gained national attention. While in progress, sight-seeing planes had flown passengers aloft to photograph and wave to the flyers.

Newsreel cameras and photographers of all sorts surrounded them, magnesium flares were lighted and flash bulbs popped as they were whisked away to the Roberts Hotel for more photographs, and to a much needed shower and a good night's rest.

Their fame had spread so far that they were even invited to meet Eleanor Roosevelt, who happened to be in Indianapolis, and to personally receive her congratulations for their accomplishment.

Both flyers used the money contributed by their sponsors to pay for their Air Transport Pilots Licenses. McDaniels went with American Airlines and Baxter to Capitol Airlines, which has merged to what is now known as United Airlines. Both became career Captains and flew as such until their retirements.

Paul Antrim Photo

CHAPTER VII

PILOTS OF NOTE

Delaware County, Indiana

James A. Belknap

J IM HAS prepared such an excellent account of his early and continuing interest in aviation that it is worth including in its entirety, just as he wrote it.

His work, first with models, soloing thirty-five years later, flying ultralights, and designing and building his own unique aircraft, is certainly worthy of inclusion in any account of aviation and aviators of East Central Indiana.

His early interest in models reminded me of a beautiful model I built of balsa wood, glue and blue silk, powered by rubber bands, with the aid of Fred Brutshien, a young Purdue engineering graduate in 1915 or thereabouts. It flew, briefly, but finally cracked up beyond repair.

And another venture: Three of us grade school classmates at McKinley School built a glider made out of discarded window blinds, wrapping paper and sticks. Bob Hutchins, who lived on North Mulberry Street, was to be the test pilot, jumping from the roof of our garage, but, fortunately, he thought better of it. An attempt at an "unmanned" flight led to a crash that demolished our glider and ended our interest in gliding.

Jim Belknap was more persistent than I, and obviously a skilled aeronaut, designer, builder and pilot. "Icarus Acres Airport" at Parker City, Indiana, is worthy of recognition in these *Ramblings*. Belknap writes:

> IN THE EARLY 1930s, model aviation was not very popular, but it was the only way an aspiring aviator could approach the romantic concept of flying. It would be thirty-five years before I soloed an airplane.
>
> At eight years old, my father (I, not my father, was eight years old), presented me with a ten cent model of a World War I Spad fighter airplane. He was a bit optimistic concerning my abilities because, although very interested, I was not able to complete the construction of this creation of balsa wood, bamboo and banana oil.

It was not until three years later that I was able to convince him that I was ready to try again. A ten-cent kit produced by Comet Models (try as I may, it is impossible to recall the airplane type, but it had a full 16" wingspan) was successfully built with Dad's help. Incidentally, he had no connection with aviation for the usual reason: lack of wealth. Have times changed?

After many years, graduating to twenty-five cent models (24" inch wingspan), then to occasional fifty cent models (36" to 40"—Wow!), my parents agreed that I could purchase a one dollar model, an Aeronca with a 54" span! It was quite impressive, and being rubber-powered (as were all my models), was flown many times from the roof of a barn south of Rockford, Illinois. It was suspended above our fireplace mantle for many years. Gas models then arrived on the scene and I delved into those momentarily, until college, followed by the armed services intervened.

Then, some eons later, marriage intervened and, during idle moments, the old hobby manifested itself. Someone in the model airplane club once commented on my prolific model aircraft output in view of two children I had produced (actually, my wife and I had produced them) in 10.5 months. Well, what do YOU do while waiting for the glue to dry?

Then, the inevitable, RC models. At first I thought it meant Roman Catholic models and considered building a small model of the Basilica on wheels with an antennae emerging from the steeple. As it turned out, it would have been more prudent to build the Basilica since radio-controlled model airplanes rarely lived up to their generic name. They were either under repair or lost for greater periods of time than they were in the air.

The radio equipment during those days was unbelievably crude and unreliable with very short range. Consider pushing a button to make the airplane turn right, which it did if the signal got through. Releasing the button caused the plane to go straight. The next push, left turn, and then straight again, etc. Imagine trying to remember which turn, right or left, was coming up next. Descend or ascend? Forget it. You would run out of fuel soon enough. Obviously, much improvement was desirable and was soon forthcoming.

The next evolutionary step was the compound escapement. Push button once and hold for right turn, release for straight flight, twice and hold for left turn, release for straight, three pushes changed the throttle from high to low or vice versa. A few years later, after the brief episode of the "Galloping Ghost" (don't ask), a stone age type of proportional control emerged. The modern day controls are electronic

miracles derived from space age technology where you fly an airplane from the ground just as you would from the cockpit.

I became friends with an electronic expert who was a fellow member of our model airplane club and he helped me build some new type radio equipment that allowed successful flights. Just when I was finally getting into this thing, my RC model flying future was rudely interrupted. This same friend broke the startling news that he was about to build a full-size airplane, a feat that I did not realize was possible.

He had researched the project thoroughly, and decided to build a Pietenpol "Air Camper" because its construction was very similar to that of a model airplane; that is, a wood framework covered by fabric and painted with airplane dope. It was designed in 1930 by Bernard Pietenpol of Cherry Grove, Minnesota, and is a parasol wing, open cockpit monoplane for passenger and pilot in tandem.

He asked me to go into partnership and, three and a half years later in July 1967, the Ruether-Belknap Pietenpol made its first flight, with someone in the cockpit, of course. Ernie Ruether, with about 600 hours of flying time in his log book, made that first flight. I did not yet have hour one, so it seemed appropriate to start taking flying instruction.

It seemed inappropriate for a green student to know much about our brand new creation, so I took lessons and finally soloed an old Piper J-3 Cub. Shortly thereafter, I soloed the Pietenpol and used it for all the solo time required to acquire my pilot's license with one exception. A flight into a controlled airport was required and the Pietenpol, of course, had no radio. A Piper Cherokee was rented. I'd rather not discuss the shambles I made out of trying to find runway 20 on a 20 degree heading at Morristown Airport in New Jersey.

Before construction of the Pietenpol was finished, I was already looking forward to my next airplane. Experience with a higher powered and faster aircraft was desired since my eventual goal was to design an amphibian. Recently, delving into my past, I found sketches of amphibians done as far back as high school, so the desire was not an impetuous passing fancy. The BD-4, designed by James Bede, seemed to satisfy my requirements, so I purchased a kit soon after acquiring my pilot's license.

A change of jobs, a move from the East Coast to the Midwest, buying out the Pietenpol from my partner, getting into sailboat racing, raising three children (excuses, excuses) probably accounted for taking twelve years to build the BD-4. Realistically, I spent the equivalent of three years of spare time on the project.

The Pietenpol is a fine airplane for fun and thrills, being open cockpit with great short field performance, but hardly a cross-country airplane. Although many, many cross-country trips have been made, it is disconcerting to be passed by cars on the Interstates with 75 MPH indicated air speed. Even a 20 MPH head wind reduces the ground speed by over twenty-five percent. Incidentally, the Pietenpol has carried as many passengers as a Boeing 747, one at a time, of course. Many of these passengers were first-time flyers and were piloted by my wife, Grace. Fifty employees of Maxon Corporation have had the dubious thrill of looking over the side at the Indiana countryside from 3,000 feet.

Some memorable trips have been made in N8001R. The first major flight was in 1967 from New Jersey to Rockford, Illinois, for the last EAA convention held at that site. An outstanding innovation was present at the fly-in: the Halsmer Safety Twin. This was, incredibly enough, a twin-engine Pietenpol.

Bernard Pietenpol designed his aircraft to accept unconventional engine installations. In 1930, aircraft engines (mainly from World War I) were rapidly becoming extinct. Consequently, Pietenpol's first design, the "Air Camper," was inspired by the most inexpensive, most common, and most available engine extent— the Ford Model "A." When I visited him in 1965 during construction of our Pietenpol, he was working on his final airplane, a Chevy Corsair powered "Air Camper." Since then, many other automobile engines have been used in this versatile design.

As an engine test bed, the Pietenpol is probably unsurpassed as evidenced in the Halsmer twin. Imagine a conventional Continental A-65 installation, except with a long propeller shaft and a free turning pulley with another propeller attached between the engine and its propeller. Now, install another A-65 directly beneath with a pulley on the propeller shaft. Attach a belt between the two pulleys, and you have two independent engines and two independent propellers with the two propellers on the same shaft.

Thus, the safety of a twin engine airplane, without the potentially unsafe offset thrust lines of a conventional twin. The upper engine was started with the time tested, although some hazardous, "Armstrong" starter, i.e., by hand. A manual clutch temporarily connected the lower engine to the running upper engine, thus starting the former. The Halsmer

brothers operated an airport near Lafayette, Indiana, for many years where they worked on their many innovations such as roadable airplanes and a wind-powered electric generating machine.

The next major flight for my Pietenpol was from New Jersey to Indiana shortly after my move here. Bruce Brenneman flew me to Sussex, New Jersey, airport in his Cherokee Six on a Saturday morning in June of 1970. After six hours of flying, heading west over the mountains of Pennsylvania, and three stops, I arrived at the eastern border of Ohio and stayed for the night.

Low ceilings prevented departure on Sunday until late afternoon, so my only progress was across the state to Madison County airport near Springfield. My wife drove over and picked me up so that I wouldn't be late for work at Maxon Premix on Monday morning. Bruce was kind enough to fly me back to Madison County on Monday evening so that I could fly my bird to its new home at Selma Airport. Three days and 10.5 hours in an open cockpit is what I would call memorable. Pietenpol "Air Camper" N8001R was twenty-five years young on June 28, 1992, and flying regularly out of Reese Airport.

In contrast, the BD-4 is in its element flying greater distances at 140 MPH. Being a true four-place airplane, two people can fly with over 300 pounds of baggage in the back seat.

Soon after the BD-4 began flying, Ultralights came into the picture. Having a suitable airstrip out here on Icarus Acres, it seemed like a fine idea to become a distributor. The KasperWing, being a true flying wing (another of my passions), was chosen. Being able to slip it into the barn spanwise was also a determining factor. A distressing factor was that pitch control was accomplished by pilot weight shift. A yoke was used for yaw and roll control via wing tip rudders. The pilot is strapped into a harness that hangs from the wing on a caribiner. Obviously, pushing on the yoke to shift one's weight back for up pitch, and vice versa for down pitch, was just the opposite of standard aircraft controls. This was somewhat worrisome until I realized that weight was not shifted by hand pressure on the yoke, but with the legs and feet on a foot rest. It proved to be a very natural and easy way to control an airplane. The idea of becoming a dealership for Ultralights was abandoned after investigating liability insurance premiums.

Ultimately, this proved to be a fortuitous decision in that, shortly thereafter, the bottom dropped out of the Ultralight industry primarily because of irresponsible reporting on the 20/20 TV program. (A more applicable name for that nationally syndicated program would be 20/600, or better, Blind as a Bat.)

Ten years later, people still ask me, "Aren't those things dangerous?" My answer is usually another question. "Would you rather run into a solid object at 15 MPH, 30 MPH, 60 MPH, or 120 MPH?" These are the stalling speeds respective of the Kasperwing (typical Ultralight), the Pietenpol (comparable to a Piper Cub), the BD-4 (similar to a Cessna 182), and a commonplace jet airliner. The speeds represent the absolute minimums at which these representative airplanes can fly. Since 30 MPH is two times 15 MPH, the force of the impact would be two squared, or four times as great. Sixty MPH is four times fifteen, so the impact is four squared or sixteen times as great. The force on one's body in a typical commercial jet passenger airliner running into something would be the square of 120/15 or sixty-four times as great as mine flying the Kasperwing Ultralight. Which airplane is more dangerous?

After flying the Pietenpol for 800 hours with control stick in the right hand and throttle in the left, I was very apprehensive about flying the BD-4 since it is flown with the stick in the left hand and throttle in the right. There was a yoke option when building the BD-4, but I believe that flying stick is a more natural way to fly an airplane. After some practice flying the Pietenpol with the left hand, it was evident that either hand could fly as well. After all, it's the same brain doing the controlling.

Then came the Kasperwing with its weight shift pitch control and yoke for yaw control. Again, more irrelevant apprehension. The most difficult thing to learn on the ultralight was ground steering. The feet are resting on a bar directly connected to the nose wheel. Therefore, pushing with the left foot results in a right turn, and vice versa. This is like steering the old Flexible Flyer sled and completely opposed to that of a conventional airplane. After a couple of encounters with the soy bean field, I became proficient; fortunately without carrying this dubious accomplishment over to "standard" aircraft. Not yet, anyway.

I believe that any pilot could fly these three very different airplanes consecutively, as I have, with the proper training. It is comparable to driving a conventional five-speed transmission immediately after driving an automatic. If you have learned both, you don't give it a second thought.

Some of the disparate statistics of these diverse airplanes may be of interest:

	Kasperwing	Pietenpol	BD-4
Wing Span–feet	36	29	26
Wing Area–square feet	180	150	100
Number of seats	1	2	4
Gross weight–pounds	350	1,100	2,200
Wing loading–# Sq. Feet	2	7	22
Cruise speed–MPH	45	80	140
Stall speed–MPH	15	30	80

Considering the versatility possible with these aircraft, what more could one desire? They all have a major deficiency. Not one will land safely on water. (Therein lies an oxymoron. If an airplane lands on land, it follows that it should water on water.) A lifelong yearning (actually since grammar school) for an amphibian is finally being realized. I am at the half way point in the construction of a Spencer Amphibian.

In 1940, Spencer designed the Sea Bee which was manufactured by a Republic Aviation on Long Island, New York. In 1970, long since retired, he designed a similar aircraft specifically for "amateur" builders. Instead of riveted aluminum construction which lends itself to factory production, the new amphibian was designed for wood and fiberglass construction. The configuration and size is almost identical to original Sea Bee, but, fortunately, thirty years of technological advancement have been incorporated into the new design. I look forward to completing the aircraft and a tour of Alaska will be the first major flight.

Paul Antrim
Jim Belknap probably working on his "Pietenpol" aircraft at his shop near Losantville and Summit Lake.

Lee Eikenberry, Jimmy Fiddler, "Sad" Sam Jones, and Everett Cox

LEE EIKENBERRY, was Muncie Aviation Corporation's star aircraft salesman. At Piper Aircraft Company's request, a separate division was set up called Piper Aircraft Cub Sales. The dealership was held in Eikenberry's name to keep it separate from the Piper distributorship, Muncie Aviation Corporation's franchise. At the meeting held in my home, April 25, 1939, attended by Clyde Shockley, A. W. Rose, Lee Eikenberry, Larry Hirschinger, secretary, recorded, "Mr. Eikenberry, Cub sales manager, reported the delivery of thirty-two new Piper Super Cruisers since the first of the year, and the company had good merchandise on hand with no used airplanes." The good year predicted was confirmed at the annual meeting of the corporation held at 7:30 P.M. at the offices of Bracken, Gray, and DeFur. Clyde Shockley, the general manager, reported the operations of the corporation during the past year; that Piper Cub sales had reached a new high, fifty-five airplanes sold and delivered in one year.

Lee was always impeccably dressed. Whenever he was out selling, he always wore a fedora hat, white shirt, necktie and dark suit, neatly pressed. The airplanes he used as demonstrators were always clean, tidy and mechanically sound.

Lee participated in several of the Annual Air Tours, including the 10th sponsored and organized by the Indiana Aircraft Traders Association. The air caravan left Indianapolis on October 10, 1939, visiting twelve cities, including Muncie, returning to Indianapolis from Muncie on Thursday. Eikenberry was well and favorably known throughout the State.

Jimmy Fiddler, Muncie's foremost radio commentator, particularly on aviation events, accompanied

R. H. Pelham Photo
Lee Eikenberry, Clyde Shockley's star Piper Cub salesman, 1940.

the caravan as commentator. Nish Dienhart of Indianapolis was the field marshal of the tour.

Another interesting Muncie pilot was "Sad Sam" Jones (formerly of Wall Field) who occasionally picked up some extra cash flying whiskey to Muncie, bootlegged from Bimini and the Bahamas. His technique was to fly to Florida, get instructions where to land on the islands to pick up his load, fly back to the mainland, land on a designated strip in a remote area of Florida. From there, he would get the assortment of liquors and fly to Muncie, always at night. He would throttle back his engine passing New Castle, at altitude sufficiently high enough to coast silently into Wall Field and unload his cargo to awaiting distributors. So much for Prohibition.

The best known air show, of course, was in Cleveland—the Cleveland Air Races, Bendix Trophy Races, and all sorts of other activities and contests of aerobatics, precision flying, and the exciting pylon closed course races and the finish of the Open Class Thompson Transcontinental Air Race. Several Indiana pilots were important participants.

I never flew competitively at Cleveland, but attended several annual races, and knew some of the participants, as related elsewhere in these *Ramblings*.

Everett Cox, who operated and ran the Winchester, Indiana, airport for many years had many fellow-pilot friends, particularly in east central Indiana. As a Piper Aircraft dealer when Clyde Shockley was manager of Muncie Aviation Corporation, he was a frequent visitor at Muncie Airport.

Everett died at the age of eighty-one December 20, 1990.

Ball Corporation's Corporate Pilots

WITH SOME justification, I believe I can claim to be Ball Corporation's, or Ball Brothers Manufacturing Company as it was known in those days, first corporate pilot. I wasn't recognized as such back in 1932 when I first started flying to outside glass plants—Okmulgee, Oklahoma, and Wichita Falls, Texas. The first time I logged these plants, for some reason, I flew my cousin Frank's Waco F-2. I logged two more flights to these same plants in September and October in my own aircraft. The company had glass plants outside Muncie besides Wichita Falls and Okmulgee in difficult places to reach by train. I flew to all of them at some time or other. They were Huntington, West Virginia; Hillsboro, Illinois; Greencastle, Indiana; Three Rivers, Texas; Sapulpa, Oklahoma; and El Monte, California. With the exception of the four years while I was away in military service, I flew many trips to outside plants, calling on customers, flying customers and company personnel, and attending all sorts of business occasions until my retirement in 1970. Even after that, I flew a few times on special occasions to corporate and business affairs in California, Colorado, Florida, New York state, and elsewhere.

My cousin Frank Ball might well be considered the second corporate pilot. As previously recorded, he was on a business trip in behalf of the company when lost his life in Findlay, Ohio in 1936, as a result of a faulty wing fitting on his new Waco cabin plane.

John Fisher correctly has established his right to be the third corporate pilot, beginning in the early 1940s. Bill Greene was the first full-time professional pilot, followed by Hank Heiner.

While others had flown part-time on call on charter flights like John Shockley, Clyde's son, who lost his life test flying an Air Commander which had been purchased by Ball Corporation. Jerry Knight was the third full-time corporate pilot ,whose excellent history is contained in these *Ramblings*. He flew from four-place, unpressurized Aztecs to modern, sophisticated, high-performance jet aircraft. As chief pilot, he literally led the corporation from prop planes to jets.

The experiences of these pilots provided an interesting history of the evolution of business-corporate flying from the early days before airlines, when it was thought to be a bizarre and dangerous form of transportation, to being accepted as an indispensable factor in the conduct of businesses.

Courtesy of Sam Clemmons, Ball Corporation
Israeli Aircraft—Westwind N75132, 1986; also N100BZ, 1987, two crew and eight passengers, cruising speed 430 knots, pressurized.

William (Bill) Greene

BILL GREENE, one of my friends and fellow pilots from east central Indiana, distinguished himself as a military aviator during World War II and also became a fine corporate pilot after the war. Bill was born and raised in Albany, in northeast Delaware County, and received most of his early flight training in the armed services.

Bill entered the Army in 1941 as a draftee. Soon convinced that the pursuit of a flying career held more interest to him than life as a soldier, Bill applied for flight training and was accepted for the aviation cadet program. He completed his flight training in 1942 and was promoted to the rank of Second Lieutenant in the Army Air Corps. He attended several flight schools and eventually was sent to a base in Florence, North Carolina, where he participated in the A-20 transition school. After completing this training, he was sent to Britain, where he joined the 410th Bomber Group flying B-25s.

Once in Britain, Bill's life took some harrowing turns. He flew many bombing missions from his post in England, including two on D-Day (June 6, 1944), an event which, as he later stated, "I will never forget." After the D-Day invasion, Bill's unit moved to France and continued to carry out bombing missions for the Allied forces. In early May, 1945, Bill completed 65 bombing missions alone as the war intensified until its conclusion on V-E Day, May 6, 1945. In recognition of his service, Bill received many decorations, including the Distinguished Flying Cross, the Air Medal with 12 clusters, and as he also later recalled, "not a few gray hairs."

Courtesy of William Greene
Combat crew: Sergeant Joseph, Captain Bill Greene, Sergeant Curry.

After leaving military service, Bill returned to Muncie, where he performed several piloting duties part-time with Muncie Aviation Corporation until he was contacted by E. Arthur Ball, one of the senior officers with the Ball Brothers Manufacturing Company. Arthur had recently purchased a Stagger-Wing Twin Beech aircraft and persuaded Bill to join him in a new business venture which he was planning in Millville, New Jersey. Bill agreed to work with Arthur on this venture but Arthur's untimely death in 1947 forced Bill to return to Muncie shortly thereafter. He then accepted a position as the corporate pilot for the A. J. Glaser construction firm.

In the 1950s, Bill joined Ball Brothers as its corporate pilot, flying the company's Twin Beech aircraft. For the next three decades, Bill worked as the corporate pilot for the company and briefly as an associate of Clyde Shockley with Muncie Aviation

Corporation. During his years as a corporate pilot, Bill was a versatile and dependable aviator, who was responsible for getting many of our executives to their various business destinations throughout the United States. He was frequently pilot for my family when visiting various places throughout the United States, and to our summer home in northern Michigan.

Bill estimates he flew something like 30,000 accident-free hours as a corporate pilot; combined with Hank Heiner's, probably over 50,000 hours. They were a great team in which all had implicit confidence.

I recall one winter several years ago when, with dubious weather conditions forecast, I wanted badly to join my family in Leland for Christmas and Bill

Courtesy of William Greene
Lieutenants Merrill and Greene (above) with A-20 in background.

J. Secrist, Crew Chief; Joseph, Gunner; Greene, Pilot; Curry, Gunner (right).
Courtesy of William Greene

Greene was the pilot. Our intended destination was Traverse City. Within twenty or so miles of Traverse City, it was snowing heavily, ceiling and visibility 0/0. Wisely, Bill returned to Cadillac where ceiling and visibility were still good, but the runway was completely iced; caution advised there was a strong crosswind from the north, and it was very cold—0°.

Bill landed with no problem and taxied carefully to the terminal. It was closed for the night, but a pay phone booth was open. Rick Shanahan, Marilyn's husband was with us and we were loaded with Christmas presents, including a large, poinsettia plant. There was another plane at the terminal which had also diverted from Traverse City as we had. I called the two taxi cab companies listed in the phone book with no luck—no answer or no drivers available. The passenger from the other plane asked our destination, and when I said, "Leland," he said, "I can get you to Traverse City if you don't mind riding in a police car." The "Good Samaritan" was "Bill" Milliken, then lieutenant governor, later to be two-term governor of Michigan. Obviously, we accepted with thanks and

Courtesy of Dick Whitney
Bill Greene and wife Marty were married a week earlier than they had planned so Bill could pilot John Fisher's DeHaviland Dove on a trip to California—a wonderful honeymoon. Left to right: Dick Whitney, Lois Whitney, Ruth Chin, Bill and Marty, Lew Jack, unidentified.

loaded up the state police car with Christmas packages including the poinsettia plant which froze and visibily wilted and died between the aircraft cabin and police car.

The conclusion to this story is that, while we were transferring our baggage and ourselves to the police car, an automobile had driven in, skidded on the ice, and badly damaged the tip of our (Bill's) plane and left without telling us. We left with thanks to Bill and wishing him a Merry Christmas. Bill didn't discover the damage until we had left, the terminal building was locked up, the airport was deserted and it was about five miles to town; only the phone booth was open, and it was Christmas Eve.

Bill finally got Hank Heiner on the telephone, explained his predicament and, without hesitation, Hank said, "Sure, I'll come and get you, but it will probably be about three hours before I can get to the airport, scrounge up an airplane, and fly to Cadillac." There was no choice. Poor Bill stood shivering in the phone booth, his only protection from a howling north wind, for three hours waiting rescue. I asked Bill later if he couldn't have gotten in the airplane, started it up, and used its heater to warm the cabin. He said he was afraid with the slippery ice, the high wind, and no brakes "it might blow into the side of the building and be further damaged."

Bill and Hank got back to Muncie about one o'clock in the morning, just in time to see Santa Claus and his reindeer disappear in the distance. Hank was Bill's real Santa Claus. Hank's only comment was, "No way I could have let my buddy spend Christmas Eve in a phone booth!"

Henry "Hank" Heiner

HENRY (HANK) HEINER enjoyed a varied career as an aviator, both as an aviation pioneer in Indiana, a military pilot in World War II, and a corporate pilot during the years from the late 1950s until his retirement in the 1980s. Although an outwardly modest and humble man, Hank was nonetheless a person who displayed considerable bravery and courage as a pilot during World War II. He also demonstrated a unique ability to pilot numerous types of aircraft during his years as a civilian aviator.

Hank Heiner was born, raised and grew up in South Bend, Indiana. He developed his attraction for aviation by "hanging around" the Bendix Airport during the late 1920s and early 1930s, where he came to the attention of Homer Stockert, a true Hoosier

pioneer aviator who ran a flying service at the airport. While still in high school, Hank worked in Homer Stockert's shop ("mostly without pay") and received flight lessons and flying time from Stockert in lieu thereof. While working for Stockert, Hank flew in a number of aircraft, including an OX-5 Waco, a Waco F, and a Kinner Bird. "Back then, you'd fly anything that you could get your hands on," Hank remembers. (And he still does!)

In May, 1936, Hank soloed in a Kinner Bird, the event which launched his career in aviation. During the summer of 1936, Stockert introduced him to Red Hunter, another aviation pioneer who had recently purchased a Ford Tri-Motor airplane. Hank and Red Hunter subsequently spent part of the summer barnstorming across Indiana and Illinois in the Tri-Motor, with their flight ending in St. Louis. Hank also received his commercial rating while still in high school and, once in possession of his license, spent many memorable autumn afternoons above Notre Dame Stadium doing "banner-towing" to the entertainment of the football crowds.

Courtesy of Hank Heiner
Lieutenant Henry (Hank) Heiner, 1942, Brooks Field, Texas, as Link Training Officer, 2nd Lieutenant.

Recalling his early years as a pilot, Hank remembered that he often labored over the objection of his mother. "My interest in flying didn't make my mother very happy because I often came home dirty and greasy after working in Homer Stockert's shop. Usually,

I'd have to crawl around on the cinder hangar floor to get under the planes and wash the bellies. My mother was all over me like a wet blanket."

In 1939, Hank enlisted in the Army Air Corps and received his first assignment, to Patterson Field, outside Dayton, Ohio. Hank possessed the necessary qualifications to apply for a Reserve Officer's Commission, which he received in 1942 after the outbreak of World War II. As a Second Lieutenant, he was reassigned to Brooks Field near San Antonio, Texas, and from there, Hank was transferred to McCook, Nebraska, where he trained the crews for the B-24 squadrons which operated in the various military theaters of the war. As World War II continued, Hank received other military duties, including some ferrying responsibilities for the Air Transport Command (ATC).

Hank's major assignment in World War II occurred in 1944–45 when he was ordered to India to participate in the China-Burma-India theater, flying B-24s "Over the Hump" to resupply American and British troops stationed in that area. Hank's unit provided support to General Claire Chenault's Flying Tigers and other air forces which were involved in combat with the Japanese. These missions were some of the most dangerous of the war.

Following the end of World War II, Hank enjoyed an assignment to ferry a small Twin Beech aircraft from Calcutta to the Allied Headquarters in Germany. This flight included stops in Baghdad, Haifa, Cairo, Rome, Marseilles, and Paris before landing in Wiesbaden, Germany. As Hank recalled, with his customary understatement: "It was a great trip!"

After Hank received his military discharge in 1946, he returned to South Bend and continued his career as a pilot. He soon discovered, however, that the postwar economy held a great deal of uncertainty for civilian pilots. After working for a brief time as a flight instructor and charter pilot, Hank took a position flying the corporate aircraft for the Northern Indiana Steel Company. Unfortunately, the postwar recession struck the steel industry first and, as Hank observed, "the company plane (and the pilot) is the first to go" when a company enters a cost-cutting period. After being laid off from Northern Indiana Steel, he went to Indianapolis, where he briefly worked for Roscoe Turner.

Hank's experience as a company pilot enabled him to land another position in corporate aviation, this time with the International Steel Corporation of Evansville. Once again, Hank's tenure as a company pilot was cut short by a recession. After leaving International Steel during the mid–1950s, he worked briefly as a Flight Inspector for the Federal Aviation Administration (FAA) at its post in Battle Creek, Michigan. Hank says he enjoyed the flight aspects of his job with the FAA but, as he later put it, he "became frustrated with the paperwork and the red tape" and soon looked forward to returning to corporate aviation.

He received another opportunity to enter corporate aviation in the late 1950s after having a conversation with Bill Greene, then the corporate pilot for the Ball Brothers Manufacturing Company in Muncie. Fortuitously, Bill and Hank had spent some time together at Meigs Field in Chicago waiting to receive clearance for return flights home, when Hank mentioned his desire to find another position in corporate aviation. A short time later, Bill called Hank and asked him: "How would you like my job? I'm going to move over to Muncie Aviation to work with Clyde Shockley. Why don't you come down here and interview for my position?" Hank followed Bill's advice and was hired as the corporate pilot for Ball Brothers, a position which he held for the next twenty-five years. Bill soon returned to Ball as corporate pilot. By that time, the company's operations had expanded so much that two pilots were kept busy.

Hank Heiner's career in aviation ended in Indiana, as it had begun almost sixty years earlier. He had, in fact, experienced much of the growth of aviation over the course of those six decades as a military flyer who encountered some of the more difficult assignments of World War II, and as a civilian pilot.

Hank and Bill Greene flew as Ball Corporation's first professional corporate pilots, totalling probably over 50,000 accident-free hours in all types of aircraft from one Twin Beechcraft Model 18, to Piper Apache, Aztec, Seneca, Navajo, and Cheyenne.

Hank was well-known throughout midwest airports and with fixed base operators, as well as other pilots. Hank's disposition was infectious. He never met a stranger and was seldom forgotten. After retiring as corporate pilot for physical reasons, he continued employment with Ball Corporation in its Transportation Department until reaching retirement age. His interest and love of aviation and for flying

continue long after this physical qualification prevented his continuing as a commercial pilot. He has been generous in passing along his experience and knowledge as a "high hour" pilot to other pilots—from beginners to old-timers like me!

Hank married Virginia Dunivant in 1942 at South Bend, Indiana. In 1992 they celebrated their 50th wedding anniversary.

Hank and I have flown together on numerous trips to New Mexico and elsewhere since his retirement. He is a good traveling companion and a consummate instructor, keeping me alert, reasonably current, and we've even had a few experiences we would just have soon not had. Hank has never been known to have turned down an opportunity to fly as pilot, co-pilot, instructor, or passenger. If anyone ever lived to fly, it is Hank Heiner!

Courtesy of Hank Heiner

Gerald L. Knight

GERALD KNIGHTS' brief autobiography is so well written, it is included in these *Ramblings* as submitted. It brings Ball's use of corporate aircraft to near the turn of the century.

I WAS FIRST exposed to flying in 1946 by a cousin who was a pilot during World War II. He would stop by our house occasionally and invite me to help him pick some tomatoes. It was our great secret that the tomato patch was just across the road from the airfield where he kept his aircraft. We would end tomato gathering with a flight over Huntington, Indiana and the surrounding areas.

In 1953, my cousin moved to northern Indiana and my family moved to a small farm south of Huntington. Aviation seemed to follow wherever I went. It seems that the Indiana Air National Guard, based at Baer Field and flying P-51 Mustangs, had chosen the airspace just south of our farm for a practice area. All summer we were treated to the sounds of those Mustangs and their Merlin engines diving and cavorting all over the sky.

After completing high school and a tour of the North Atlantic with the United States Navy, I returned to Huntington where I was employed by the Erie-Lackawanna Railroad as a locomotive engineer. In September, I rediscovered flying and began taking lessons at the Scott Ranch Airport.

By spring of 1964, I had moved my training to Baer Field at Fort Wayne and progressed through private, commercial, instrument and flight instructor ratings. From 1964 until June 1969, I flew as a flight instructor for Consolidated Airways.

During this period of time, the Korean War G. I. Bill came into effect and there was no shortage of students. One of my students stands out in my mind. He was a B-47 pilot in the Air Force and when he got out of the service, he did not convert his military rating over to civilian. He was a very accomplished pilot in every way, but before the second training flight, actually just a familiarization flight in a Piper Cherokee trainer, we were discussing stalls and stall recovery and I sensed some apprehension on his part. His questions were about parachutes and the proper method of getting out of the aircraft. I answered that the Cherokee had a very docile stall performance and there would be no need for chutes or getting out of the airplane in a hurry.

We then proceeded to the practice area and, after climbing to about 3,000 feet above the ground, I took

control of the aircraft to demonstrate the stall entry and proper recovery techniques. The student then moved his seat fully aft, tightened his seatbelt very tight, and firmly held onto the bottom of the seat. I again reassured him there was nothing to worry about, and we went on with the demonstration.

Afterward, having seen the maneuver, he was visibly relieved and sweating profusely. He related to me the stall procedure for the B-47 which explained why he was worried. The stall in a B-47 was performed at 35,000 feet and if recovery was not completed by 15,000 feet, the crew bailed out. Quite a difference.

In June 1969, I accepted a pilot position with Warner Gear and moved my family to Muncie. We flew two Cessna 411As to outlying plants and to customer and vendor locations.

In 1971, Warner Gear's flight department closed and I went to work for Muncie Aviation as a charter pilot and flight instructor. During my stay at Muncie Aviation, I met many interesting people, including Ed and Virginia Ball. I instructed Mrs. Ball for her multi-engine rating and I found her to be a very exacting pilot, both in her performance and for her instructor. We performed many maneuvers repeatedly until she was satisfied, well beyond my requirements.

Charter flying, both passenger and freight, was doing great. At on time, we were flying seven Aztecs with fourteen full- and part-time pilots.

In April 1974, I was hired by Ball Corporation to join Hank Heiner and Bill Greene flying the Cheyenne and Aztec. The Cheyenne was the first turbine-powered aircraft built by Piper Aircraft and was a real learning experience for all. Our aircraft was Serial Number 4, and the first production model delivered to a customer.

Being a new aircraft and a new model, there were always bugs to be worked out. We'd break something and Piper engineering would send us the latest version of the part and ask for feedback on its operation. It seemed we did a lot of field test and evaluation for them.

The Cheyenne brought both speed and comfort to corporate travel, and our trips began to lengthen and become more frequent. As the demand for transportation increased, so did the Ball Corporation fleet—first a Navajo Chieftain added to the original Cheyenne and Aztec; then a second Cheyenne to replace the Chieftain in 1979. Until the Chieftain was sold, this was the first time the fleet was at four aircraft.

Of course, if you increase the number of aircraft you fly, you have to increase the number of pilots. During this period of time, 1975 through 1979, Ed Bristow, Dan Hillman, Larry Miller, and Tom Greene joined the staff and all would leave for greener pastures. Bristow, Hillman, and Miller went to major airline carriers and Tom Greene joined an Indianapolis flight department. In April 1980, after Hank Heiner and Bill Greene had retired, I was designated Chief Pilot for the corporation.

The corporation had acquired two larger models of the Cheyenne, The IIXL. Its larger engines and longer fuselage made for quicker and more comfortable travel. Around 1979–80, we started to evaluate the various models of jet aircraft on the market.

Trying to match the corporation's travel needs and coast-to-coast operations was quite a challenge, but eventually the Israel Aircraft, Inc.'s Westwind, Model 1124, Serial Number 226, was purchased from "The Limited, Inc." and put into service.

Doug Colbert, who joined the staff in 1980, and I proceeded to FlightSafety, Inc. for initial training. After a period of twenty-five hours flying with a FlightSafety instructor, to satisfy our insurance carrier, we began operations.

In the first three months, October, November, and December 1982, we covered most of the United States and had one trip to Mexico. With the Westwind and the two Cheyennes, a lot of miles were traveled and a lot of passengers carried.

In 1985, Israeli Aircraft completed the last five airframes in their inventory and offered them for sale. Ball Corporation purchased Serial Number 426 in January 1986, bringing the fleet once more to four aircraft. Because of the age and flight with another of the newly-manufactured aircraft. Serial Number 438 was purchased in January 1987 and number 226 was traded in. As the requests for longer travel increased for the Westwind, the Cheyennes were no longer able to fulfill the role they had carried so well. The last Cheyenne was sold in 1989.

The present fleet of two Westwinds and staff consisting of myself, Doug Colbert, Dave Readle, Dan Pankey, Dave Providence, and Ray Rideout, flew almost 1,200 hours and almost 500,000 miles in 1992.

In April 1993, we will complete the second year of our in-house maintenance program. Phil Stuckey, Chief of Maintenance, and his assistant, Rob Johnson, oversee the maintenance and inspection procedures for both aircraft. Through their skills and efficient operation, there are very few days that the aircraft are not available for flight.

I never would have guessed, sitting in the cockpit of that Piper Colt in the fall of 1962, that my career would have been so fulfilled. I'm very proud of my association with Ball and with the fine group of aviation professionals who are the 'Ball Corporation Aviation Department.'"

Use of aircraft throughout these sixty years of recorded history have saved the corporation untold thousands of dollars and has become an indispensable form of transportation throughout all its operations.

Courtesy of Sam Clemmons, Ball Corporation

(Left to right) Piper Cheyenne II, N80BC, 1974, two crew and six passengers, cruising speed 240 knots, pressurized; Piper Chieftain (Navajo), N96BC, 1972, two crew and six passengers, cruising speed 210 knots, non-pressurized; Piper Turbo Aztec F, N20BC, 1970, two crew and four passengers, cruising speed 180 knots, non-pressurized; Piper Cheyenne II, N10BC, 1978, first Cheyenne of the line at Lockhaven, Pennsylvania, plant and first high-performance aircraft owned by Ball Corporation, two crew and six passengers, cruising speed 240 knots, pressurized.

Lawrence "Larry" Hirschinger

LAWRENCE (LARRY) HIRSCHINGER enjoyed a career in aviation which encompassed over fifty years as a pilot, flight instructor, manager of an aviation business, manager of an airport, lecturer, broadcaster and consultant. Larry's commitment to aviation safety, both from the standpoint of the pilot and of the ground personnel, serve as hallmarks of his career.

Courtesy of Lawrence Hirschinger
Larry Hirschinger

Larry was born in 1914 and grew up in Elwood, Indiana. Even as a youngster, he developed a fascination for flight, building a number of successful airplane models and entering them in various contests which were held around east central Indiana during the 1920s and 1930s. In 1935, Larry took his first solo flight after completing his training course in Indianapolis. Shortly afterward, he became a flight instructor. In 1937, Larry taught for a while as a flight instructor for several of Weir Cook's "Flying Cadet" students. Also, during the late 1930s, Larry served as an Air Mail pilot.

During World War II, Larry moved to Muncie where he became an instructor for the military flight school operated at Ball State. This program, known as the Civilian Pilot Training Program or CPTP, enabled Larry to instruct over 1,200 pilots who then went on to advanced training as Air Force or Navy pilots. Also, during the war, Larry provided flight instruction to many other prospective military pilots at bases in the south and southwest.

After World War II, Larry pursued a career as a commercial aviator, flight instructor, and consultant to airlines and aviation companies. A vigorous proponent of air safety, Larry worked to institute such procedures as regulated airport traffic patterns, flying with lights on both day and night, and hemispheric cruise altitudes, and making them standard operating procedures. He also became an advocate of such in-flight safety procedures as encouraging passengers to keep their seat belts fastened while in flight.

In 1964, Larry became the general manager of the Muncie Aviation Company and the manager of Muncie Airport, positions which he held until his retirement in 1985. During those twenty years, Larry managed the sales and service operations of Muncie Aviation while also working on the expansion of the Muncie Airport. Observers of aviation in Muncie and east central Indiana have long recognized that the Muncie Airport serves as one of the best examples of how a privatized public service can be administered for the benefit of the public.

In 1967, Larry suffered a major heart attack, the effect of which forced him to suspend his career as a pilot. Nevertheless, he subsequently volunteered for a heart research program conducted by the Federal Aviation Administration to test the suitability of previous heart attack patients for the resumption of flying. Following his participation in that study, Larry became one of the first six pilots recertified with a license waiver petition. By 1991, Larry had logged over 21,000 pilot in-command hours and over 15,000 flight instructor hours.

Both during his working career, as well as in retirement, Larry remained active as a lecturer and writer on aviation topics. He has written columns on aviation for two newspapers as well as being a regular contributor to such monthly publications as *Michigan Flyer, Ohio Flyer, Indiana Flyer,* and *Fly Paper.* He currently writes and publishes *AAI Flightlines*, a quarterly magazine for Hoosier aviation enthusiasts.

Currently, Larry is the Executive Director of the Aviation Association of Indiana, an organization with over 500 members. He is also a charter member (in 1935) of the Indianapolis Pilots Association (now the Indianapolis Aero Club), one of the oldest of such organizations in the country. Finally, he was deservedly inducted into the OX-5 Aviation Hall of Fame.

Hirschinger has been instrumental in continuing the tradition Clyde Shockley began in the early '30s of having an annual Rotary meeting at the Muncie Airport. Larry was president of the Muncie Rotary Club in 1976–1977.

Courtesy of Lawrence Hirschinger
Larry Hirschinger (above) at his desk, Muncie Aviation Corporation 1942.

Larry Hirschinger and group of "MAC" flight instructors (right), World War II, 1942.

Courtesy of Lawrence Hirschinger

Vernon Thomas Hitchcock

ALTHOUGH Vernon Hitchcock was born in nearby Selma, Indiana, and has had long-time family roots in that area, I never new him until sometime in the late 1980s. He telephoned me and introduced himself as a Delaware County pilot who had a wide range of flying experiences. He had heard that Virginia and I had flown in Australia and Africa and thought it might be interesting to exchange experiences. This first conversation and correspondence resulted in several visits to my office.

Courtesy of Vernon Hitchcock
Lieutenant Hitchcock in cockpit of VR-11 N.A.T.S. NAS, Honolulu, September 22, 1945.

As an airline and executive aircraft pilot, he has had a number of fascinating experiences; some he has drafted into a fantasy story based on some of his flying in Africa. I've had the privilege of reading the draft which he says he doesn't intend to publish.

The following brief résumé is based on information he gave the San Francisco Quiet Birdmen Hangar when he was initiated in January 1983.

Vernon Thomas Hitchcock was born Route 1, Selma, Indiana, in 1919. As a small boy, he flapped his arms and jumped off a rock trying to fly. He never got the hang of it until several years later. When Lindbergh was flying the Atlantic in 1927, he was playing in airplanes sitting in a barn owned by Robert Retz next to his grandfather's farm in Farmland, Indiana. Retz' brief biography is included in these *Ramblings.* Hitchcock confirms Retz' airplanes were powered by converted automobile engines—Chevrolet and Ford. Across the road from Vernon's home farm, barnstormers operated in JN-4s from the farm of Ansel Tony, the master kite-maker, who recently died just short of reaching 100 years of age.

Hitchcock appeared on a program of Amelia Earhart's at Purdue University in 1936 where he graduated from the School of Agriculture in 1940.

He tried to enlist in the Army Air Corps but was rejected because he was too tall. He enrolled in the Indiana University Law School, but soon enlisted in the Naval Aviation Cadet training program. His first ride was in a Navy airplane doing loops, snap rolls, spins, etc. He soloed December 9, 1941, Navy aircraft designated N3N, and received the Naval Aviator Certificate Number C-64 September 3, 1942.

Courtesy of Vernon Hitchcock
*Photograph used on Christmas card 1966
showing oil well rig in the background
representing the company's major business, the
LAVCO Hitchcock flew, and the camel used for
ground transportation.*

*Hitchcock (right) with faithful DC-3 number
9896F he flew for Libyan Aviation Company
serving oil wells and crews in the Sahara Desert*

He instructed in the Navy's primary training school, then went to the American Airlines transport school in 1943. He was assigned to Naval Air Transport Service Squadron VR-2 at Alameda, California; then to VR-4 at Oakland; and finally to Olathe, Kansas, to the VR-3 school for Training Plane Commanders.

At Olathe, he met Jim Richter from Selma whose brief biography is also included in these *Ramblings*. His next station was NAS Moffitt in 1945 for training to the R5D school and then to Honolulu.

He was relieved from active duty in the Navy in December 1945 but continued in the Naval Reserve until 1969.

In 1946, for a year, he flew as captain with National Air Transport Service in Miami, and then flew Southwest Airways out of San Francisco with TWA until 1951.

He resigned and entered the Stanford Law School, graduating in 1953, and began private practice in Healdsberg, California. Shortly after, he was appointed Deputy Attorney General for the state, serving until 1956. During that time, he represented California's Aeronautics Commission as Deputy Counsel for Sonoma County and was influential in developing the Sonoma County Airport.

This airport was the locale for making aviation movies. Paul Manz and Frank Tallman were stunt flyers, the latter of whom was one of Hitchcock's DC-3 (Navy R4-D) students. Tallman flew through a hangar in the movie entitled *It's a Mad, Mad, Mad, Mad, World* which was made there. (Virginia and I met Frank Tallman when he was one of the luminaries and honorary officials at the Great Australian Trans-Continental Air Race in 1976.)

In 1966. Hitchcock resigned to become Executive Director of the Libyan Aviation Company which had operated throughout the Sahara Desert, supporting their oil exploration programs and development of production. He was caught in the June 1967 Six-Day War after which he accepted a position as legal counsel for Sonoma County schools back in California. It covered forty-four districts including junior colleges.

He retired July 1, 1982. During his varied and exciting experiences as an aviator, he accumulated some 7,500 hours of flying time. Since then he has continued an active life pursuing his various interests including the operation of his family farm near Selma.

Courtesy of Vernon Hitchcock
Hitchcock in Brisbane, Australia, posing in tri-motor Fokker, June 28, 1983, in which Kingsford-Smith was the first to fly from Oakland, California, to Australia in 1982.

David M. Meeks

LONG-TIME friend David M. Meeks was one of my "frequent fliers."

We flew to Florida a couple of times, 1934. He was my "co-pilot" of sorts in that "rigged air race" in Columbus reported elsewhere in these *Ramblings*.

Dave has also supplied me with bits and pieces of recollections that he has saved and given me sources and clues of events and experiences long forgotten.

I persuaded him, somewhat reluctantly, to record the short history of a local flying club, members consisting of Dave, Andy Rose, John Oesterle, and Gordon Lockwood. He recorded it as follows:

IN THE SPRING of 1934, Andy Rose, John Oesterle, Gordon Lockwood and I formed a flying club and purchased an airplane for $250. It was a Waco 10 with an OX-5 motor—an open cockpit plane. It had been stored in a barn for many years and, since the covering on the fuselage and wings was badly cracked, we stripped it, put on new fabric and painted it.

Andy had already learned to fly. Gordon Lockwood never got into the plane, and John Oesterle and I learned to fly it.

One hot afternoon in August, John was practicing take-offs and landings. While approaching the field for a landing, he realized he was much too high, decided to go around again to lose altitude and make a proper approach. In order to stretch his glide, he inadvertently raised the nose of the plane, lost flying speed, stalled the craft and crashed to the ground.

In the crash he suffered two broken ankles and various other injuries, including a hole in his windpipe. Since the plane didn't burn, he really lucked out.

A few days later it was discovered that John had trench mouth which caused infection in his windpipe injury, badly damaging his vocal chords. As a result he nearly lost his voice and to this day is unable to speak normally.

As a sidelight, at about the time of the accident my uncle, Ernest Meeks, and I were having dinner at the Delaware Hotel. He said, 'Dave, I wish you guys would get rid of that old crate before someone gets hurt.' At that very moment we heard the siren of an ambulance which we later discovered was heading for the crash site northeast of the airport.

Andy, Gordon, and I claimed that John owed us for what we had spent on the plane. He claimed we owed him for cracking it up first and, to this day, the argument has never been settled.

But they are still great friends and both entitled to membership in the OX-5 Aviation Pioneers organization.

Gordon Lockwood, son of George B. Lockwood, was on the staff of the *Muncie Star* and *Press* publishing company, at one time served as its publisher.

John Oesterle and Andy Rose both rose in the ranks of Warner Gear and then went on to important positions with Borg-Warner, Andy to Chicago and California, and John to Detroit and Chicago. John's voice, as a result of the accident, was well-known throughout the Borg-Warner organization and the automotive industry. He was highly respected as a top executive in Borg-Warner's management team, as well as with its customers, particularly Ford and Chrysler Motor Companies.

Gordon Lockwood died many years ago, but Andy, John, and Dave have remained close friends over the years, in spite of distance (Andy in California; Dave and John still in Muncie), and that old Waco 10 experience back in 1934.

William "Bill" Moffitt

R. H. Pelham Photo
William Moffitt, 1937

THERE WERE several aircraft owners in Muncie in the 1930s, including Bob and Bill Moffitt.

Together they owned and flew what we all considered to be a very "high powered," open cockpit Hisso Travel Air, Model 3000.

Bob taught Bill to fly. Bill accumulated enough hours in that Hisso to earn his commercial license and became one of the first corporate pilots in this area, flying for Warner Gear and manager Jack Simpson. I believe the brothers sold their airplane at that time. Bob did very little flying after that, but Bill continued as Warner Gear's pilot. The company first purchased a Beech Bonanza and later acquired a twin Beech model number 18. Bill flew the latter for many years out of Muncie, mostly for executives back and forth from Muncie to Chicago and Detroit.

Bill developed the first instrument landing procedure for Muncie airport. It was quite ingenious, but I'm sure it was never approved by FAA or whatever authority was in charge in those days. He used WLBC's radio tower south of Muncie, for what would be called today an NDB (a non-directional beacon) approach. He describes it more accurately in his own recollections which follow.

Several other pilots used the same procedure. Although I sometimes "homed" on the WLBC signal with my ADF, I don't recall ever actually using it under instrument conditions.

Bill Moffitt's letter, in response to my inquiry, is so interesting and informative, I include it in these

Ramblings verbatim:

IN ANSWER to your letter, here is some information that might be of interest.

My brother, Bob, learned to fly at the Curtiss-Wright School in Chicago and graduated with a limited commercial license. In an approved school this only required 35 hours of solo flight time.

After he returned to Muncie it became obvious that if he wanted a job in aviation, he would have to build up his flight time and experience. Dad decided the least expensive way to do this was to purchase a used airplane. However, he made one condition, that Bob teach me to fly.

We bought a used Travel Air, Model 3000, powered with a 180 HP Hisso Model E Engine. This was about double the power of most of the engines in use at that time in civilian airplanes. Also, most of all the engines being used by the aircraft manufacturers were surplus from World War I. Our Travel Air was built in 1927. The liquid cooled V-8 Hisso saw extensive use in the Spad France single seat fighters.

As events turned out, I was the only person Bob ever taught to fly. He never built up more than about 70 hours total flight time and then completely dropped out of the aviation business.

I had spent several years building model airplanes in grade school and high school along with reading everything I could find on aerodynamics and applied this to the design of my models. Then suddenly, I found myself alone up in the great big beautiful sky—what a thrill it was—the airplane and its response felt like it was just a part of me. I always felt this way when flying and ended up spending over 50 years in the aviation business.

My early training was at Wall Airport on south Hackley Street in Muncie. I soloed in about nine hours and received some advance instruction from a commercial pilot named J. R. (Pete) Williams. He was one of the best instructors I ever had. He was not only a very skilled pilot, but a good aircraft mechanic with a fine understanding of aerodynamics.

A short time later it was decided to convert Wall Airport into a housing addition. The new Muncie Airport was under construction and not usable so we continued flying at Wall Field as long as possible. However, the area was platted and streets were bull-dozed in to a depth of 18 inches. To roll off the sod surface into the street was certain to end up wrecking an airplane. All that was left for the airplanes was the old hangar at the north end of the airport sitting on a 650 foot square of the original sod. Since the old airplanes did not have wheel brakes or wing flaps this condition made flying hazardous. However, this proved to be excellent training for me when landing in some of the small airports of the early days.

Clyde Shockley offered to hangar our Travel Air at his old airport near Kokomo until the new airport was to the point where we could fly out of the new Muncie field.

In a couple of months, Clyde told me the roof on the original hangar was half completed and I could bring my plane back to Muncie, if I did not mind having it moved outdoors every day so the rest of the roof could be finished.

I took Clyde up on his offer, and as a result I became the very first paying tenant for hangar space at $15.00 per month.

During the depression days of the early 1930s, the Davis Aircraft Company in Richmond, Indiana, ceased all production of their two seater Monoplanes. When the assembly line stopped, it left several airplanes in various stages of completion. I bought one about seventy-five percent finished and hauled it to Muncie after arranging to use a small part of the empty Bell Piano factory on Kilgore Avenue. I finished the work on the plane, then took it to the Muncie Airport for final assembly. After having it inspected by the Department of Commerce, it was licensed and ready to fly. I test flew it on April 4th 1934.

It was a very attractive airplane with maroon body and yellow wings and tail. However, it proved to be slightly underpowered with a LeBlond 80 HP radial engine. Walter Davis liked it so well that I traded it back to him for some cash and another one on the assembly line which was only about forty percent finished but was

stressed for a 125 HP Warner radial engine. I finished this plane also at the Piano Factory and test flew it in mid summer 1935. It was painted light blue body and yellow wings and tail.

This one was a very good performer. Highly maneuverable—cruise 125 MPH—and climb to 10,000 feet above sea level in 10 minutes. I kept this airplane until late 1937 and then sold it to Jeannette Lempke who was a charter member of the '99s women pilot organization. She flew the plane in a cross-country race from Los Angeles to Cleveland, Ohio.

Minnetrista Cultural Foundation, Incorporated, Gift of Laverne Ables
Bill and Bob Moffitt with their Hisso Travel Air.

About this time I became an employee of Muncie Aviation and was flying many different types of airplanes. I also had sold my Travel Air to three new local pilots: Robert McDaniel, Al Heath and Russ Morris. All three men later became senior airline pilots with American, TWA, and Penn Central Airlines respectively. All have been retired for some time now. As you know McDaniel became well known for his endurance flight with Kelvin Baxter at the Muncie airport.

Prior to all this the three boys used my Travel Air and a J3 Cub to operate the Richmond, Indiana, Airport. The Piper J3 Cub was the one used in the endurance flight that set quite a record.

In regard to my developing the first instrument landing procedure, it was a matter of necessity for the Muncie airport as my home base of operations. It worked like this—when I was within 5 minutes of my ETA of WLBC, I would descend to 2,500 feet above sea level until the ADF indicated passing over the radio station. I would reduce speed to 120 MPH and then headed directly south for two minutes. At that point made a 180 degree left turn and headed back for the station on a true north track. Again after passing over the WLBC tower, I would fly outbound tract of 355 degrees for 90 seconds while descending to 2,000 feet. At this point, I would be past the two high smokestacks at the light company power plant on north Walnut street. Then started the final descent to 400 feet within the next 30 seconds. If I did not then have visual contact with the ground near the airport I would climb up to 2,500 feet and either try it all over again or proceed getting a clearance from traffic control to proceed to my alternate airport, usually Fort Wayne, Indianapolis or Dayton.

This system worked pretty well and got us back home most of the time. The real secret of success depended on precision in execution and on being thoroughly familiar with the airport and all the close-by surrounding territory. Of course the procedure had to be adjusted to existing weather such as wind direction, visibility beneath the cloud cover, and the airport surface condition. When I first started using this approach there were no hard surface runways but there was a bright rotating beacon and a lighted wind sock on top of a tower right beside the hangar. However, there were few boundary lights."

Minnetrista Cultural Foundation, Incorporated, Gift of Andrew W. Rose
Warner Gear's Twin Engine Beech 18 (right) flown for several years by Moffitt and Lew Jack.

Bill Moffitt (below) taking deliver of Warner Gear's first aircraft, a Beechcraft Bonanza, at Wichita, Kansas, 1938.

Minnetrista Cultural Foundation, Incorporated, Gift of Andrew W. Rose

Lewis Reese, Thomas Reese and the Reese Flying Service

LEW REESE and Tom Reese were brothers who built a successful private aviation business in Muncie after World War II and, in the process, earned a well-deserved reputation as pioneers in the entrepreneurship of aviation in east central Indiana. Lew and Tom were both born and raised on their family farm in Selma, a short distance southeast of Muncie. The farm had been in the family for several generations and Lew and Tom, along with their father and older brother Revere, helped with chores and other duties during their boyhood years. Interestingly enough, both brothers eventually came to use the family's parcel of farmland as the site of their aviation venture.

The older brother, and Lew became interested in flying before Tom and was a regular observer of the flight activity at Wall Field in south Muncie during the late 1920s. In 1927, Lew took his first flight, which cost him $25 for an hour's worth of flying time. "I was making $24 per week at my job and here I was spending $25 for an hour's worth of flying. No wonder that my Dad thought I was crazy. But I was hooked," Lew recalled. "All I could think about was flying."

Like his brother, Tom took to aviation "right away" and, after his graduation from Selma High School in 1931, pursued his interest in flying. During the 1930s, Tom obtained his commercial pilot's license after flying successfully at Weir Cook Field in Indianapolis. He purchased a J-3 Travel Air which he kept on the farm, but when World War II broke out, he entered active military service. Eventually stationed at an air base in San Angelo, Texas, Tom served as a flight instructor and also occasionally ferried aircraft to the theaters in Europe or the Pacific. During the war, Lew remained back home in Indiana to operate the farm, a lonely occupation at the time, since a shortage of farm laborers existed.

During the war, Lew was given the opportunity to purchase an additional forty acres from a neighboring farm, land which proved useful in constructing the aviation business which the two brothers envisioned for the postwar years. After Tom received his discharge from the armed services in 1946 and returned to Muncie, the two brothers set out to build their air field and begin operating their business. Lew began to clear the field at the air strip, located just north of Inlow Springs Road south of Muncie, a task which took several months of hard labor. In addition, he purchased a small Cub coupe aircraft during the war, which he offered to Owren Kirklin, a Muncie building contractor, as partial payment for the construction of a hangar. In this deal, Kirklin thereby acquired an aircraft and Lew got his hangar, or at least the trade

Courtesy of Tom Reese
Lew Reese became involved in flying before his brother Tom in 1946.

covered a good deal of the cost of the hangar's construction. Eventually, the Reese Flying Service's buildings and runways were finished without, as Lew noted proudly, "having to go into debt. Both Tom and I were raised very conservatively."

In the beginning years of the business, Tom did much of the flight instruction and Lew managed the facilities. In 1947, however, Lew obtained his commercial pilot's license and became an active instructor. The Reese Flying Service engaged in a number of aviation-related activities, including flight instruction, airplane storage and maintenance, piloting local businessmen to their various destinations,

Courtesy of Tom Reese
Tom Reese, his airplane, and his dog, Lucy, 1984.

Courtesy of Tom Reese
The Reese Airport (above) in the winter, late 1980s.

Reese Flying Service first hangar and office, 1946.

Courtesy of Tom Reese

running charter flights, and even occasional crop dusting. "We were always a small operation but that was all right," Lew observed. "A good friend of ours was Clyde Shockley who ran Muncie Aviation Corporation and he told us to be careful and not try to outgrow our pants. Still, every dime we earned went back into the airport."

The passage of the GI Bill in the late 1940s provided some of the initial impetus for the success of the Reese Flying Service. "Suddenly, everybody wanted to learn to fly," Tom remembered. Their training of pilots under the GI Bill continued well into the 1950s. Then, during the 1960s, the brothers received a contract from the Air Force ROTC unit at Ball State University to offer flight instruction to seniors enrolled in that particular military program. Their work with the ROTC students occurred during the Vietnam War and many of these young men later became pilots of advanced aircraft. "I enjoyed working with those students," Tom explained. "Many of them became doggone good pilots. They were tough. They had to be." Furthermore, one of the special highlights of the flight instruction for the Reese brothers involved the career of Bob Ruddick, who went on to become a pilot for Air Force One.

Courtesy of Tom Reese
Lew Reese; left, Bob Ruddick and son; center, and Tom Reese; right. 1990s. Ruddick was a Reese graduate who became a pilot of "Air Force One."

In 1970, the Reese brothers made a substantial investment in their business when they constructed a 2,800 foot paved runway, running east and west, on their air strip. "We knew that if we were going to continue in the business that we had to have a paved runway," Lew explained. The runway made it possible for the Reese brothers to offer flight instruction year-round, and not lose valuable days when the ground was either too wet or too soft to fly their aircraft. The brothers were obviously also thinking about the future, as today the company is managed by Steve Reese, Tom's son, who is also a corporate pilot.

The story of Lew Reese and Tom Reese, however, is an account of how two brothers, both raised in a farm family, followed their dream of building and running an aviation business. The fact that the Reese Flying Service has now entered its second generation of management shows how skillfully the brothers have managed their business. For those many years, it has been an important facility and service to the north central Indiana community. Its convenient location was an important factor in the Academy of Model Aeronautics' decision to locate in Muncie.

Courtesy of Tom Reese
Tom Reese, Steve Reese with his daughter, Kara, and Lew Reese, 1980s.

Robert R. Retz

Pioneer of Home-Builder Aircrafts

A NOT-TOO-WELL remembered but important historically as a pioneer pilot, aircraft designer and builder as well as designer and producer of aircraft propellers, is Robert R. Retz of Farmland, Indiana.

From his first close-up view of a World War I airplane which landed close to his father's farm in Farmland when he was a boy, to his untimely death in an aircraft accident in 1937, he devoted his entire life to aviation.

During high school, he made the acquaintance of John C. Edwards who became a life-long friend. After graduation from high school in 1925, he hitch-hiked to California, earning his way even during Depression years by working as a carpenter and developing woodworking skills that would be important as a designer and builder of aircraft frames.

He and his friend Edwards entered the Sweeney Aviation School in Kansas City in 1927. They couldn't put together enough money to take flight training, but both studied and became experts as engine mechanics, welders and in "stick, wire and frame construction, and rigging of aircraft."

They returned to Farmland where Retz became acquainted with a barnstormer, hired out as his mechanic, and learned to fly in partial payment for his skills, and services.

Courtesy of Vernon Hitchcock
Retz Airport and Hangar, 1935

Through his mechanical abilities, he became acquainted with and serviced the movie star Ken Maynard's Travel Air bi-plane which he used for sport flying. They maintained a close lifetime friendship.

In 1929, Retz, in his parent's home near Farmland, began building his first airplane—a single seater of wood, wire, and linen construction. He made his own jigs, fixtures, spars, and ribs. Youngsters in the area, including his friend John Edwards, assisted and retained their interest in aviation as well as their friendship with Retz.

He only built three airplanes with approved modifications and different engines on each. The first was an air-cooled converted, four-cylinder Chevrolet passenger car unit rebuilt by Fred Rathel of Daleville. This engine never developed sufficient horsepower and reliability resulting in numerous forced landings including on the famous kite maker, Tony Ansel's, nearby farm.

The next engine used on Retz' aircraft was a converted four-cylinder Ford Model A which increased the aircraft's speed and carrying capacity. This aircraft was advertised in Popular Aviation magazine in 1934 and sold. Final disposition is unknown.

In the meantime, Retz' friend Edwards entered Purdue University as a mechanical engineering student. He shared his knowledge of propeller designs gained from information contained in the University's library with his friend. Back at Farmland, Bob successfully built propellers for amateur aircraft builders. Propellers were both three- and four-bladed, all hand-carved, and with professional workmanship.

During 1935, the Retz Air Shop located on the Farmland Airport enjoyed some success repairing and rebuilding damaged aircraft. Among several purchased and repaired was and

American Eagle which he intended to use for student instruction.

The third and final Retz-built aircraft, according to the article dated April 26, 1937, from which the above information has been summarized, was "a beautiful, single-place tapered wing bi-plane with an eighteen foot wingspan. The wings were cantilevered and tapered, both plain, form and thickness. A pair of streamlines straight-legged struts supported the landing gear. Power was provided by a LeBlond sixty horsepower engine. Airplane writers commented that it climbed rapidly and flew beautifully, resembling a tiny pursuit ship in the air. Unfortunately, it experienced very little flying before its builder met an untimely end on May 29, 1937, while instructing. The airplane fell a few hundred yards short of the runway. Both teacher and student died instantly.'

One speculates on what Robert R. Retz might have been able to contribute to the advancement of light aircraft had he lived longer.

Quoting again from the *Sport Aviation* article, "his silver and black, taper-wing bi-plane was last heard of in California in the late 1940's. Its original likeness is inscribed on Robert Retz' tombstone in the Maxwell Cemetery slightly east of Farmland, Indiana."

Courtesy of Vernon Hitchcock
Bob Retz, left, and Fred Wrathel, the engine designer, with "R–1" powered by a four-cylinder converted Chevrolet engine.

Jim Richter

JIM RICHTER from Richmond, Indiana at the age of seventeen, soloed in a Piper Cub from the Centerville Airport near Richmond on July 18, 1937. Exactly fifty years later he commemorated the event by flying the same type of aircraft from the Richmond Municipal Airport. By that time he had logged over 28,000 hours of flying as an airline pilot, in the Navy during World War II, and back to the airlines following the War and then as a corporate pilot.

Jim had washed airplanes in exchange for flying lessons. After graduating from Tri-State College in Angola in 1941, he got his first job as an airplane pilot. After completing his service in the War as a Navy pilot, he returned to the airlines and terminated his flying career in 1984 as Chief Pilot and Manager of Pacific Gas and Electric Company's aviation department.

Like all us old-timers, he is keenly aware of how things were in the Halcyon Years of flying—no rules, no regulations, flying for fun, thrills, excitement, and earning sufficient money to support it all.

His comments about crowded air traffic lanes and landing facilities, particularly for the commercial airlines, is typical of all airlines pilots. But there is still plenty of room up there in the great skies above us if we use common sense and don't abuse our prerogatives.

Richter had a wide range of experiences and assignments. He flew for Trans Ocean Airlines and TWA prior to World War II.

A particularly unique experience was flying devout Arabian pilgrims to Mecca for Hadjj. On a flight, detecting the smell of smoke in the passenger cabin, he found a group had started a small fire to heat up some tea. Needless to say, the tea party came to an early conclusion.

Courtesy of Vernon Hitchcock
Jim Richter (left), Norm Mahaffey, and Ray Thomas.

Andrew "Andy" W. Rose

Gordon Lockwood, the third "non-flying" partner with Dave Meeks and John Oesterle and Andy Rose in the photograph. Gordon had a great sense of humor and was always laughing about something. Andy was a perfect foil.

ANDREW "ANDY" W. ROSE, son of Fredrick, President of the Merchants Trust and Savings Company, and Gladys Rose, graduated from Kenyon College, joined the Navy in World War II after learning to fly with MAC, and served as a flight instructor at Bunker Hill Naval Base, later named Grissom Air Force Base, terminating with the rank of Commander. Before and after the war, he worked for Warner Gear Division and later became a group vice president for Borg Warner in Chicago and Detroit.

Andrew Rose, originally of Muncie, enjoyed a productive and interesting career as an aviation pioneer, taking on challenging assignments as an entrepreneur, military aviator and flight instructor, and pilot who flew company-owned planes for business travel. In the process, Andy belonged to that rather small but close-knit fraternity of Hoosier aviators who began their careers in east central Indiana but then branched far afield during the 1930s and during World War II.

He took his first airplane flight at Wall Field in south Muncie during the summer of 1927. It was not until 1931, however, after he had graduated from Kenyon College in Ohio and returned to Muncie to work at the Warner Gear Corporation, that he became a certified pilot. In April 1931, he took a demonstration ride at the Silver Fox Airport near Yorktown with Paul Peters, flight instructor, and then, on May 21, 1931, made his first solo flight. As Andy recalled the date of his solo flight, it was the fourth anniversary of Charles Lindbergh's transatlantic flight, an occasion which gave the event a unique personal significance.

On July 29, 1931, Andy took his flight test at Wall Field in the presence of Joe T. Shumate, a CAA inspector who was making his scheduled visits of regional air facilities. Andy received Private License number 21335 at the same time that Bill Moffitt, another aviation pioneer in Muncie, successfully passed his flight test.

In 1932, at the age of 21, Andy became a minority partner in the establishment of Muncie Aviation Corporation, joining Frank Ball, Clyde Shockley, Jim Kennedy, Abbott Johnson, Fred Petty, Frank Hanley, Victor Hutzel, Lester Milligan, Frank Reed and myself in this new venture. Andy served as the secretary of this new business venture during the days of the Great Depression.

In 1933, another opportunity in the aviation field presented itself to Andy. Convinced that an article on local aviation would command an enthusiastic readership in the local press, Andy approached Paul Harrold, the managing editor of the *Muncie Morning Star,* with the idea of writing such a column. Harrold accepted Andy's suggestion and he immediately began writing a column entitled "Skylines by RPM" which became so successful that, within a year, Gordon Lockwood, publisher of the *Muncie Evening Press,* asked him to write a column for his newspaper. Andy left the *Star* for the *Evening Press* and wrote a column entitled "Airport Beacon by The Observer" which appeared weekly for the next seven years.

During the 1930s, the effects of the Depression often made business exceptionally slow at several of Muncie's industrial companies, and Warner Gear did not escape the effects of the slumping business conditions. Andy took advantage of many of the slack times at Warner Gear to assist Clyde Shockley in the work of the company, often accompanying him to pick up airplanes or to charter corporate passengers to their destinations throughout the midwest. These flights led to some interesting occurrences, such as the time in 1933 when Andy and Clyde were forced by weather to land in a large pasture near Hardyville, Kentucky, and passed the time until the weather cleared by giving rides to the nearby bystanders for two dollars per flight.

In 1935, Andy purchased a C–3 Aeronca plane and subsequently participated as a pilot in the *Aeronca Aircruise,* a group flight from Cincinnati to Miami at the time of Miami Air Races in December 1936. Despite a few harrowing incidents on the flight to Florida, Andy arrived safely and also made the return trip without incident. After the event was concluded, aviation enthusiasts concluded that the *Aeronca Aircruise* was the first time such a large caravan of

Courtesy Andrew W. Rose
Andrew W. "Andy" Rose as Instructor at Bunker Hill, Indiana, Naval Base (later Grissom Air Force Base).

private planes had ever traveled such a distance. Twenty-six airplanes comprised the fleet that took off from Lunken Field in Cincinnati, and all twenty-six of them arrived in Miami, on time and without needing repairs. The cruise established a new cross-country record: twenty-six planes flying a total of 70,200 miles (each plane traveling approximately 2,700 miles round trip) without repairs or engine trouble.

The outbreak of World War II for the United States in December 1941 changed Andy's life considerably, as it did for other civilian pilots in Indiana. In the summer of 1942, Andy followed up on a Navy program designed to recruit civilian pilots as flight instructors to train prospective Naval aviators. In August 1942, Andy flew to Chicago with Bill Moffitt, where he completed the preliminary exams necessary for him to become eligible for active military service in the Navy. Andy postponed the completion of some of his final paperwork until after his wife Janet (whom he had married in 1939) gave birth to their first child, Chris, in mid-September. On October 15, 1942, Andy was sworn in by a notary in Muncie and reported for active duty in Chicago on October 21.

Andy's first assignment for the Navy was to report to the Muncie Airport to take the Secondary Instructor Refresher Course in the Civilian Pilot Training contract school. He received his instruction from Larry Hirschinger who, along with Clyde Shockley, was responsible for administering the school. Following the completion of his course in Muncie, Andy underwent a prolonged training period which took him in 1943 to Chicago (for Navy Indoctrination School), then to Corpus Christi, Texas,

next to the Naval Air Station in Dallas, and finally to the Naval Air Station, New Orleans. In June 1943, Andy's class graduated and he received his designation as Naval Aviator and certificate of Instructor Rating.

At the end of June, Andy was assigned to the Naval Air Station at Bunker Hill, Indiana (now the site of Grissom Air Force Base), a short distance from Kokomo. Andy's family was able to join him, ending their prolonged absence while he underwent his training. At NAS Bunker Hill, Andy was involved in the flight training of approximately 800 cadets, using a Stearman as the training aircraft. In 1944, Andy was appointed Outlying Fields Officer and then, later in the year, Operations Officer for the station. In 1945, Andy received his final assignment of the war when he was reassigned to the station in Dallas, where he served as Wing Commander until he received his discharge in late September.

Following World War II, Andy returned to Muncie, where he resumed his business career with Warner Gear. He also continued his aviation interests and flew often on his business trips for the company. In 1953, Andy and his family moved to Los Angeles, where they made their permanent home. Nevertheless, in the short span of about fifteen years from 1931–1946, Andy had contributed significantly to the development of aviation in our area.

Richard "Dick" Whitney

DICK WHITNEY was one of the original aviation pioneers in east central Indiana who typified the flying careers of a number of Hoosier aviators who began their flight experience during the 1930s. Dick grew up on a dairy farm south of Muncie, then attended city schools where he studied at Eugene Fields Elementary School, Wilson Junior High, and graduated from Central High School. Dick's family operated a successful dairy business where he was employed as a

Courtesy of Richard L. Whitney
Richard L. Whitney, who gave up on his family's dairy farm, said, "The dairy business wasn't for me; all I wanted to do was fly."

teenager. With his customary candor, Dick admitted that the dairy business "wasn't for me; all I wanted to do was fly."

Whitney nourished his enthusiasm for aviation by visiting the rudimentary air fields around Muncie and watching the local flyers do their takeoffs and landings. He spent many hours at the Muncie Airport ("I hitch-hiked to the dedication when I was 12 or 13") and observed such local aviators as Bill Moffitt, Mike Murphy, Eddie Bridges, Al Heath, Kelvin Baxter, Bob McDaniel, and Russ Morris. But Dick also liked to visit neighboring air fields in Yorktown, Winchester, and Richmond to follow the flight activity in those places.

In 1935, Dick took his solo flight in a Kinner Bird at the Silver Fox Airport in Yorktown and, for the next several months, flew a number of aircraft out of that field, including Wacos, OX-5s, and OX-9s. Shortly after he graduated from Muncie Central in 1937, he purchased his own airplane for $600 and moved it to Richmond, where he often flew with Heath, Morris, and McDaniels.

Dick's closest brush with death occurred in Muncie on Sunday, October 2, 1938, when he was flying with Charlie Brown, a local insurance salesman. Both men were flying in Brown's aircraft when suddenly the engine went dead, and despite the pilots' efforts to land the plane safely, the aircraft plummeted to the ground from a distance of about 200–300 feet. Brown, seated in the front seat, was killed instantly in the crash. Dick, seated to the rear, was seriously injured and rushed immediately to Ball Memorial Hospital in Muncie with numerous

Courtesy of Richard L. Whitney
On October 2, 1938, an accident almost ended his flying career and his life.

wounds, a fractured leg, and a fractured ankle. Dick spent the better part of the next week fighting for his life. At first, his physicians believed that his right leg would need to be amputated, but his mother managed to obtain an examination by a prominent orthopedic surgeon from Indianapolis, who then operated on the ankle and managed to save Dick's leg. Dick spent the next six weeks in the hospital before he was released and then resumed his flying career.

During World War II, Dick's injuries prevented him from active military service, but he nevertheless managed to contribute to the war effort anyway. By this time, Dick had acquired his commercial rating, then went to Louisville, Kentucky, to take a refresher course in order to obtain an instructor's rating. During the early years of the war, Dick worked for a company, known as Anderson Air Activities, which had a contract with the Army to train glider pilots at its facility in Antigo, Wisconsin. In this job, Dick worked with a number of Army officers and gave them lessons equivalent to a private license as well as pre-glider training. Many of Dick's students at this school later went on to participate in the Allied invasion at D-Day in 1944.

Following the experience in Wisconsin, Dick went to McBride, Missouri, where the Anderson firm had obtained a contract to train Army cadets in flight training using Stearman aircraft. Many of the students trained by Dick in this assignment later went on to fly missions for the Air Transport Command (ATC). Before World War II ended, Dick had also participated in flight training programs for the Army at Indianapolis, Milwaukee, and Dayton.

After the end of the war, Dick returned to Muncie where he continued his career as a pilot. Dick's first job after the war involved becoming the personal pilot for William Ball, then a senior executive with the Ball Brothers Manufacturing Company. William had recently purchased a twin-engine Cessna and later a

Courtesy of Richard L. Whitney
Dick Whitney, front row on right, with a group of fellow instructors at Antigo, Wisconsin, working for Anderson Air Activities to train pilots for military service.

Twin-Beech, which also functioned as company aircraft. Dick literally flew across the United States and North America, both for William Ball and for the company, to such destinations as New York, California, Nassau in the Bahamas and a host of other places in between. As Dick remembered that particular period: "I got to see a lot of original Broadway shows (with William Ball and his family) that way."

In 1950, Dick began a lengthy period which extended for the next thirty-five years when he continued to work as a pilot for several Indiana companies. Between 1950–1961, he piloted the company aircraft for Acme-Lee, an industrial company located in Muncie, but which was part of a larger midwestern corporation. In 1961, Dick worked briefly for Dwyer Products, Incorporated, located in Michigan City, but chose to return to Muncie and resume flying for William Ball.

In 1965, Dick received an offer from Charles Rothhaar, a senior executive with Maxon Corporation in Muncie, to become the company pilot for that firm. Dick accepted that position and piloted the Maxon aircraft, first a Piper Aztec and later a Navajo, until his retirement in 1984. Maxon Corporation had sales

Courtesy of Richard L. Whitney
After the war, Dick returned and became personal pilot for William H. Ball and his family.

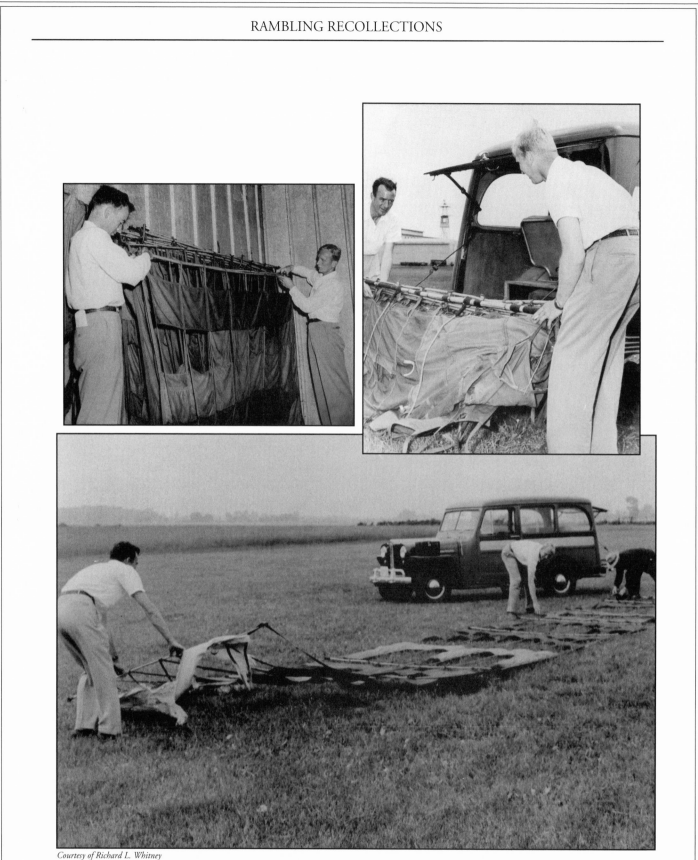

Courtesy of Richard L. Whitney
A series of photographs illustrating how banners were prepared to be towed carrying advertisements. Bill Greene, another young pilot, helping Dick get his banner ready for towing—not a simple task. Carelessness could mean disaster.

offices in numerous major cities around the United States and Dick frequently flew the company's sales engineers to "trouble-shooting" assignments at those locations. During his years with Maxon, Dick was occasionally joined by Steve Reese, the son of Tom Reese of Reese's Flying Service, who became Maxon's company pilot after Dick's retirement in 1984.

Although now retired, Dick Whitney still continues his love of flying. He lives less than a mile from the Muncie Airport, a convenient location to fly occasionally and also to observe air traffic at the airport.

Dick and his wife, Lois. Lois, herself, became a fully qualified pilot, an instructor, and flew as a charter pilot with all the necessary ratings. She was a 99er and good friend of Olie McCormick and Margaret Petty, also 99ers. Lois soloed December 1, 1948, and earned her commercial pilots license August 16, 1951. At that time, she was one of only six Indiana women holding that rating.
Courtesy of Richard L. Whitney

Courtesy of Richard L. Whitney
Christmas in Mexico. George Young, pilot; Ann Eckerson (on step); Judith Eckerson (doorway of aircraft), grand-daughters of William and Agnes Ball; and Dick Whitney, co-pilot,. Mr. & Mrs. Sam Moxley would join them. Lucina's first husband, Dr. Ed Eckerson, serving on board a hospital ship in the Pacific during World War II, was killed when the ship was struck by a Japanese bomb.

J. Raymond "Pete" Williams

Pete Williams held a transport pilot license, number 9816, and an A&E certificate (aircraft and engine). He was the first pilot Clyde Shockley employed when he moved to Muncie and became his all-around "Man Friday" in those earlier years. He could do 'most anything—fly, repair aircraft, fix and repair balky engines, work on the troublesome hangar door, fix the boiler and do just about everything. As related earlier in these *Ramblings,* he flew to help diagnose my engine problem in "Black Cat Roy" and piloted the plane to advise me of "Wheel Off Ed" in that incident.

Also recorded earlier in these *Ramblings,* Pete flew co-pilot with "Sad Sam" Jones, as pilot of the short-lived Continental Airlines' first round-trip flight from Muncie to Chicago.

He was popular, friendly and always smiling, no matter what the situation might be.

Ironically, Pete was killed instantly in an automobile accident on his way from the airport to his home in Yorktown on August 7, 1938. It occurred at an intersection blind from all four directions by tall corn growing to the corner on both sides of the intersecting roads. The young lady driving the other car was seriously injured, but Pete, we believe, never knew what hit him.

Pete played an important part in those early days of Muncie Aviation Corporation, Muncie Airport and had a fine career ahead of him in aviation, had he survived.

CHAPTER VIII

CONCLUSION

From Fruit Jars to Satellites

*I*T WAS MY intention at the outset to simply record some of my personal flying experiences, adventures and misadventures. But then, as it became more and more involved, and included a broader field of events and people than I originally intended, the material seemed to fall rather clearly into two general categories. One, more of historical events and individuals, likely of greater general interest. The second of more personally related events and individuals.

The result has been two volumes.

Volume I attempts to give a flavor of what I like to call the Halcyon or Golden Years of Aviation. It begins only seven years after the Wright brothers flew at Kitty Hawk, when Muncie citizens built an aircraft modeled after Blieriot's successful monoplane. A Muncie citizen, George Kemp, developed one of the first a widely-used, air-cooled engines. An aviation club was started in Muncie.

It was my good fortune to have participated in some of the events that followed and to have known many of the individuals personally through more than six decades of aviation history.

It's amazing to think back over the events that have transpired in aviation in that period of time.

Following Octave Chanute, who conducted his successful glider flights in 1896 on the Indiana Dunes on the shores of Lake Michigan, Blieriot, Langley, Lillienthal, the Wright brothers, who lived in Indiana, and Glen Curtiss, the really first pioneers, came those of my era, many of whom I knew.

Lindbergh flew solo across the ocean in 1927 and sparked a monstrous leap forward in the general public's interest in aviation.

These were the swashbuckling knights of the sky who emerged after World War I. In Indiana, they were people like Colonel Weir Cook, Clarence Cornish, "Cap" Aretz, Mike Murphy, Herb Fisher and Milo Burcham. They were the barnstormers, stunt flyers and self-made—out of necessity—mechanics, aircraft riggers and designers without the benefit of proven aerodynamic formulae, of formal engineering

The "Ball Mason Jar" Satellite (left), Ball's entrance into NASA's space program, literally "From Fruit Jars to Satellites," the title of Edmund F. Ball's address to the Newcomen Society in Chicago in 1960, led to much creative publicity.

training, of access to wind tunnels and computers. They staked their lives, testing their ideas and innovations most by trial and error, and sometimes they lost.

Others of the early barnstormers like Clyde Shockley, with whom I was associated many years in Muncie Aviation Corporation, "Cap" Aretz of Kokomo and Lafayette, Homer Stockert of South Bend, John Ruzicka and others moved their bases from small fields and farmers' pastures to established airports and became Fixed Base Operators, serving and storing local and transient aircraft, taught students to fly, sold airplanes, and flew passengers.

Walter Davis, Cessna, Stinson, Walter Beech, and even Henry Ford, began manufacturing airplanes. The Friedlanders built Aeroncas in Cincinnati. Wallace Friedlander started the Aeronautical Corporation in Cincinnati in 1935 building Aeronca aircraft and was its president until he died in 1939. Carl Friedlander took over as President until 1943 when John Friedlander was elected President, serving until 1948. The company discontinued building airplanes in 1950. Muncie Aviation Company was Aeronca distributor for Indiana until Aeronca went out of business, and Taylor Aircraft, soon to become Piper Aircraft, took over the small aircraft market. Waco Aircraft with Clayt Brukner built Waco aircraft in Troy, Ohio. Belancas were built with controls like those on an automobile so that, theoretically, anybody who could drive a car could fly an airplane, and Mr. Piper with his Cubs strove to make air the preferred means of travel for the common man and woman.

Women in aviation go back to the earliest days. I recall, for instance, Jacqueline Cochran, who was one of the first to enter the field of professional pilots competing in national air races and who went on to

head up the WACs, Women's Aviation Corps, in World War II, Amelia Earhart, and Katherine Stinson, Olive Beech, and Indiana had its own Jean MacElroy, Clarence's wife, the first Indiana woman to hold a transport pilot's license.

History records that the first American woman to fly as a passenger was a sister of the Wright brothers who flew with her brother Wilbur in 1907, aloft for two minutes and seven seconds at the height of thirty feet. The Wright brothers, one of whom was born in Indiana.

The first woman to become a licensed aircraft pilot in the United States was Harriet Quimby who, after thirty-three lessons totalling four and a half hours in the air, was granted her license by the American Aero Club, there being no Federal agency at that time, on August 2, 1911.

John Friedlander (left), and Carl Friedlander, circa 1939.

Katherine Stinson, mentioned previously, was the fourth woman pilot to be licensed in 1912. She taught her brother, Ed, to fly and helped build and design Stinson airplanes such as Muncie Aviation Corporation sold and were used during World War II for training pilots and for spotting artillery targets. I flew one after I returned from overseas during maneuvers in the

Louisiana and thoroughly enjoyed the assignment.

While I didn't know them personally, I was well aware of the deeds of many of the famous aviatrix within my span of recollections.

Ruth Long, who brought all kinds of cross country records, using hand-drawn maps and even railroad timetables for distances between towns used as checkpoints in the middle teens.

Phoebe Omlie performed sensational tricks in the air wing-walking, parachute jumps, won air races, and was the first woman appointee by Franklin D. Roosevelt during his first term to the Civil Aeronautics Authority, now the Federal Aviation Administration.

Ruth Nichols flew her Lockheed Vega to speed, altitude and long distance records.

Louise Thaden was the first woman to win the prestigious Bendix Air Race in 1936, had many thrilling experiences, helped Phoebe Omlie in her campaign to identify towns and cities by painting their names on rooftops and wrote a book entitled *High, Wide and Frightened,* appropriate to all of us at some time or other.

We, here in Muncie, knew about Mae Hazlip through her more famous husband's visits here.

Of course, everyone knows about Ann Lindbergh and Amelia Earhart. As always, mentioning a few does injustice to many others.

Certainly one who should be mentioned is "Josie" Orr, wife of two-term Governor Robert Orr. She flew with the WAFs during World War II for Nancy Love and Jacqueline Cochran. Stories she tells of her experiences are fascinating and often hilarious. Then, of course, there were the giants like Douglass, Boeing, Sikorsky, Curtiss, Lockheed. They strove to out-do each other in building passenger-carrying airliners, forerunners of our modern passenger transports.

Those were exciting, heady times and the future for the aviation industry seemed unlimited.

The ubiquitous Jimmy Doolittle set the continental air record for cross-country flight in 1931 of eleven hours, sixteen minutes, and ten seconds, with two en route fuelling stops to capture the first Bendix Trophy. He was the first to experiment with blind flying, based on reference to instruments only with no visual contact with the outside world, flew across country and made the first completely successful instrument landings.

Bill Lear developed his auto-pilot, which was used so successfully in World War II and was the forerunner of the sophisticated auto-pilots we have today.

"Speed Merchants" vied with each other to set new records.

Doug Davis, no relation to Walter, whose Travel Air Mystery Ship, powered by a souped-up 400 HP Wright Whirlwind engine, won the first Thompson Trophy race in Cleveland in 1929, averaging almost 200 MPH over a fifty mile, closed-circuit course, for which he won a prize of $5,000.

Chuck Hollman in his Laird Solution averaged over 200 MPH in a hundred mile, closed-circuit course, winning the Thompson Trophy race in 1930.

The epitome of all swashbuckling "Speed Merchants," Ambassador of Aviation throughout the United States and abroad, and perhaps the most skillful pilot of them all, Colonel Roscoe Turner, with his sharply pointed, waxed moustache, his powder blue uniforms, boots, diamond studded wings and his pet lion cub, Gilmore. He exceeded the 300 MPH mark in a Turner-Laird Special powered by a twin Pratt and Whitney Wasp engine, over a three hundred mile, closed-circuit course, winning the Thompson Trophy race in 1939.

"Tex" Johnson and his Bell-80 Airacobra, powered by an Allison engine, averaged 374 MPH over a three hundred mile, closed-circuit course, the last of the Thompson Trophy races in 1946.

Races such as the Thompson Trophy were no longer feasible.

World War II brought tremendous changes in aircraft design and capabilities. Chuck Yeager broke the sound barrier, over 600 MPH, on October 14, 1947, and another aviation frontier had been crossed.

This montage presents a panoramic view of Ball's projects in space.

Development and uses for jet engines relegated internal combustion, piston engines, driving propellers, to smaller aircraft, like those for business and pleasure, executive flights and special operations from short fields, student's training, crop dusting, and advertising.

Ball Corporation entered the space age in 1957 by way of acquiring a small operation in Boulder, Colorado, with only fourteen employees and literally expanded from "Fruit Jars to Satellites." By 1962, it was producing its own series of satellites, the very successful Orbiting Solar Observatories, leading to important high-tech aerospace contracts, with NASA, Department of Defense and numerous civilian projects in the United States and abroad. A model of OSO and of IRAS are displayed in the National Air and Space Museum, Smithsonian Institution, Washington, D.C.

The operation has grown to over 3,000 scientists and engineers and is recognized as one of the tops in the industry. Current evidence of its versatility is a $40,000,000 contract awarded to repair, in orbit, the faulty Hubbell Space Telescope.

Men walked on the moon in July 1969 and shuttle flights to outer space have become almost routine to study from afar our fragile planet, our space ship Earth, on which we are passengers. Scientists look to Mars and beyond to heretofore unknown galaxies to learn more of the infinite universe in which we are but a tiny speck.

All this in a mere lifetime. I'm awed in retrospect by what has been accomplished in the field of aviation and aeronautics, am excited by the opportunities that lie ahead, and envious of those who will be participating.

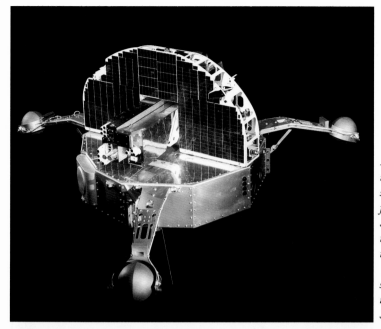

Ball Brothers Research Corporation, BBRC was incorporated in 1956 and integrated as a subsidiary in Ball Corporation. In 1962, Ball's first of a series of seven highly-successful Orbiting Solar Observatory satellites (left) was launched, the final in 1971. Their assignment was to study the relationship between the Sun and Earth. Their discoveries were crucial to the safety and success of astronauts' ventures into space. A model is displayed in the Air and Space Museum, Smithsonian Institution, in Washington, D.C.

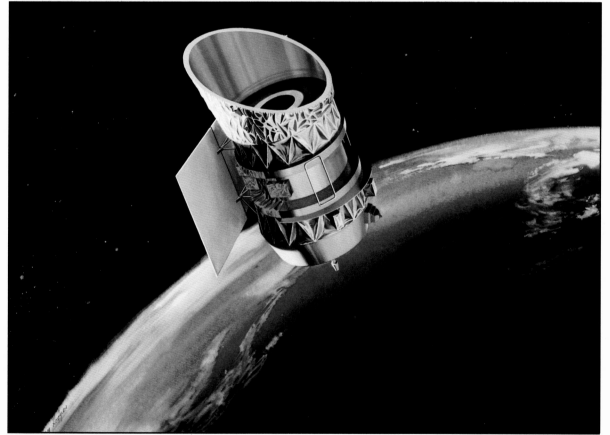

In 1983, the Infra Red Astronomical Satellite (IRAS) was launched, carrying Ball's telescopic system. Ball's expertise in cryogenics and electro–optics became recognized in the project leading to numerous other applications in NASA projects. A model of IRAS is displayed in the Air and Space Museum, Smithsonian Institution, in Washington, D.C.

Courtesy of Edmund F. Ball
Cecelia Aragon, Muncie Airport September 12-13, 1992.

Perhaps not typical, but a good example of the role young men and women will be playing in the future of aviation as it moves into the next century, is Cecelia Aragon.

Cecelia has roots in Indiana. Her parents are both on the faculty of Purdue University. She holds a B.S. degree in mathematics and literature from Purdue, and an M.S. in computer science from the University of California-Berkeley. She credits much of her success to her parents who told her she could do anything she wanted to do, but that she would have to work hard to achieve any worthwhile goals.

Her visit here was under the auspices of Minnetrista Cultural Center, featuring aviation, at that time. Her Saber 320, is a custom-designed, high-performance, aerobatics monoplane with a 320 HP engine. She also owns a Pitts S1T.

She says that, as a little child she always wanted to fly. Her first flight was with a pilot friend who offered to take her for a ride. She was afraid, but figured she should try it at least once. She didn't expect to love it as much as she did. It was an experience of freedom she'd never experienced. She promptly signed up for flying lessons, has accumulated over 3,300 hours.

One of the smallest aerobatics pilots in the business, she is only 100 pounds and five feet tall. She operates an aerobatics flying school in Vacaville, California.

Early in her career, she became interested in aerobatics and began training with all the vigor of Olympic athletes, sometimes, "landing with bloodshot eyes and bruises from high negative G's." Her ambition was to be selected one out of eight final contestants to represent the United States in the World Aerobatics Contest held every two years. She was one of four chosen.

She holds an impressive record: nineteen International Aerobatics Club trophies; International Aerobatics Club "All Ten" Special Achievement Award, only twenty-nine in the history of aerobatics; Unlimited Championship Southern California Regional Aerobatics; in 1990 Unlimited Champion Northwest Regional Aerobatics Competition; in 1991-92, selected a member of the United States Aerobatics Team, and won fourth place among all international pilots.

It is fitting to conclude these *Rambling Recollections* with this recording of the accomplishments of a remarkable young lady, as she continues the legacy of the early "barnstormers."

INDEX

Rambling Recollections of Flying & Flyers